Babylon and the Brethren

*The Use and Influence of the Whore of Babylon Motif
in the Christian Brethren Movement, 1829–1900*

JAMES HARDING

WIPF & STOCK · Eugene, Oregon

BABYLON AND THE BRETHREN
The Use and Influence of the Whore of Babylon Motif in the Christian Brethren
Movement, 1829–1900

Unless otherwise stated Scripture quotations are taken from the *Holy Bible: King
James Version*. 1611 edition. Peabody: Hendrickson, 2003.

Wipf & Stock
An Imprint of Wipf and Stock Publishers
199 W. 8th Ave., Suite 3
Eugene, OR 97401

www.wipfandstock.com

ISBN 13: 978-1-62564-885-3

Manufactured in the U.S.A.   10/15/2015

Babylon and the Brethren

Dedicated to my mum, Joan Harding

Contents

Acknowledgments

Several individuals and institutions have assisted me in the course of this work. All may be assured of my most sincere heartfelt gratitude, though space permits that only a selection of the debts may be here acknowledged. My PhD supervisor, Rev. Prof. K. G. C. Newport, is due a particular mention for the guidance, inspiration and meticulous attention to detail he has brought to the project. His commitment to my development as a researcher has often gone above and beyond my expectations.

The staff at St. Mellitus College, in particular the dean, the Rev. Dr. Graham Tomlin, for his support, and my office "roommate," Dr. Chris Tilling for encouragement to publish.

Additionally, Liverpool Hope University College and the Panacea Society provided financial assistance during my years as a PhD student, for which I am very grateful.

Dr. Graham Johnson the Christian Brethren Archivist in the JRULM must be thanked for his tireless assistance in making archival material available.

I must acknowledge the practical and emotional support provided by friends and family throughout the course of my postgraduate studies, in particular those who have patiently listened to me "thinking out loud" over the course of dinner and drinks. Special thanks are due to Alan Smith who carefully read through the provisional draft, Joel Gutteridge who helped with formatting and typesetting, and Karl Coppock from Wipf and Stock for his careful attention to detail.

Finally, I express my gratitude to Katie Jane Harding, my wife, and my children, Agnes, Noah, and Elsie, to whom (along with my mum) this book is dedicated, for unwavering support, depth of love and awesome patience shown throughout.

Whilst all those mentioned above, and more, have each imputed something to this book, it must be stated that this work is entirely my own as are any deficiencies or mistakes contained therein.

Abbreviations

LW   Pelikan, J., and H. T. Lehmann. *Luther's Works*. 55 vols. St. Louis: Concordia and Philadelphia: Fortress/Muhlenberg, 1955–86.

NC   Darby, J. N. *Notes and Comments on Scripture*. 7 vols. Bath: Humphrey, 1884–1913.

NIDOTTE   VanGemeren, W. A. *New International Dictionary of Old Testament Theology and Exegesis*. 5 vols. Grand Rapids: Zondervan, 1997.

NIGTC   Marshall, I. H., and D. A. Hanger. New International Greek Testament Commentary. 13 vols. Grand Rapids: Eerdmans, 1978–2005.

NJ   Darby, J. N. *Notes and Jottings from Various Meetings*. 5 vols. London: Foreign Gospel Book Depot, 1931.

n.d.   date of publication not known.

n.pubs.   publisher not known.

n.pl.   place of publication not known.

NPNF   Schaff, P., and H. Wace. *A Select Library of Nicene and Post-Nicene Fathers of the Christian Church*, series 1 and 2. 28 vols. Edinburgh: T. & T. Clark, 1886–1900.

NW   Ross, D., and J. R. Caldwell. *The Northern Witness: A Monthly Magazine of Biblical Literature*. Vols. 1–16. Glasgow: Publishing Office, 1870–1886.

PS   Newton, B. W. Patmos Series. Vols. 1–43. Aylesbury: Barnard, n.d.

PPPS   Trotter, W. *Plain Papers on Prophetic Subjects*. London: Partridge & Oakey, 1854.

SC   Wolston, W. T. P. *Ten Lectures on the Second Coming and Kingdom of the Lord Jesus*. London: Nisbet, 1891.

TIESS   Sills, D. L., and R. K. Merton. *The International Encyclopaedia of the Social Sciences*. 1st ed. 17 vols. New York: Free Press, 1968–1979.

WBC   Hubbard, D. A., and G. W. Barker. Word Biblical Commentary. Vols. 1–59. Dallas: Word, 1982–2005.

Introduction

At the very back of the Bible, lurking suspiciously just before the maps and the concordances, is a very strange book indeed. Of all the books in the New Testament, the book of Revelation, or the Apocalypse as it is often referred to,[1] stands out from the crowd as being somehow different. It is a book of wild imagination, of vivid pictures and terrifying visions. It is a book of many-headed beasts, of dragons and angels, of seas of blood, blazing stars, earthquakes and plagues. It is a book ripe for imaginative interpretation.

Although the place of Revelation within the canon of Scripture has been heavily debated,[2] the book has, nevertheless, been highly influential in the Christian tradition. Indeed, as will be seen throughout this book, the influence of Revelation has often been highly significant as interpreters are able to draw on the rich, heavy, descriptive images, and apply them easily to the world in which they live. Sometimes this has been very positive. For example, for black South Africans struggling against the Apartheid regime in the second half of the twentieth century the text has brought hope of a better world to come,[3] while for Christian women subjugated and oppressed by men in a patriarchal society, the Apocalypse has been a source of strength and hope.[4]

---

1. The word Apocalypse comes from the Greek word *apokalypsis* meaning "unveiling" or "revelation." The fact that the book is called "revelation" does not go unnoticed by the kind of commentators under discussion in this book, who argue, reasonably enough, that the meaning of the mysterious images contained therein have been "revealed" and can therefore be understood.

2. It is not important here to discuss the history of the disputed text since this book is concerned with the text as it has been received. For a brief summary of the main points see, Mounce, *Book of Revelation*, 21–24.

3. Mwombeki, "Book of Revelation in Africa," 145–51; see also Boesak, *Comfort and Protest*, 126.

4. See for instance, Schüssler Fiorenza, *Revelation*, 101.

However, the text has not always been put to such positive use and in some circumstances interpreters have used the text to have a far less savory impact. The leaders of some Christian sects, for example David Koresh, whose community the Branch Davidians in Waco Texas suffered catastrophic fire in 1993, have used the Apocalypse to justify and give validity to a number of beliefs and practices, which, so some have argued, have led to death, destruction and the suffering of many.[5]

In this book some other interesting uses of the text are brought into focus, with particular reference to the way in which the symbol of Babylon the Great has been interpreted by a number of commentators, and with particular emphasis being placed on the exegesis of the Whore of Babylon passages in the Christian Brethren movement.

The book of Revelation has of course proved to be a source of great fascination and attraction to those on the margins of any society. Its magnetism and natural appeal is due in part, even allowing for the difficulty of interpreting the text in detail, to the central idea that the author is seeking to convey: that although one may suffer in this life it will be for but a moment as the end of all things is coming, maybe just around the corner. The *parousia* of Christ will right all those wrongs, and usher in a new age where God shall live with his people: "And he shall wipe away every tear from their eyes; and death shall be no more; neither shall there be mourning, nor crying, nor pain, any more: the first things are passed away" (Rev 21:4). Furthermore, as many have pointed out, the hope that is offered in such texts as Revelation does not pertain to the *eschaton* only, but rather it seems to be the case that the author is seeking to reassure his readers in their present experiences. Even though it may look as though the devil has the upper hand, in fact God is in control "behind the scenes."[6] Such a message has an obvious application to those who perceive this world to be a threatening and dangerous place and it matters little whether those perceptions are accurate or not.[7] As we shall see, this was the case with the Brethren.

One very prominent image in the book of Revelation is that of the Whore of Babylon. This image can be seen in Revelation 14:8, 16:19, 17:5, 18:2, 18:10 and 18:21. Although Babylon is mentioned six times in other

---

5. Such a view is argued extensively for example in Newport, *Branch Davidians of Waco*, especially chs. 13–15. While the details of the exegetical scheme that was in place at Waco are not directly relevant in this book, we note in passing that according to Newport, Koresh interpreted the figure of Babylon as, among other things, the American Government and this was a factor in the catastrophic outcome that resulted from the siege.

6. Rowland, *Open Heaven*, 425, 427, 429–30.

7. Ibid., 413.

New Testament writings, five of these six references outside of the Apocalypse clearly refer to Babylon in a historical, geographical, and literal way and not as an image or symbol at all.[8] The sixth occurrence of the word Babylon, in 1 Peter 5:13, is generally accepted as being used figuratively as a cryptogram for Rome,[9] although it was understood by some of the Brethren authors to refer to the literal geographical place called Babylon.[10] Thus the Petrine text is not relevant here. It is clear, therefore, that as half of all New Testament biblical references to Babylon are to be found in Revelation, and it is here that the figurative sense of that term is found, that "Babylon," whatever that might mean in this context, plays an important role in the author of the Apocalypse's vision of the end. It was not understood even by the author as a literal, historical place only.

As we shall see in this book, this symbolic or figurative representation of Babylon becomes an important image for many commentators, no more so than in the Protestant tradition from the mid-sixteenth century onward.[11] It was an important image too in the narrower confines of the Brethren movement, and indeed became central to their ecclesiology[12] and eschatology.[13] Both the Reformers in general and the Brethren movement in particular, then, turned to the book Revelation and found there a church with a *Sitz im Leben* not unlike their own and found in that book images easily transferable to their own situation. It was in the same text too that they found enemies like their own enemies.

THE *SITZ IM LEBEN* OF THE BOOK OF REVELATION

Although historical-critical issues, such as determining the authorship and date of Revelation, are largely unimportant for a book such as this, which is an examination of the *Wirkungsgeschichte* or "history of impact" of a particular part of that text, it is important to note just one historical-critical

8. See Matt 1:11, 12, 17 (two occurrences), and Acts 7:43, for literal references to Babylon.

9. See, e.g., Cullmann, *Peter*, 86.

10. William Kelly, e.g., writes: "Peter was in Babylon, the literal Babylon on the plain of Shinar, when he wrote the First Epistle." Kelly, *First Epistle of Peter*, vii. Note that the Brethren authors upon which the majority of this book is focused held a literalistic interpretation of Scripture. This enabled them to identify Babylon in 1 Pet 5:13 as a literal woman: "a well known sister," in the literal geographical location of Babylon. See, e.g., Darby, "Short but Serious Examination," 108.

11. See ch. 3 below.

12. See chs. 4–7 below.

13. See chs. 8–9 below.

issue in passing, namely the *Sitz im Leben* of the book.[14] This is so since, as we shall see, it was the *Sitz im Leben* of the book that probably made it particularly relevant to the Brethren movement, the focus of this study.

Within the book of Revelation there is strong, if not incontrovertible evidence, that the text had been written for a group that was either experiencing persecution or at least expecting it: a maltreated group perhaps, and a community whose members were being told to stay strong and retain hope in the midst of suffering.[15] The author was offering hope to his community. Even though in the present the "locusts and scorpions" may be tormenting and hurting them (Rev 9:1–12), this will be only for a finite period of time (Rev 8:10); even though the seven-headed, ten-horned monster from the sea wages war on the saints (Rev 13:1–10), they must endure and have faith (Rev 13:10). Similarly, while the two-horned dragon-like monster from the land killed anyone who did not worship its statue (Rev 8:11–18), John[16] calls for endurance from God's people (Rev 14:12). The Rider called "faithful and true" will soon destroy these enemies (Rev 19:11–21), and the saints will live forever with God in the New Jerusalem (Rev 21:1–7; 22:4). Here is a group which is being urged to remain faithful and pure, uncorrupted by the social and religious evils of the world around them. They must not bow down and worship the beast or his statue, neither must they receive his mark or fornicate with the Great City. Their robes must remain white; they must be unpolluted, a spotless virgin bride waiting patiently for their eschatological groom (Rev 21:8). The text hence appears to be written by a member of a persecuted community (anticipated or actual), a community whose members are both at odds with the world and in enmity with the world.

In the context of this book, this apparent *Sitz im Leben* of the book of Revelation is significant, for it provides an important potential link and commonality of experience between the author of Revelation and the Christian

14. The German phrase *Sitz im Leben* literally means "situation in life," but it has a more technical meaning within the historical-critical examination of scripture. In this context *Sitz im Leben* means the whole historical, social, religious, political, cultural, and linguistic context that the author writes in and the reader reads in.

15. It must be noted here that it is entirely possible that the book of Revelation was not written by one author to be read by a group of readers. Such a view is posited by many source-critical authors of the twentieth century. However, it is the view of the present author that it is entirely reasonable to speak of the *Sitz im Leben* of the original reader or readers of the Revelation, or at the very least the *Sitz im Leben* of an implied reader of the Revelation as the Brethren, the group in focus here, would indeed have understood that the book of Revelation was written by an author both to the earliest Christian readers and also to themselves.

16. For the purposes of this book the author of Revelation is referred to simply as "John," a name he gives himself in Rev 1:9. Specifically which "John" this might have been is unimportant in the context of the focus of this book.

Brethren authors discussed here. Both perceived themselves as persecuted groups, groups who needed to stand against the world, who needed to maintain faithfulness in suffering, and hopeful of a better world to come. This book explores some of that dynamic as readers and text interact.

DESCRIPTION OF REVELATION CHAPTERS 17 AND 18

The references to Babylon in Revelation chapters 17 and 18 present an image of Babylon as an anti-Christian power. Babylon is a symbol of something highly unpleasant. She is portrayed as both a woman and a city. Yet she is no ordinary woman; she is a whore and a fornicator. This use of sexual corruption and promiscuity fits well enough into the Old Testament world with which the author was so familiar, as one finds there, in books such as Hosea, that prostitution and promiscuity are used as metaphors to represent unfaithfulness to God.[17] "Babylon" has not only prostituted herself, but is responsible also for giving birth to all forms of whoredom, being identified as the "Mother of Harlots" and the "mother of the abominations" of the earth. Yet, intriguingly, the precise identity of this Babylon figure is also something of a mystery and a paradox. John tells us what she looks like as a woman. She is adorned with precious and costly materials, but yet she is also filthy. She rides the scarlet-colored beast with seven heads and ten horns symbolizing her authority over them; and yet she is hated by the ten horns of the beast she is riding. The horns of the beast shall make her desolate and naked, and they shall eat her flesh and burn her (Rev 17:16). She has glorified herself, lived deliciously, yet despite her judgment she still believes in her heart that she is a queen and not a widow.

John also identifies Babylon as a place, not just a woman. She is a city, a great city, which reigns over the kings of the earth. John also tells us the nature of her sins. She has deceived the nations by her sorcery; she is drunk on the blood of the saints, the martyrs, the apostles, the prophets, God's servants and "all that were slain upon the earth." She has fallen, she has become the place were devils, foul spirits and unclean and hateful birds reside. She is a center of trade not only for all luxury items but also she trades in the souls of men. John tells us of her ultimate future: she will be judged severely. God's judgment will be the plagues of death, mourning, famine and fire, which shall all come in just one day. The very kings who destroy her will mourn over her destruction because they were made rich by her. Her destruction will be rejoiced over by the people of God for they have been avenged. Finally, John tells the reader of how the people of God must

17. On this, see "'Whoring' in the Book of Revelation and the Old Testament" below.

respond to Babylon. They are to "come out of her" and must not partake of her sins lest they "receive her plagues" (Rev 18:4).

It is apparent then that in the book of Revelation the figure of Babylon is a force opposed to God and the church and, whatever it might have meant in its original context, such rich and enticing symbolism is easy to apply to different situations. Thus it is hardly surprising that the Christians of the first few centuries of the Common Era applied it to the pagan, imperial Roman Empire, the entity that was opposed to their own life setting,[18] whereas the Protestant Reformers of the mid-sixteenth century found in such rich symbolism an image of Rome Papal, the source of suffering in their own experience.[19] As is shown in this book in some detail, the Brethren of the nineteenth century also took up the symbol of Babylon, in which they too saw something that they perceived as important in their own *Sitz im Leben*.

BABYLON IN THE OLD TESTAMENT

It is now well-established that the author of the book of Revelation was steeped in both the language and the literature of the Old Testament.[20] This being so, some account must be taken here of the appearance of "Babylon" in that material since a study might aid in understanding the use of the Babylon motif in Revelation and also the use that is made of the concept by the commentators here under review. This is not to say that the way in which "Babylon" is used in the Old Testament necessarily acted as a restraint on the use to which it could be put by the author of Revelation,[21] nor that the use of Babylon in Revelation restrained the imaginative use of it by later commentators. It might, however, provide some broader context of the study presented here.

18. See ch. 3 below.

19. See ch. 3 below.

20. While detail is not here needed it is relatively obvious that the author of Revelation used the Old Testament a great deal. The intertextuality is picked up by, among others, Brethren interpreters, as we shall note throughout this book. For a summary of some of the more general issues, see Charles, *Critical and Exegetical Commentary*, 1.xxi, and Ford, *Revelation*, 26–27. The question of exactly how the author of Revelation used the OT is a much more debated question. For recent studies, see Beale, *John's Use of the Old Testament*, and bibliography.

21. For the purposes of this book the point made by Moyise is relevant: "Every quotation is out of context because it has been relocated. It cannot possibly mean the same thing as it did in its old context because most of the factors that affect interpretation have changed," Moyise, *Old Testament in the Book of Revelation*, 140.

"Babylon" is mentioned throughout the whole of the Old Testament some 287 times.[22] A historical-critical examination of the use of the word "Babylon" in Old Testament Scripture reveals that while the concept begins chronologically as simply a geographical and historical entity, a kingdom that occasionally is friendly towards Israel but more often than not at war with her, in later Old Testament writings the meaning changes significantly, symbolic overtones have begun to develop, and Babylon begins in some way to become an archetype of the enemy of Yahweh's people.

In the Torah we read of the mythological accounts of how and why Babylon came into existence. The Yahwist writer tells us the story of the "Tower of Babel," the name given to the tower built in the land of Shinar after the Deluge. The writer hence provides a mythological narrative to account for the fact that his geographical neighbors speak a different language, and also why it is that humankind is divided into nations. This part of the biblical account states that it was as a result of Yahweh's anger that "confusion" came about, for it was Yahweh who defeated the design by "confounding" the builders' language. "Babylon" here is used with the meaning of "confusion." The ancient story also acts as a picture of human rejection of the rule of God and rebellion against the divine will. As we shall see, Brethren writers picked up on both of these Old Testament themes. "Babylon" was still "confusion" (but this time doctrinal) and it still represented a rejection of and rebellion against the word of God in Scripture.[23]

In the Hebrew Writings and Historical Books, we find information about the warfare of Babylon with Israel and also general historical and geographical information about the kingdom of Babylon. This is only to be expected, for, as von Rad has so convincingly demonstrated, from the earliest days of Israel's existence as a people, holy war was a sacred institution undertaken as a cultic act of a religious community.[24] While the Brethren writers make numerous references to Israel's warfare with Babylon, little importance is placed on such texts for the Brethren church, as the growing dispensational hermeneutic of, for example, John Nelson Darby, William Kelly, George Wigram, James Bellett, Edward Dennett and William Trotter,[25] consigned the importance of such scriptures to the Jewish people only and

22. This figure is based upon a key-word search of the KJV using the *Master Christian Library* software CD-ROM, version 6.02. Note that while most modern biblical scholars would not use the KJV in the context of an academic book, it is entirely appropriate to use that translation herein as the KJV would have been one of the translations used by the Brethren themselves during the time period this book is examining.

23. See ch. 7 below.

24. Rad, *Holy War in Ancient Israel*, 41–51.

25. Biographical details on these major Brethren authors can be found in ch. 4 below.

placed a great emphasis on distinguishing between the spiritual hopes and promises of the church in the present dispensation and the earthly hopes and promises of Israel in the past dispensation.

In the Prophets, for example, Isaiah, Jeremiah, Ezekiel, and Daniel, "Babylon" has begun to be understood in a highly symbolic way, prefiguring later Christian exegesis. The authors' understanding of Babylon clearly changes from being either a precritical explanation for semantic variety or a literal and geographical kingdom which threatens national security, to something more figurative and symbolic. This is hardly surprising of course given the *Sitz im Leben* of this material. The exilic and postexilic writers speak with a clear prophetic voice that utters a scathing indictment against the prevalent contemporary civilization in which they find themselves captive. The utter desolation of the city of Babylon is foretold by the prophets. Babylon will be destroyed by Yahweh. The destruction of the first temple, the ensuing captivity and desire for Israel to remain ethnically and religiously pure while subjugated in a foreign land and forced into idolatrous religious practice, found described in the Prophetic and Historical books of the Old Testament, leads to the identification of Babylon primarily as the one who destroyed the Jerusalem temple and took the people of God captive. Protestant Reformer Martin Luther of course famously picked up on this theme of exile in Babylon in his work *The Babylonian Captivity of the Church* (1520).[26] The Brethren writers also picked up on this theme. Hamilton Smith (1862–1943) writes that "the professing Church, as a whole, was, and still is, enslaved in Babylonish captivity."[27] As will become clear in this book, however, while the Brethren writers did pick up occasionally on such Old Testament references, it was without doubt the book of Revelation that was the primary source for their views on present-day "Babylon," a subject on which they had much to say.

For John, the author of Revelation, clearly drawing on the older traditions and writing after the year seventy Common Era and the destruction of the second temple in Jerusalem, the way that Babylon was understood changed yet again. Babylon became a code name for Rome, because Rome was the second city to destroy the temple. And as Babylon became "Rome," so, for Brethren writers, "Rome" became, among other things, "Apostate Christianity." Hence the symbolism is once again transferred.[28]

26. See ch. 3 below for more details.

27. Smith, *Haggai*, 4. See also Darby, "Notes on the Apocalypse," 101. See also Darby, "Thoughts on Romans 11," 499.

28. The use of the word Babylon as a cryptogram for Imperial Rome is examined in some detail in ch. 3. Whereas for Papias, Hippolytus, and Tertullian, Babylon was a symbol of Pagan Rome, in Brethren exegesis, Babylon becomes a symbol for Papal

"WHORING" IN THE BOOK OF REVELATION AND THE
OLD TESTAMENT

There is another concept in Revelation which, as we shall see, becomes very important to later interpreters, this is the concept of "whoring." This is particularly important since John often uses this concept in conjunction with the word Babylon. Hence it is not just "Babylon" that we read of, but the "Whore of Babylon." This is picked up by Brethren writers who conflate references to "Babylon," the "Great Whore," and the "harlot."

There is a clear Semitic context that needs to be kept in mind here and it was not lost on Brethren writers. The issue is however a little complicated for, as Charles has noted, in the book of Revelation in general, Hebraic as well as Greek or Aramaic linguistics are at work.[29] It is hence often difficult to be certain of the relevant semantics when dealing with the text. What is relatively plain, however, is that the author of Revelation is using the concept of "whoredom" and general sexual immorality in the well-worn Old Testament sense of religious apostasy.[30] Such language in Revelation takes the reader back to a number of Old Testament passages where Israel, Yahweh's chosen people, are described in similar terms and language because of their unfaithfulness to Yahweh (which will later be seen as the church's unfaithfulness to God). In Jeremiah 3:1–9, 5:7–31, and Ezekiel chapters 16–23, for example, the concept of harlotry became "a picture of Israel's apostasy from Yahweh."[31] The concept of whoredom and prostitution had here already taken on religious connotations and became a common form

---

Rome. See ch. 5 below.

29. Charles, *Critical and Exegetical Commentary*, 2.56. For Rev 17:1–10, the order of words is "Hebraic," for Rev 17:11–17 the order is "decidedly non-semitic . . . we are obliged to attribute [them] to a Greek or Aramaic linguistic sources."

30. Perhaps the best example of "whoredom" as religious infidelity to Yahweh in the Old Testament is to be found in the book of Hosea. Israel's unfaithfulness to Yahweh is described as fornication in Hos 2:2, 4; 3:3; 4:11, 14; and 6:11, and the act of following after false gods is described as "a-whoring" in Hos 2:5; 4:10, 12, 13, 14, 18; and 5:3. It is clear that by the time that John authored his apocalypse the concept of whoredom as an illicit activity, not only in a sexual but also in a spiritual and religious sense, was well established as a term of description. As many scholars have noted, John was clearly aware of the Old Testament antecedents found in Hosea, Jeremiah, Ezekiel, and elsewhere, which described Israel's religious infidelity as whoring after false gods, and it is even possible that in linking the words "whore" and "Babylon" together, John was aware of Babylon being the place where cultic prostitution was first found as a religious practice. This gave the opportunity to later writers to follow up on this Old Testament theme and use the link between religious infidelity and prostitution to castigate their own religious communities and the communities of those around them.

31. Reisser, "Porneuo," 499.

of description for the nation's religious infidelity. This will become important to later Christian commentators.

SUMMARY OF BOOK

Having sketched in some of the very general issues that are important in
dealing with this area of study into the *Wirkungsgeschichte* of Revelation
chapters 17–18, the rest of this book will be devoted to examining the use
made of these chapters and the Whore of Babylon motif in particular in
later Christian sources with an emphasis upon Brethren commentators.

The first chapter examines the five major approaches taken by those
who have sought to interpret Revelation.

Chapter 2 examines the closely related issues of the relationship between "texts and meanings." The purpose here is to give the broad history-
of-interpretation framework within which the interpreters examined in this
book were working and also to raise some of the critical issues related to the
use made of the text by those who read it, in this case the Brethren interpreters in particular.

Chapter 3 is an overview of the history of the exegesis of Revelation
chapters 17–18 which gives a more precise account of the trajectory leading up to the Brethren material. Here we shall note that in many ways the
Brethren did break some new ground, though in others they stayed within
the broad Protestant paradigm.

Chapter 4 provides a brief history of the Brethren movement including
an introduction to some of the key authors and some key doctrinal beliefs
held by the movement.

The archival section contains five chapters (chs. 5–9). It is here that
much of the original work of this book is presented. These chapters contain
a comprehensive and systematic survey of Brethren publications relating to
the Whore of Babylon theme. The chronological scale is ambitious: the work
stretches from the time when the first publications from Brethren authors
containing the word "Babylon" appeared (1829) until the turn of the twentieth century when interpretative exegetical principles operative within this
community had been established as fixed and normative (which is rather
surprising given that the movement had by now become rather fragmented).
The material surveyed here has primarily come from the Christian Brethren
Archive in the John Rylands University Library, Manchester, England, but
some material was also procured from the Sovereign Grace Advent Testimony Publishers in Chelmsford, England, the Chapter Two bookshop in
London, England, the Echoes of Service publishers in Bath, England, and

also three publications pertaining to Kelly not found in the archive were available in electronic format from Stem Publishing.

Throughout this book I argue that the Christian Brethren use the Whore of Babylon motif as a form of vituperative rhetoric. The Brethren vilify all other Christian traditions as "Babylon" in order to define the "self" on a religious level (chs. 5 and 6). On an epistemological level those with divergent doctrinal beliefs, both *extra muros* and *intra muros*, are defined as "Babylon" (ch. 7). On a secular level Babylon is used to vilify the "extreme outsider": the world, a place of pollution and contamination (ch. 8). The Brethren "secret rapture" doctrine developed as the direct result of a biological "fight or flight" response and a psychological "fear and fantasy" response to the Babylon motif (ch. 9). The ultimate application of Revelation 18:4, "come out of her," is not merely to leave the above noted interpretations of Babylon, but to be "raptured," to quit the earth altogether to meet Christ in the sky.

1

The Five Different Approaches
to Interpreting Revelation

Since the very earliest attempts to interpret the book of Revelation
through to the present day, expositors have differed not only with regards to the interpretation of specific motifs, words, phrases and concepts,
but also regarding the general hermeneutical framework that should be
used to interpret the book in the broadest sense. It is generally accepted
within the realm of New Testament studies that these various approaches to
exegesis can be classified into five main categories.[1]

A survey of the five main approaches to interpretation will enable us
to place Brethren exegesis in a historical context, and determine how their
method of interpretation is similar to or different from the broad stream of
interpretation that went before. It will also enable the Brethren to stand out
in more sharply focused relief against the background of other groups who
engaged in the exegesis of Revelation during the same time period.

CONTEMPORARY HISTORICAL-CRITICAL APPROACH

The first category is generally known as the contemporary historical-critical
approach. This mode of interpretation has been the dominant academic approach to the exegesis of the Apocalypse from the mid-nineteenth century
to the present day. Historical criticism is, in short, the attempt to see the text

---

1. See, e.g., Newport, *Apocalypse and Millennium*, 1–23. Kovacs and Rowland,
Revelation, 7–11. Wainwright, *Mysterious Apocalypse*.

within its own historical, social, political, cultural and intellectual setting, commonly referred to as the text's *Sitz im Leben*. The origins of the contemporary historical-critical approach are located within the broader context of changing views concerning the nature and place of Scripture that emerged during the Enlightenment period.

The approach is widely regarded as entering fully onto the academic agenda at the University of Tübingen when F. C. Baur was appointed professor of theology in 1826.[2] The historical-critical approach to Scripture generally, and the book of Revelation specifically, dominated academic and scholarly works on Revelation for most of the twentieth century, and even today continues to be a normative scholarly approach to biblical exegesis. Charles, for example, took just such an approach when, writing in the first quarter of the twentieth century, he noted that Revelation was not written by a single author, but that the book was written by two writers "related to each other, either as master and pupil, or as pupils of the same master, or as members of the same school."[3] These proto-authors he called "the Evangelist and the Seer."[4] The sources they compiled were woven together by the editor of the final redaction of the Apocalypse: "The author of J[ap] was a Palestinian Jew . . . a great spiritual genius, a man of profound insight,"[5] who died after editing together only the first twenty chapters of the book, leaving "a series of independent documents . . . put together by a faithful but unintelligent disciple in the order which he thought right"[6] to construct the final two chapters. For Charles, Babylon is to be identified quite simply as Rome,[7] since the source behind Revelation chapter 18 was written during the Vespasianic period, soon after the destruction of Jerusalem,[8] when "a considerable body of the faithful is presumed to be actually present in Rome."[9]

The source-critical form of historical-critical exegesis used by Charles emerged during the nineteenth and early twentieth century, and sought to uncover the various sources behind the Apocalypse. Such exegesis is generally rejected in recent studies in favor of reading the book as a work

---

2. For a study, see Harris, *Tübingen School.*

3. Charles, *Critical and Exegetical Commentary,* 1.xxix.

4. Ibid., 1.xxxiii.

5. Ibid., 1.xliv.

6. Ibid., 1.l.

7. Ibid., 2.87.

8. Ibid., 2.88.

9. Ibid., 2.93.

with inner cohesiveness, literal integrity and ideological unity,[10] which was certainly the way in which the Brethren commentators read it. However Massyngeberde Ford's *Revelation: A New Translation with Commentary* (1975) shows similarity to the earlier work of Charles in dividing up the text into its preexistent units. It is Ford's view that the Babylon motif has a historical application and relates to John's own day; it is a symbol of Apostate Jerusalem.[11] Her identification of Babylon as Jerusalem has not found widespread acceptance within the academic community.[12] David Aune, for example, continuing in the historical-critical tradition, in the *Word Biblical Commentary*, identifies Babylon as Rome, particularly in the form of the worship of *Dea Roma* and her cult.[13] Adela Y. Collins also suggests that Babylon is Rome, "not only the historical and physical city, but also what it stood for in the author's point of view: the goddess *Roma*, the claim of the Roman Empire to dominion over the earth, the inequities and violence" of Rome.[14] Richard Bauckham identifies Babylon in light of the historical-critical purpose of Revelation and *Sitz im Leben* of the group to whom it was originally addressed, suggesting that the Babylon motif is a

> prophetic critique of the political idolatry and economic oppression intrinsic to Roman power in the late first century, and as a call to its readers to bear witness to the truth and righteousness of God in the specific circumstances—religious, political, social and economic—in which they lived in the cities of the Roman province of Asia.[15]

Thus for Bauckham, Revelation chapter 18 is not only a religious and social polemic, but also a political and economic critique of Rome and in fact "one of the most effective pieces of political resistance literature from the period of the early empire."[16] Gregory K. Beale's *New International Greek Testament Commentary on the Book of Revelation* (1999) follows the trend suggesting that the Apocalypse was written during the reign of Domitian, around 95 CE,[17] and he concludes with Bauckham that Babylon is the Rome

---

10. Bauckham, *Climax of Prophecy*, x.

11. Ford, *Revelation*, 27, 54–55.

12. See, however, Beagley, *Sitz im Leben*, 179–80.

13. Aune, *Revelation*, 928, 1012.

14. Collins, "Apocalypse," 1012.

15. Bauckham, *Climax of Prophecy*, xii–xiii.

16. Ibid., 338.

17. Beale, *Book of Revelation*, 4, 27.

of that time noting that in "John's day the Roman Empire represented this wicked system."[18]

Further examples of historical-critical interpretations of the Babylon motif in the book of Revelation could easily be assembled. However, such is not necessary to this book, for already the broad contours of the historical-critical exegetical method have been outlined and it is thus possible already to set the Brethren rejection of such an approach in context. The kinds of interpretation that have been sketched in above were coming into prominence during the period with which this book is concerned. The historical-critical approach was by definition critical and antisupernaturalistic and did not appeal to Brethren writers, indeed, the Brethren writers saved some of their most vitriolic and polemical words for an attack upon it. They were certainly aware of contemporary historical-critical interpreters: Prominent Brethren author William Kelly names Strauss, Baur, Weizsacker and Meyer [*sic*, Meier].[19] Regarding Old Testament historical-critical exegesis he wrote,

> The learned follies of Tübingen have justly aroused in all foreign countries a dislike of German-knowledge! . . . Of the new school of critics generally, we may say without exaggeration . . . that their principle consists in believing everything but the truth, and exactly in proportion to want of evidence; or, to use the words of a poet, "In making windows that shut out the light, and passages that lead to nothing."[20]

Kelly's mentor and friend Darby completely rejected the historical-critical method, too. His disdain for the hermeneutics of the Tübingen School can be clearly seen as he states,

> The writers of the Baur or Tübingen school . . . [are] merely part of a progressive effort, not simply to undermine the authority of the New Testament history, but to do so by the invention of a system already seen through and refuted as alike historically unfounded and absurd . . . [it] has demonstrated the animus of the inventors and their untrustworthiness in every respect.[21]

Clearly, then, the Brethren movement strongly rejected such an approach to interpreting the Apocalypse. They are not alone, throughout the

---

18. Ibid., 924. We may conclude that Babylon, as a symbol of Imperial Rome, is the standard view in historical-critical circles; see also Sweet, *Revelation*, 264, and Bauckham, *Climax of Prophecy*, 345.

19. Kelly, *Exposition of the Gospel of John*, 482–83; see also 178. Kelly, *Exposition of the Gospel of Mark*, vi. Cf. Harris, *Tübingen*, 44, 133, 147n26.

20. Kelly, *Exposition of the Book of Isaiah*, 77.

21. Darby, "Miracles and Infidelity," 307, 301.

history of the Christian church, expositors have sought to find a hermeneutical method that will effectively unravel the meaning of Revelation
and make its abstract and at times strange images applicable to everyday
Christian life including their own. As Luz has noted: "A major problem of
historical-critical exegesis today lies in isolating a text in its own time . . .
thus preventing it from speaking to the present . . . to keep historical-critical
distance is . . . an attempt at avoiding the reality of life."[22]

HISTORICIST OR CHURCH HISTORICAL APPROACH

The second type of exegetical framework for interpreting Revelation is generally known as the Historicist School of prophetic interpretation, or sometimes as the "Church-Historical" method. This method of interpretation
suggests that Revelation is an outline or panorama of the whole of world
history from the start of Christianity until the end of time. The sequence
of events in the Apocalypse are a prophetic blueprint outlining the major
events of world history from the time of its authorship until the end of time
itself, the judgment of the world, the establishment of the New Jerusalem
and eternal life for the saints. The historicist interpreter sees a "progres-
sive and continuous fulfilment of prophecy, in unbroken sequence, from
Daniel's day and the time of John, on down to the Second Advent and the
end of the age."[23]

This method of interpretation is generally accepted as originating in
the late twelfth century from the Calabrian monastic Joachim of Fiore (ca.
1135–1202).[24] Joachim perceived world history according to the pattern
of the Trinity, that is, as divided into three distinct ages or dispensations.
He called the three dispensations the "Age of Law," under the rule of God
Father, the "Age of Grace," which began with the birth of Jesus and ended
with the birth of St. Benedict (ca. 480–550), and the "Age of the Spirit," the
age in which Joachim lived, which was inaugurated by the establishment of
the Benedictine order, but would fully arrive in 1260 CE as the final chapters
of the apocalypse began to unfold.[25] In his three main works, *Expositio in*

22. Luz, *Matthew 1–7*, 96–97.

23. Froom, *Prophetic Faith*, 1.23. It is important to note at this stage of the book
that Froom was himself a Seventh-day Adventist, and it was his opinion that the "anti-
papal" interpretation of Rev 17–18 was right. Although some allowance must be made
for such views, the wealth of evidence that Froom brings to bear on the exegesis of these
chapters is impressive and the broad outline of what he suggests seems entirely secure.

24. See, e.g., Reeves, *Joachim of Fiore*, preface; Froom, *Prophetic Faith*, 1.690; Wainwright, *Mysterious Apocalypse*, 49; Cohn, *Pursuit of the Millennium*, 108.

25. See plate 21. Joachim, "Seven Headed Dragon," from the *Liber Figurarum*, MS.

Apocalypsim (1527),[26] *Liber Figurarum* (1953),[27] and *Liber Concordia Novi ac Veteris Testamenti* (1519),[28] it is clear that Joachim read the whole of the Bible, from Genesis to Revelation, as a chart of human history. The Apocalypse was considered by Joachim to be a blueprint with which he could outline the major events of world history. So, for example, Joachim found in the seven-headed dragon of Revelation 12:3–4, references to Muhammad (d. 632) as the fourth head and Saladin (ca. 1137–93) as the sixth head.[29]

The Historicist method of interpretation laid down by Joachim developed into the hermeneutic of choice within the later Protestant tradition. The reader of the Apocalypse, able to look at the signs or portents occurring in their own day and life experience, could turn to the Apocalypse and identify each contemporaneous event as an image or motif within the book. The images within Revelation thus act as "signposts" on the roadmap, to find out exactly where one stands in the course of world history; what has past, and what events are left to unfold before the end comes.[30] So, for example, in 1369, when Konrad Schmid was burned at the stake for heresy, his followers, the Thuringian flagellant movement, turned to Revelation 11:3–11, and, using the Historicist method interpreted the event as being the fulfillment of the prophecy concerning two witnesses who were to preach against the antichrist, be killed by him and resurrected.[31] Then, later, in the eighteenth century the prophetess Joanna Southcott, upon receiving heavenly revelations concerning the war in France, naval mutinies and rotten harvests, turned to Revelation and used a Historicist method of exegesis to identify herself as the "Woman Clothed with the Sun" in Revelation chapter 12. She believed that she would give birth to "Shiloh" a "man child who would rule with a rod of iron" (Rev 12:5), and seal the 144,000 elect of Revelation chapter 7.[32]

255A, f.7r. in Reeves and Hirsch-Reich, *Figurae*, plate 21. For explanation, see 146–50.

26. I will be using Reeves, *Joachim of Fiore*; McGinn, *Calabrian Abbot*; and West and Zimdars-Swartz, *Joachim of Fiore* for references to Joachim's *Expositio in Apocalypsim* (1527) in this book.

27. I will be using the 47 plates attached as appendices in Reeves and Hirsch-Reid, *Figurae of Joachim of Fiore*, when referring to Joachim's *Figurae* in this book.

28. Joachim of Fiore, *Concordia Novi ac Veteris Testamenti*. This is a facsimile of an edition originally published in 1519.

29. Wainwright, *Mysterious Apocalypse*, 51.

30. Cornelius of Lapide in the early seventeenth century called Joachim "the founder of the method of historic parallels" and was aware of Joachim's interpretation of Revelation as foretelling "the whole history of the Church down to the Last Judgement." Lapide, in Reeves, 120.

31. Cohn, *Pursuit of the Millennium*, 145–46.

32. Brown, *Joanna Southcott*, 135–38, 252–58. Weber, *Apocalypses*, 114.

This view of Revelation, as a panorama of the whole of world history, has often been combined with a hermeneutical technique known as the "year-day" principle.[33] This interpretative method was based on a number of Old Testament passages such as Numbers 14:34: "forty years—one year for each of the forty days," and Ezekiel 4:6: "I have assigned you 40 days, a day for each year." Interpreting Revelation in light of such Old Testament texts as these led many people to try and calculate precisely when the end will come. So, for example, using the "year-day" principle Joachim predicted the culmination of the Apocalypse as occurring between 1200–1260 CE taking the "1,260 days" of Revelation 11:3 and Revelation 12:6 to mean 1,260 years (mistakenly taking the year zero for the birth of Christ as his starting point).[34] Whereas in 1452 CE Nicholas of Cusa predicted the End of the Age for the year 1741 CE by using Daniel 8:14, "Unto two thousand and three hundred days; then shall the sanctuary be cleansed," which according to the "year-day" principle means 2,300 years. Cusa calculated that the 2,300 years began in 559 BCE when he presumed Daniel's vision had taken place, thus when the latter is subtracted from the former, a date 1741 CE is achieved.[35] William Miller, founder of the Seventh-day Adventist movement, interpreted the 2,300 days of Daniel 8:14 according to the "year-day" principle as 2,300 years, the seventy weeks of Daniel 9:23–27 as 490 years, and the 1,260 days of Revelation 11:3 and 12:6 as 1,260 years. This led him to predict first 1843 CE then 1844 CE as the year of Christ's return.[36]

A second common feature of the Historicist school of prophetic interpretation is that many interpreters who use this model try to identify the Antichrist according to their own *Sitz im Leben*. As this hermeneutical framework was a predominantly Protestant tool, the Antichrist was usually identified as Rome in either pagan but more usually papal forms,[37] although Muslims, Jews, Napoleon and Hitler were all identified as the antichrist by Historicists who sought to understand the evil actions of individuals in their own day in light of the Apocalypse's prophecies. So, for example, during the sixteenth-century Reformation, Martin Luther believed both the pope and the Turk to be the antichrist,[38] whereas Serafino da Fermo (1469–1540 CE), reformer of the Canons Regular of the Lateran Congregation, drawing

33. Froom, *Prophetic Faith*, 4.206.

34. Reeves and Hirsch-Riech, 137. Reeves, 35.

35. Weber, 36.

36. Froom, *Prophetic Faith*, 4.689–93.

37. Ibid., 3:252–53; 4:1191.

38. Luther, *Luther's Works*, 54:46, 346.

directly on Joachim's Historicist hermeneutic,[39] in an interesting counter-historicist twist, suggested that Luther was the star which fell from heaven in Revelation 8:10, which turned the waters bitter and caused many to die, and also the Beast from the land in Revelation 13:11 who "spake like a dragon."[40] In the twentieth century, Otto Pankok and Nathaniel Micklem identified Hitler and Nazi Germany as the Antichrist during World War II.[41] More recently, the eschatological "Jews for Jesus" group identified Saddam Hussein as the Antichrist in the 1990s. They suggested that the ancient city of Babylon would be literally rebuilt and the Jews would be led back into Babylonian captivity,[42] a view that some of the Brethren authors held themselves a century earlier.[43]

The final common feature of the Historicist school of biblical interpretation is that it presupposes a belief in the literal visible bodily second coming of Jesus. Such belief comes from the literal acceptance of such eschatological passages as Matthew 26:24, 2 Thessalonians 1:7, 2 Peter 3:10, and 1 John 2:28. In particular 1 Thessalonians 4:16–17 may be noted:

> For the Lord himself shall descend from heaven with a shout, with the voice of the archangel, and with the trump of God: and the dead in Christ shall rise first: Then we which are alive and remain shall be caught up together with them in the clouds, to meet the Lord in the air: and so shall we ever be with the Lord.

Regarding the above verses, Adam Clarke, a prominent biblical scholar of the Wesleyan Holiness tradition, writing between 1810 and 1826 CE, commented, "Jesus Christ shall descend from heaven; shall descend in like manner as he was seen by his disciples to ascend, i.e. in his human form, but now infinitely more glorious."[44] This view is reflected both in the fourth-century Nicene Creed and the sixteenth-century Augsburg Confession, article 17. Joachim in the twelfth century, accepting the biblical account as literal, believed that Christ would physically return to the earth to personally destroy the antichrist.[45] The same adventist beliefs, that is, belief in a literal, physical and visible return of Christ at the end of the age, are held in the twenty-first century by Seventh-day Adventists, Jehovah's Witnesses

---

39. Reeves, 125.

40. Wainwright, 61.

41. Ibid., 175.

42. Boyer, *When Time Shall Be No More*, 330.

43. See ch. 8 below.

44. Clarke, *Commentary on the NT*, 8.34.

45. Froom, *Prophetic Faith*, 1.709.

and many fundamentalist or evangelical Bible-believing Christians in the Western world.[46]

There are elements of the "Church-Historical" method of exegesis that can be found in the exegesis of the Brethren interpreters, the most obvious being that of dispensationalism. Key Brethren author John Nelson Darby renewed the tendency to divide the history of the world up into distinct eras or epochs in his day, just as Joachim had in his own day.[47]

The Brethren also had some commonality of exegesis with the "Church-Historical" school in their adherence to the belief in a literal, physical and visible advent of Christ. Thus Darby writes, in concord with Wesleyan interpreter Adam Clarke, that Christ will visibly appear: "looking for that blessed hope, and the appearing of the glory of our great God and Saviour."[48] The view is reiterated by Brethren author William Trotter who writes of the Second Coming as "the descent of the Lord Jesus into the air,"[49] and "the second coming, the appearing in glory, of our Lord Jesus Christ . . . the grand event which is before us; an event to which the Christian indeed and the Church may look forward with intense desire and expectation."[50] As we shall see in chapter 9, the literal belief in a second coming of Christ in the Brethren movement took a novel expression and was influenced in part by the group's exegesis of the Babylon motif.

It must be pointed out though that a belief in a literal physical advent was commonplace in the nineteenth century and that a literal interpretation of Revelation was accepted without critical question regardless of hermeneutical method at that time (with the exception of those within the Historical-Critical School). The Christian Brethren cannot be adequately described simply as belonging to the Church-Historical School of interpreters since they differ from the Protestant hermeneutical method on a number of important points, for example, the Brethren interpreters refrained both from attempting to identify the Antichrist and predicting possible dates for the end of the world. Perhaps more importantly, however, many Brethren

---

46. In the Seventh-day Adventist church: "The Saviour's coming will be literal, personal, visible, and worldwide." See General Conference of Seventh-day Adventists, *Seventh-day Adventists Believe*, 332. The Jehovah's Witnesses believe that Christ's Second Advent has already occurred in 1914 but this was an invisible event. The sect awaits a third visible return of Christ some point in the future and in America. See Longley, *Chosen People*, 254.

47. See, e.g., Darby, "Evidence from Scripture," 149–50. Extensive commentary on Darby's dispensational exegesis found throughout the latter part of this book.

48. Darby, "Fragmentary Thoughts," 357–58.

49. Trotter, "Apocalyptic Interpretation," 356.

50. Trotter, "Approaching Judgments," 25.

interpreters simply did not believe that Revelation was being fulfilled in the present Dispensation. For Brethren authors like Darby, the present age was devoid of any prophetic fulfillment for the church. Darby writes that "the Revelation treats of no part of the present dispensation which is yet fulfilled, though the things spoken of be distinctively characteristic of it; and that which thus distinctively characterizes it as altogether future."[51]

Those interpreters who do apply the fulfillment of Revelation's prophecy to their own time, such as the interpreters in the "Church-Historical" School, are according to Darby, adhering to a perverse outlook. He writes, "I deprecate a morbid disposition to apply all things to our own times."[52] While prominent Brethren author William Kelly, aware of Edward Bishop Elliott's *Horae Apocalypticae* (1844), a standard and comprehensive exegesis of Revelation according to the Historicist schema, stated that such an interpretation is clearly wrong. As the "Church-Historical" method tends to see Revelation as being continuously fulfilled throughout time, such a view led Elliott to believe that the discovery of America and Australia had been predicted in Revelation 10:2. Concerning this Kelly writes, "The late Mr. E. B. Elliott . . . imagined that there is a more direct allusion to the discovery of America, if not of Australasia, in Revelation 10:2 . . . He naturally says little, and is somewhat indefinite, but as usual confident."[53] Kelly clearly believed that the "Church-Historical" hermeneutic was an exegetically false system, stating that "no ingenuity can make these revealed facts fit into the Protestant interpretation, as I showed many years ago in reviewing the last edition of Mr. Elliott's *Horae Apoc.*"[54] Brethren exegesis of Revelation does not neatly fit into this hermeneutical model of interpretation.

PRETERIST APPROACH

The third method of interpreting the Apocalypse is known as the Preterist School of prophetic interpretation, taking its name from the Latin *praeter* meaning past. The method of exegesis first appeared in connection with the Spanish Jesuit Alcazar (1554–1613 CE) who initially developed some of its details as a Catholic counter-reformation response to the growing popularity in Protestant circles of the historicist framework in his work *Vestigatio Arcani Sensus in Apocalypsi* (1615).[55]

51. Darby, "Examination of the Statements," 12.
52. Darby, "On 'Days' Signifying 'Years,'" 60.
53. Kelly, "Answers to Questions," *BT*, N1.47.
54. Kelly, "Answers to Questions," *BT*, N1.319.
55. Alcazar, *Vestigatio Arcani Sensus in Apocalypsi*, in Froom, *Prophetic Faith*,

Alcazar, drew attention to the words of Jesus as found in Luke 21:32, "This generation will not pass away, till all be fulfilled," and used this text to argue that most of the prophecies in the Apocalypse had been fulfilled in the first few Christian centuries. Thus, for many Preterists, the prophetic meaning of Revelation is principally only applicable to the early church,[56] although some Preterists would argue that a small percentage, that material contained in the closing two chapters of the book, awaits fulfillment in the future.

For the Preterist, Revelation had its primary function in counseling and encouraging the needs of the early Christians through the suffering and persecution that they were experiencing, as such there is little future eschatology in the book whatsoever and hence, the Preterist, sees little meaning in the Apocalypse for the church of today.

Although Preterism was mainly a Catholic method of interpretation, for the Dutch theologian Hugo Grotius (1583–1645 CE) and the English commentator Henry Hammond (1605–1660 CE), both of whom were Protestants, the millennium had begun with the conversion of Constantine and ended in 1300 CE and as such the period they lived in was one devoid of prophetic fulfillment.[57]

The Christian Brethren interpreters were not Preterists, although they, for different reasons, understood the present dispensation as an age devoid of any prophetic fulfillment for the church. They were, however, looking forward for a future millennium to begin. Such a "Catholic" hermeneutic could never be accepted by a community who believed Catholicism to be utterly corrupt and such incorrect doctrine to be highly contagious. William Kelly, for example, writes, "Why then waste time in the shallow fields of Germanising Praeterists?"[58] In fact Kelly considered the Preterist School of interpretation to be worse than the Historicist, and regarding the correct identification of Rome as the Whore of Babylon, rejected both "Church-Historical" and Preterist hermeneutics, stating, "There is therefore much truth in the Protestant application of the chapter, as compared with the Praeterist theory of pagan Rome. Yet it will be found imperfect, for reasons which ought to be clear to unbiassed and spiritual minds."[59] Further, Kelly comments on Preterist interpreter Bousset's entry on "antichrist" in *The*

2.507–10.

56. Kovacs and Rowland, *Revelation*, 10.

57. Wainwright, 63.

58. Kelly, *Lectures on the Book of Revelation*, 183.

59. Kelly, *Lectures Introductory . . . Acts*, 542.

Encyclopaedia Britannica and states that "any preterist or historical interpretation is out of the question."[60]

Thus it is clear that the Christian Brethren interpreters rejected the contemporary historical-critical approach, the "Church-Historical" approach and the Preterist approach to interpreting the book of Revelation, although elements of each are found in later Brethren writers.

FUTURIST APPROACH

The fourth approach to understanding Revelation is known as the Futurist School of Prophetic Interpretation. This interpretation locates, either in a consecutive or recapitulatory way, the fulfillment of prophecies from Revelation 4:1, "things which must be hereafter," onward in the time of the end, when antichrist will personally appear and there will be a last great apostasy. The prophecies of Revelation from chapter 4:1 to the very end of the book are all projected into a remote age to come.[61]

This interpretation is widely regarded as being founded by Jesuit priest Francisco Ribera (1537–1591 CE). Futurism was a method of exegesis developed by the Jesuits as a counter response to the historicism of the Protestant Reformation which sought to place all the negative symbolism of the Apocalypse, such as "Whore of Babylon," and "antichrist," on the pope and Roman Catholicism without falling into the counter-historicism of such Catholic exegetes as Serafino da Fermo.[62] The Historicist account of the Apocalypse had become a form of antipapalism, an exegetical stick in the hand of the Protestant interpreters with which to bash the bishops of Rome. The "year-day" principle in association with the historicist model had also led to the historicists trying to calculate the day of the *parousia*. This was a pitfall that the futurists tried to avoid, and in doing so drew attention to such scriptures as Matthew 24:36, "But of that day and hour knoweth no man, no, not the angels of heaven, but my Father only," and also Matthew 24:42, "Ye know not what hour your Lord doth come."[63]

Rather than antichrist being a succession of popes throughout the ages, as held in the historicist schema, Ribera suggested that an individual antichrist would reign for three and a half years at the end of time, just before the end of the age would come. The antichrist would be an individual Jew from the tribe of Dan who would set himself up as the Messiah in the

60. Kelly, *Exposition on the Gospel of John*, 505.

61. Froom, *Prophetic Faith*, 1.89.

62. See the "Historicist" approach above.

63. See also Mark 13:32 and Luke 12:46.

temple at Jerusalem.[64] Ribera believed Rome was mentioned in the Apocalypse but that this referred only to a final apostasy by the Jewish antichrist in Rome (definitely not the pope) at the end of time.

Cardinal Bellarmine (1542–1621 CE) developed the futurist interpretation of Ribera through his vehement opposition of the "year-day" principle that seemed so integral to the historicist framework of interpretation. Bellarmine turned his attention to the much-cited text of Ezekiel chapter 4, which was commonly used as an evidence for the principle. Bellarmine replied to the historicists that Ezekiel could not have remained on his side for 390 years as this time period was outside the life period of one man. In the same way, antichrist could not reign for 1260 literal years as this is again outside the parameters of a single man's life, and must refer symbolically to three and a half years. Antichrist must be, therefore, an individual figure and not a millennium of papal antichristian rule, as suggested by the Protestants, as the length of his rule is in harmony with the life of an individual, not 1260 years. The antichrist would be, maintaining Ribera's view, an individual Jew, but his time had not yet arrived. Bellarmine turned to Daniel 12:11: "And from the time that the daily sacrifice shall be taken away, and the abomination that maketh desolate set up, there shall be a thousand two hundred and ninety days." Antichrist would destroy the daily sacrament of the Roman mass, thus he would be an anti-papal figure, but this would not occur until the very last three and a half years of world history.[65]

Another Jesuit scholar, Cornelius of Lapide (1567–1637), suggested that the popular Protestant identification of the pope as antichrist was ridiculous, and that if antichrist really meant "vicar of Christ," as suggested by a number of Protestant interpreters, then Saints Peter and Paul, and all the Apostles were all antichrists too![66]

Thomas Malvenda (1566–1628 CE), a Dominican scholar, appealed to the authority of tradition, citing the church fathers such as Jerome, Cyril, Augustine, Bede and others, who were all expecting an individual Jewish antichrist to arrive on the scene just before the world ended. He also strongly resisted the Protestant penchant for using the "year-day" principle as a method of guessing when the end would come.[67]

Although, in general, futurists understand prophecy as projected into a remote age to come, some events may have occurred or may be already

64. Froom, *Prophetic Faith*, 2.488.

65. Newport, *Apocalypse and Millennium*, 76; Kovacs and Rowland, *Revelation*, 212; Froom, 2.496–98.

66. Froom, *Prophetic Faith*, 2.504.

67. Ibid., 505.

occurring, and as such, for some, the futurism is in some sense inaugurated. For example, Ribera, while maintaining a highly futuristic exegesis of Revelation, followed in the footsteps of Augustine in suggesting that the millennium had already been inaugurated, beginning with Christ's birth and extending until the last days.

The Benedictine Bishop of Rama, Charles Walmesley writing under the pseudonym Signor Pastorini, published his *General History of the Christian Church, from her Birth to her final triumphant State in Heaven, chiefly deduced from the Apocalypse of St. John the Apostle* (1771). In it he developed further the futurist view of Revelation. We read:

> The Book of the Apocalypse, according to that learned interpreter of the Scriptures, St. Jerom [*sic*], contains an infinite number of mysteries relating to future times . . . Some modern writers hold the same opinion. Besides these authorities, our own study of that mysterious book, diligently pursued, has entirely prevailed upon us to expound the same sentiment.[68]

Walmsley, although generally holding a futurist hermeneutic, believed that some events of the Apocalypse were being fulfilled in his own time and that other events were to be fulfilled imminently, thus he writes, "Every Christian must take in that part of the history which relates to the present time, and to those scenes which are approaching."[69] Thus although it is clear that Walmsely was a futurist, his futurism was in some sense inaugurated, that is, the future events had already begun to unfold in the present.

In the modern period futurism has become the predominant hermeneutical framework in twentieth-century North American fundamentalism. On a popular level this kind of "inaugurated futurism" can be seen in the multimillion selling novels by Hal Lindsey, of which *Late Great Planet Earth* (1970), the first of twelve, is probably the most well known. Here he interprets the narrative of Revelation, according to the inaugurated futurist hermeneutic. Such events as the tension between America and Arab nations in the Middle East was seen by Lindsey as an indicator that the Apocalypse is shortly to be fulfilled. With regards to the creation of the Jewish State of Israel in 1948 CE, Lindsey refers to the words of Jesus in Matthew 24:34: "This generation shall not pass, till all these things be fulfilled." Lindsey then comments,

68. Pastorini, [pseud.] Walmsely, *General History*, iii. Newport describes Walmsley as "counter-historicist," although, as will become apparent, the term "inaugurated futurism" is perhaps a better way of describing his interpretive scheme. See Newport, *Apocalypse and Millennium*, 81.

69. Pastorini, xxiii.

What generation? Obviously, in context, the generation that would see the signs—chief among them the rebirth of Israel. A generation in the Bible is something like forty years. If this is a correct deduction, then within forty years or so of 1948, all these things could take place. Many scholars who have studied Bible prophecy all their lives believe that this is so.[70]

Regarding the nuclear capabilities of Russia and the political aspirations of Communist China, identified as the nations Gog and Magog of Revelation 20:8, Lindsey writes, "The current build-up of Russian ships in the Mediterranean serves as another significant sign of the possible nearness of Armageddon."[71] Lindsey follows Ribera, Bellarmine and Malvenda in identifying the antichrist as a discreet individual and identifies two intriguing figures who will rise up at the end time: the Antichrist and the False Prophet. One will rule over the United European Powers and the other will be found in Israel. They will make a treaty with each other and bring in a peace for a short time. Lindsey, like Ribera, believed that the antichrist would rebuild the temple in Jerusalem: "Obstacle or no obstacle," he writes, "it is certain that the Temple will be rebuilt. Prophecy demands it."[72]

Such "popular" apocalyptic futurism still captures the public imagination. Currently, LaHaye and Jenkins, whose *Left Behind Series* has spawned a movie, an official website, a clothing company, and audio, video and DVD products, promote the inaugurated futuristic interpretation of the Apocalypse to an enormous fan base. Throughout the series we see events occurring with "apocalyptic" undertones: precursors to a final and future end of time. Overall LaHaye and Jenkins paint a picture in their novels of an imminent but "not quite yet" end of the world. The antecedents to the final end have begun to occur, but the worst awaits the reader in the future. These novels represent the most recent significant occurrence of the inaugurated futurist exegesis of Revelation.

The Brethren interpreters followed a modified and inaugurated Futurist method of exegesis. As has been mentioned earlier, the Brethren community divided the world up into epochs or eras, which is the heart of the dispensational view of history that they adopted. However, as will become clear in this book, the Brethren approach to prophecy as a whole is considerably more complicated than has been traditionally allowed. As we shall see later, the Brethren understanding of the Whore of Babylon motif in particular, introduces clear historicist elements into the exegetical

70. Lindsey, *Late Great Planet Earth*, 54.

71. Ibid., 145–46.

72. Ibid., 56.

methodology, hence, while futurism was in general the approach adopted, on some particular points other approaches to the book of Revelation can be seen to have had their influence. What is more, the precise details of the futurism adopted by Brethren authors were relative to their own historical context, and in places quite unique. This included a belief in the restoration of the Jewish nation, and most particularly the development of the doctrine of the secret rapture of the church. They also had a particularly nuanced version of the anti-papal identification of Babylon which will become clear in what follows.

IDEALIST APPROACH

The final way that biblical expositors have attempted to interpret Revelation is known as the Idealist School of prophetic interpretation. This method of exegesis is also known as the Triumphalist or Symbolic interpretation. It is marginally unimportant in the context of this book, since it was not a method that appears to have had much impact on Brethren authors.

The idealist interpretation of the Apocalypse understands the narrative as offering abiding moral and spiritual principles which are applicable in every age of the history of Christianity. The whole of the book is an allegorical and symbolic message of the struggle between the forces of good and the forces of evil in the world. It describes in symbolic language the struggle between Christianity and her religious and social enemies, yet ultimately, throughout all the symbolism of oppression the book contains a message of hope; that Christ is the victor. In this understanding, the contents of the book are not seen to relate to any historical events at all, but only to symbolize the ongoing struggle between good and evil during the church age until Christ returns. Among the kinds of interpreters dealt with in this book idealism has never achieved the popularity of the four other schools (contemporary historical-critical, historicist, preterist and futurist).[73]

73. On idealism, see further Newport, *Apocalypse and Millennium*, 15; Wainwright, *Mysterious Apocalypse*, 13, 38, 203–11; and Kovacs and Rowland, *Revelation*, 28–29, 56–57, 144–45. The method goes back a long way, perhaps as early as Victorinus of Pettau (d. ca. 303 CE), who in *De Fabrica Mundi* encourages the development of an allegorical and spiritual interpretation of Revelation. Tyconius (d. ca. 390 CE) also promoted an idealist interpretation of Revelation in which he focused on the narrative as a metaphor for the relationship between Christ and the Church. See Simonetti, *Biblical Interpretation*, 97. The method continues to inform the work of some contemporary scholars: e.g., Maier, *Apocalypse Recalled*, x, 38; Boesak, *Comfort and Protest*, 38; and Schüssler Fiorenza, *Revelation*.

2

Texts and Meaning

As has been shown above one of the many ways in which the figure of Babylon has been interpreted is as a symbol of "confusion."[1] It is perhaps ironic, then, that the variety of interpretative methods which one might apply to the Apocalypse have themselves led to a great deal of confusion over the very meaning of this text!

As has also been shown, there are five basic methods which have been adopted by those seeking to interpret the book of Revelation. All of which have all been put forward as the "correct" way to interpret the text. Expositors representing each of the above hermeneutical models claim that they know the truth; that they have the key to understanding what the text really means. The implications of this are that either one method is correct and the others are wrong, or, in some way, the variety of interpretative models means that the text is somehow flexible and open to more than one, or potentially any number, of various interpretations.

Here attention will be given to theories of interpretation and hermeneutics, and to two key questions which need to be addressed: is it the author who places the meaning into the text (which the reader then needs to unlock in order to discover the meaning)? Or is it the reader who decides or imposes the meaning on the text? Seeking to address these questions will help to determine the relationship between the text of Revelation, its author and its readers. In the immediate context of this book such a theoretical discussion will help to determine whether Brethren readers of the text can

---

1. See above, "Babylon in the Old Testament."

be said to be truly involved in exegesis (that is bringing the meaning "out" of a text) or in *eis*egesis (that is reading the meaning "into" the text).

Possibly the earliest example of how words and language have been understood is known as the "referential theory" of meaning; a hypothesis that postulates that the meaning of a word lies in the object to which it refers. Meaning is not merely a matter of subjective perception, or even of interpretation.[2] While the Enlightenment saw the rejection of Scripture and Tradition as sources of authority preferring experience and intellect as the basis of meaning, noncritical, nonacademic, popular biblical exegesis was often still based, in the commentaries and sermons of interpreters such as the Brethren, on the referential theory of meaning. The Brethren believed that it was not only the author who had placed meaning into the text, which the reader could actually extract, but also, through the belief in the dual-authorship of Scripture, that God himself had placed the meaning there.

READER-RESPONSE THEORIES OF MEANING

In the postmodern age the way biblical texts have been understood has radically changed. It is no longer possible for modern biblical scholars simply to believe, as did the Christian Brethren interpreters of the nineteenth century, that a text has a single fixed meaning which God placed there.

One of the methodological responses to the challenge of postmodernism to traditional biblical interpretive theory was that of reader-response theory. This approach contends that "readers" or "interpretative communities" are the ultimate determiners of the text's meaning and not the original author's intention in that text. Hence McKnight writes,

> This approach [reader-response] views literature in terms of its reader's values, attitudes and responses, thus supplementing or displacing approaches to literature that focus on either the universe imitated in the work, the author, the original audience, or the work itself. The nature and role assigned the reader may vary however according to the critical theory being used and the implicit or explicit worldview of which the theory is a central part.[3]

Reader-response theory is a postmodern hermeneutical method insofar as the notion that there is one correct meaning contained within a text is rejected. Instead it is held that texts are open to more than one meaning.

2. Evans, "Meaning," 436.
3. McKnight, "Reader-Response Criticism," 370–73.

Each of the hermeneutical methods of interpreting the Apocalypse sketched in above approach the text with a form of cognitive absolutism and objectivism. In other words, the interpreter takes a metaphysical stand and claims to recognize absolute truth, historically invariable and unconditioned. Whereas the contemporary historical-critical approach might reduce this interpretation to several statements, such as representatives of each epoch, or each culture, are the possessors of their own truth, according to reader-response theory, truth as a whole, in a postmodern world, is always open and incomplete; no one can claim that his or her hermeneutical method is exclusive.

The literature devoted to such issues is significant and no attempt to deal with it all is here made. One example is Richard Rorty's *Objectivity, Relativism and Truth* (1991) in which Rorty ridiculed such "representational" truth claims—claims of objectivity or finality—as fictional "sky hooks," and advocated an abandonment of "the search for Truth" altogether.[4] Such a position has obvious consequences for those interpreting the book of Revelation. Thus for example it would not be possible for Alcazer to assert confidently that the Preterist method of interpreting the Apocalypse is the only way to unlock the truth within, or for Ribera to contend that the Futurist hermeneutic is the key to discovering the meaning of the Apocalypse. Even the historical-critical interpreters, in their endeavor to discover the meaning of the text in its historical *Sitz im Leben*, are attempting to find the mythical Archimedean place outside of the phenomenological realm and assert that their hermeneutical method is essentially the key to finding meaning.

Gadamer's Hermeneutical Approach

The twentieth-century German hermeneutical philosopher H. G. Gadamer never wrote a commentary on the book of Revelation, but his insights into the intangible and normative transcendental character of truth, and his analysis of the understanding of texts, can prove useful to those who would discover meaning within the Apocalypse.

Gadamer suggests that in trying to understand a text, that is, in taking part in the hermeneutical exercise, we are engaging in an event or process geared towards finding truth. However, Gadamer goes on to note that when we arrive at a conclusion we are, as it were, too late. The truth is transcendent, beyond our grasp. As such Gadamer understands "the act of understanding itself as the movement of transcendence, of moving beyond

---

4. Rorty, *Objectivity, Relativism and Truth*, 13, 24.

things."[5] Building on K. Jaspers existentialist postmodern rejection of the Archimedean vantage point over truth, Gadamer writes, "The very idea of a situation means that we are not standing outside it and are hence unable to have any objective knowledge of it."[6]

One of the reasons is that the truth of particular statements always depends on the truthfulness of our own worldview which may change as frequently as the next paradigm shift in thought comes along. That is why from the hermeneutic point of view the task of understanding and interpretation which leads to meaning and truth always involves communication and dialogue among individuals, groups and cultures.[7] Yet Gadamer also highlights the idiosyncratic and intrinsic nature of truth and meaning when he states "all understanding is ultimately a self understanding."[8] Truth, for Gadamer, has an existential and personal dimension. His semantic examination of the German verb *Verstehen*, "to understand," uncovers its forensic origins and the original legalistic sense of the word used in asserting one's own standpoint in a law court. Therefore, Gadamer concludes, to understand is not only a dialogical process but also a personal process. Thus he suggests that a person who "understands" projects themselves into the text according to their own possibilities and experiences.[9]

The importance of Gadamer's hermeneutical theory in helping us elucidate how an interpreter might read Revelation goes beyond simply highlighting the transcendental and communicative yet simultaneously existential dimension of understanding texts. He has shown how the individual's understanding occurs in a larger historical and hermeneutical context. To do this Gadamer developed the notion of "effective historical consciousness" (*Wirkungsgeschichtliches Bewusstsein*). It is the conscious act of the fusion of old and new interpretations, of past and present understandings. It is "the fusion of horizons" that is the task of effective history, and it is only through this process that one arrives at an answer of "living value," an answer that is able to overcome the problems of hermeneutics noted above.[10] Effectively, Gadamer is putting forward a hermeneutical approach that takes seriously and gives sufficient weight and importance to both the variety of effects that a certain text may have had upon a tradition or individual and the multiplicity of interpretations that may have arisen

---

5. Gadamer, *Truth & Method*, 230.

6. Ibid., 269.

7. Ibid., 331, 347, and 419.

8. Ibid., 231.

9. Ibid.

10. Ibid., 273.

within that tradition diachronically. Thus the reader of the Apocalypse learns from Gadamer to both take seriously the effects that the text has had on its readers and also to listen to the variety of interpretations that have arisen from the reading of that book.

The starting place of understanding texts in this way is, for Gadamer, to be found in tradition. He accords great importance to the role of tradition and prejudice (*Vorurteil*) in any interpretation. Thus, for example, Gadamer writes,

> It is true that the interpretation process has to start somewhere, but it does not start just anywhere. It is not really a beginning . . . the hermeneutical experience always includes the fact that the text to be understood speaks in to a situation that is determined by previous opinions.[11]

Gadamer notes that "the prejudices we bring with us"[12] and the very traditions and backgrounds that we come from have an essential role to play in our understanding of texts. We cannot escape or get away from the past to read or interpret a text in a vacuum or isolation, but rather, as Warnke has noted concerning Gadamer's work, the effect and influence of the past has a realigning effect on our understanding in the present. She writes,

> We find ourselves in historical and cultural traditions that hand down to us the projections or hypotheses, the prejudices, in Gadamer's terminology . . . our understanding is oriented by the effective history or history of influences of that which we are trying to understand.[13]

Each prospective interpreter, each individual who seeks to understand and find meaning, must look to their own tradition. Each tradition has texts and works that belong to it. For the Catholic tradition this may include the Old and New Testament, the Apocrypha, the work of the church fathers and papal encyclicals. For the Christian Brethren this may include the biblical Scriptures as with Catholics, perhaps with a particular emphasis on prophetic parts, but involve a rejection of Apocryphal, Patristic and papal works, perhaps replaced with some of the publications that will be examined below by their highly esteemed founders, such as Kelly and Darby.

An interpretation of Scripture cannot simply involve an individual reading of the text but must include an awareness of every effect that that text has had on a tradition and the ways it has influenced the thoughts,

11. Ibid., 429.

12. Ibid., 273.

13. Warnke, "Hermeneutics, Ethics and Politics," 81.

beliefs, worldviews and practice of its members. The interpretations of the texts that we read do not arise out of the idiosyncratic autonomous will of the individual but are effectively bequeathed to us as a legacy of the tradition we stand in. They are an intrinsic part of our identity. As Taylor states in his work on Gadamer, "We are part of the 'effective history' (*Wirkungsgeschichte*) of this past, and as such it has a claim on us."[14]

If the insights Gadamer has given concerning truth and meaning are applied to the general question here of the relationship between the text and the reader, and to the specific question of the relationship between the Christian Brethren interpreters and Revelation chapters 17–18, one might conclude that it is not possible to limit the meaning of the text to the presumed opinion of its author. We must reject the referential theory of meaning. One cannot simply say, for example, St. John meant Imperial Rome when he described Babylon, or even Papal Rome for that matter. Finding the "real" meaning of a text is an existential act which involves both self-understanding and an awareness of our own experiences. One's history, tradition and prejudices will all effect the way in which the text is approached and understood. Thus Brethren writers will understand the text specifically within the context of their own worldview, a conceptual scheme which involved seceding from the established Anglican and Roman churches as well as segregating from Non-conformist and Dissenting movements. Discovering meaning involves awareness of the relationship between the reader and the world in which they read.

Above all to understand fully the text we need to be aware of the "effective history" of the text, the "history of the interpretation" of that text and then begin to develop a new horizon which fuses together both old and new interpretations. All understanding is in itself actually interpretive and hermeneutical, for "understanding and interpretation are ultimately the same thing."[15] To understand fully what the author of Revelation meant by Babylon one must take into account all the ways the text has affected readers throughout time and the variety of interpretations that have been arrived at. We cannot escape the effects the past has had on our understanding of texts in the present, for as Gadamer asks, "Is it not the past which has stamped us permanently through its effective history?"[16]

14. Taylor, "Gadamer on the Human Sciences," 142.

15. Gadamer, *Truth & Method*, 350.

16. Gadamer, *Philosophy*, 95.

Luz's Hermeneutical Approach

The Tübingen New Testament scholar Ulrich Luz, in his works on Matthew, has highlighted the importance of Gadamer's "history of effects" in the general area of New Testament studies. As Sheppard has correctly noted, Luz has "built significantly on Gadamer's stress on the 'effective history' of texts and reopened important questions about the role of the history of interpretation and its methodological implications for biblical scholars."[17]

The first thing that Luz identifies as an important consideration in the interpretation of biblical texts is that the reader who approaches the text can never read in an isolated or independent manner as we "are not independent from the history of the effects of the Bible."[18] To explain what he means by this statement Luz uses that analogy of a small boat in a river where the unchanging water represents the biblical text, the stream represents the history of the effects of that text and the boat represents the reader. He uses this analogy to explain why a text can be open to a variety of interpretations while still remaining the same text according to where the reader stands in history:

> Interpretations change because situations and interpreters change. There is no uniquely true interpretation of a text . . . the attempt to understand a biblical text always includes a stable element, namely the text itself, and a variable element, namely, the interpreter and his or her situation.[19]

Such an observation makes the text come to life. It is living insofar as it is moving, replicating, travelling along the stream of its own effects. The text itself interacts with the reader in a relational and dialogical way:

> The texts come from life, witness to life, and want to produce life . . . the biblical texts have a history of effects, which is the history between them and us. The history of effects . . . cannot be separated from texts, because it is an expression of the texts own power. It belongs to a text in the same way that a river flowing away from its source belongs to its source.[20]

Here Luz is borrowing and developing Gadamer's earlier metaphor in *Text and Meaning* of a moving river to describe the interplay between the openness and the closed-ness of hermeneutics. The act of exegesis holds the

---

17. Sheppard, "Biblical Interpretation," 417.

18. Luz, *Matthew in History*, 25.

19. Ibid., 26.

20. Ibid., 24.

reader in tension within the boundaries of "a continuous tradition that is already completed" a "unified steam of historical life."[21]

Using language reminiscent of postmodern philosopher Rorty, Luz informs us that the text cannot be understood as "an objectively confronted entity which can be scientifically investigated" but rather, maintaining the nautical analogy, he suggests, "The interpreter is like a person who must investigate the water of a river while sitting in a little boat which is carried and driven by this same river. Thus the interpreter is carried by the texts."[22] This is where Luz begins to use and develop Gadamer's concept of *Wirkungsgeschichte*. Luz draws our attention to the usefulness of the "History of Interpretation" in determining the original meaning of the text, yet also in a Gadamerian way simultaneously highlights the existential "being" dimension of determining meaning, hence we read as interpreters with all our history, understanding, tradition and prejudice. Luz writes,

> The history of interpretation and the history of influence are meant to help us understand how each interpreter is influenced by the text, it illuminates the prehistory of one's own preunder-standing . . . our distinctiveness—what we are—makes necessary a distinctive, situational listening to the original meaning of the text.[23]

Luz does make an important and often neglected distinction between *Auslegungsgeschichte* (simply History of Interpretation) and *Wirkungsge-schichte* (History of Effects or Impact), that is, the difference between simply plotting a chart, or writing a list, highlighting the variety of ways that a biblical text has been interpreted and going further to suggest that the same text has had a profound effect or impact on the way that the reader has acted or behaved in real life. Luz clarifies the distinction between the two forms of interpretation by writing that by *Auslegungsgeschichte*, or "history of interpretation" he means simply "the history of the interpretations of a text in commentaries and other theological writings" whereas by using "history of influence," or *Wirkungsgeschichte*, Luz means

> the history, reception, and actualizing of a text in media other than the commentary, thus, e.g., in sermons, canonical law, hymnody, art, and in the actions and sufferings of the church. The history of influence and the history of interpretation are

---

21. Figal, "Doing of the Thing Itself," 121.

22. Luz, *Matthew 1–7*, 96.

23. Ibid., 97.

related to each other like two concentric circles so that "history of influence" is inclusive of "history of interpretation."[24]

Thus for Luz, Gadamer's concept of Effective History, when applied specifically to biblical texts, is the history of the impact or influence that those texts have had on people. Such a concept raises the question, "If a specific text were missing from the Bible, would the reader still act in the same way as he or she would after reading the text, or is it a case of simply the reader acting in a certain way then looking back into scripture to find some kind of divine authority for acting in such a way?"[25] Luz seems to think that, at least in some cases, biblical texts can and do have an effect on the reader: "Biblical texts have a history of effects, namely, the history of the churches and their confessions after them and, through them, the whole history of the human world."[26]

Luz's use of *Auslegungsgeschichte* in his commentary on Matthew shows how the Gospel is a text which provides for the reader a rich source of subsequent readings, demonstrating its *Sinnpotential* or potential to effect the senses. Thus his aim is no longer to discover the literal or original meaning of the text but to demonstrate and explain the sources of the "multivalency" of the text and this is why he writes,

> The history of interpretation and the history of influence remind us of the fullness of the potential of meaning which is inherent in biblical texts. It reminds us of the fact that biblical texts do not simply have a closed, set meaning but are full of possibilities.[27]

The Christian Brethren, the group this book is focused on, as will become apparent in what follows, did try to discover the literal and original meaning of the book of Revelation, but they were not bound to this task alone, for the *Sinnpotential* of the Apocalypse influenced them to arrive at a multivalency of interpretations. The Brethren were able to find meaning and fulfillment within the context of their own life and times. The Apocalypse then, like the Gospel of Matthew, is a text which has provided a rich source of subsequent readings, and the Brethren exegesis of that text adds to the richness of its history.

24. Ibid., 95.

25. A Texan Snake Handler's reading of Mark 16:18 and, as Newport has suggested, a Jehovah's Witnesses' view on blood transfusions are probably safe examples of History of Effect, whereas Catholic evidence for papal authority through reading of Matt 16:18: "You are Peter . . . I will build my church" is probably History of Interpretation. See Newport, *Apocalypse and Millennium*, 6.

26. Luz, *Matthew in History*, 23.

27. Luz, *Matthew 1–7*, 98.

Räisänen's Hermeneutical Approach

Finnish New Testament professor Heikki Räisänen takes on the subtle distinction between *Auslegungsgeschichte* and *Wirkungsgeschichte* to which Luz has drawn our attention and develops it further. He too believes that a distinction should be made between the history of effects and the history of interpretation and as such he writes, "In my opinion the decisive line should be drawn, not between reception in different media [for example in sermons, art, actions of the church etc.], but between the actual 'effectiveness' of a text and such 'reception' as does not let it be effective."[28] There is thus a distinct difference between an interpretation of a text that has had an effect on the interpreter and an interpretation of a text that has not had any effect on the interpreter. Although the interpreter in both instances has engaged in the same act, namely the act of exegesis, the results and outcome of that exegetical activity are in reality different. Hence Räisänen suggests that the history of reception is different to the history of effects. The deciding factor in determining if the interpretation of a text belongs in the category of *Auslegungsgeschichte* or *Wirkungsgeschichte* is, according to Räisänen, "if it can be shown that a particular allegorical interpretation has actually brought about a *new* idea or a new practice, and not just legitimated an existing one, that would belong to effective history."[29]

Essentially Räisänen is asking here, "If a specific biblical text had not been written, would the interpreter who cites such a text as the reason for his or her actions still behave in the same way?" If the answer to that question is "yes" then that interpretation belongs to the "history of effect." However, if the answer is "no," that is, rather than the text exerting an influence over the interpreter, the text is simply being used retrospectively to add validation to an action, then that interpretation belongs to the "history of interpretation."

Räisänen's question is raised in this book in a very specific way. A central concern here is: "Exactly how was the Whore Of Babylon image used by the Brethren movement, and did the text have any significant influence on the thought and practice of the movement?" Did the image of Babylon as a bloodthirsty whore impact the Brethren readers to such an extent that the text had an effect on how the community perceived themselves, the denominations from which they seceded, and the world around them? Or did that image simply provide a useful tool to give divine authority to doctrines of sectarianism and exclusivity that had been developed anyway, and was that motif simply used retrospectively to provide divine sanction to existing

28. Räisänen, "Effective History," 311.
29. Ibid., 312.

notions? It is argued here that the Brethren reading of the Babylon motif belongs both to the "history of effects" (as seen for example in their development of the "secret rapture of the church" doctrine) and to the "history of interpretation," as seen for example in the identification of Babylon as the papal system and as "Worldliness."

Boxall's Hermeneutical Approach

Ian Boxall explores the specific link between *Wirkungsgeschichte* and the Babylon motif found in Revelation chapter 17.[30] He examines the way that this image has been interpreted in Dürer's woodcut of 1482 CE, Cranach the Elder's woodcuts which accompany Luther's *New Testament* (1522 ed.), and Holbein the Younger's woodcuts of 1534 CE. He goes on to extrapolate a history of interpretation of the Babylon motif, citing the way it has been understood by Tertullian in the late second / early third century CE, by Cyprian in the third century CE, and Beatus of Liebana in the Middle Ages. However Boxall fails to make the important distinction that both Luz and Räisänen have made of the nuanced difference between *Auslegungsgeschichte* and *Wirkungsgeschichte*. He clearly sets out a whole variety of interpretations throughout history, such as, Babylon as Imperial Rome or as the world in opposition to the church and the anti-papal tradition etc. but fails to ask the question "If Revelation chapter 17 were missing from the Bible, would Cranach and Holbein have created woodcuts of the Pope as a great harlot, or would Tertullian and Cyprian have warned women against wearing luxurious feminine attire?" As such Boxall's chapter should be located not in the area of the *Wirkungsgeschichte* of the Whore of Babylon motif but in the area of the *Auslegungsgeschichte* of the whore of Babylon motif.

Fish's Hermeneutical Approach

There are three reader-response theories that will help shed light on the specific way that interpreters within the Christian Brethren community read and understood Revelation chapters 17–18 that will be briefly examined in the remaining section of this chapter. The first is that of Stanley Fish and his theory of "interpretive communities." In *Is There a Text in This Class? The Authority of Interpretive Communities* (1980) Fish argues that the most important consideration when one begins interpreting any text is that of the reader's membership of a particular institution. The same we may

---

30. Boxall, "Many Faces of Babylon," 51–68.

assume for the reading of religious texts within religious institutions which themselves may be defined as "interpretative communities."[31] Such social affiliation predisposes the reader to a shared interpretation rather than the imposition of an individual subjective and idiosyncratic reading of the text. Fish's work into the role of the reader in making literature has enabled people to realize that readers do not interpret texts by self-consciously trying to figure out an idiosyncratic response, but rather, that interpretation is a collective and sociological phenomenon bound within the context of communities.[32] Fish suggests that "getting texts right is a matter of negotiation within a community, not arriving at the Holy Grail of the text itself or at fixed rules of interpretation."[33]

Having simply a shared language in common between author and reader is not enough to be able to understand another person; rather, a commonality of life is needed. Fish uses the analogy of an argument with a fellow academic. If he and his peer disagree on the nature and style of a poem it is only possible because "poem" is a "possible label of identification" within shared and set parameters of what counts as an identifying mark and what does not. Such observations are of direct relevance to this book. For example, within the Western Christian Protestant tradition, the commonly held view within that "interpretative community" is that the Whore of Babylon is the pope of Rome, and this view can be seen for example in Luther, Calvin, Adam Clarke, etc., and within all who belong to that interpretive community. Using Fish's social theory of language, "Whore of Babylon" can be interpreted and understood, not because the meaning is placed there by the author John of Patmos, or because Luther or Clarke simply share a language, but because "Whore of Babylon" is a phrase that has identifying marks of what it "is" and what it "is not" stipulated within a defined interpretative community.

31. Graff, headnote to *Is There a Text*, 38.

32. Of course Fish is not without his critics. Criticism of Fish's work can be found in Olson and Worsham, *Postmodern Sophistry*. Within this edited work, Bérubé, "There is Nothing Inside the Text," 11–26, is of particular relevance, noting that "on theoretical grounds the term 'interpretive communities' has been beset by problems at every point in its existence" (11), and draws reference to Iser's criticism of Fish's "denial of determinate meaning, the insistence on the ubiquity of interpretation, and the anti-voluntarist, strong-constructionist account of 'communities' that constrain any individual's activity of interpretation" (17). See also Freund, *Return of the Reader*, 108, 110. Freund raises the ethical problem of interpretative communities becoming "grimly coercive" (110). Such criticism does not, however, weaken the central argument being made here, namely, that meaning is determined by interpretative communities and the Brethren are one such interpretive community who interpret the text within a collective and sociological context.

33. Graff, headnote to *Is There a Text*, 38.

Fish claims that "communication only occurs within a community." In order to argue that communication is not possible between disparate communities he suggests that there exists a radical distance between such discrete communities. It would not be enough to just "give someone 'on the outside' a set of definitions" because, going back once again to Rorty's postmodern epistemological stance,

> an understanding that operates above or across situations— would have no place in the world even if it were available, be- cause it is only in situations—with their interested specifications as to what counts as a fact, what it is possible to say, what will be heard as an argument—that one is called on to understand.[34]

If an interpreter is not part of the interpretive community in which the act is done, written, spoken or uttered they have no access to its "intention" nor can they gain "understanding." Thus we are sealed off from the utter- ances of history, bound to interpret them based on our cultural assumptions and "prejudices," to borrow Gadamer's language, and unable to penetrate into the mindset of the past. This though is as far as the Gadamerian her- meneutic goes in Fish's work as he denies that an individual, idiosyncratic interpreter could find the meaning of the text. Rather the meaning can only be what the interpretive community understand it to be, not what the au- thor originally intended the text to mean. As such Fish defines the "text" simply as whatever the interpretive community says the "text" is. Because "the intentions of the author are unavailable and the responses of the reader too variable,"[35] Fish concludes that the "correct" interpretation

> is not constrained by something in the text, nor does it issue from an independent and arbitrary will; rather it proceeds from a collective decision as to what will count as literature, a deci- sion that will be in force only so long as a community of readers or believers continue to abide by it.[36]

The "true" interpretation of the text is based on a community's shared beliefs about the world, texts, and reading behaviors. Those beliefs establish legitimate and illegitimate categories of behavior for readers, and define unacceptable or acceptable interpretations.

The Christian Brethren of the nineteenth century are one such inter- pretive community. As such they will find the "true" explanation of Revela- tion chapters 17–18 through their shared belief about the world, through

---

34. Fish, *Is There a Text*, 304.

35. McKnight, "Reader-Response Criticism," 370.

36. Fish, *Is There a Text*, 11.

their reading behavior, and what they themselves as a community define as acceptable and unacceptable interpretations. For a person who dissents and secedes from a Christian tradition to belong to the Brethren community, and in order to define themselves as "Brethren," they must share a mutual understanding of the perceived correct and incorrect interpretations of Scripture. When a member of the Brethren community diverges on an issue of the correct interpretation of Scripture, then that individual is placing themselves outside of the boundary of Brethren "community interpretation" or the Brethren hermeneutical circle, and the result is that they can no longer be classed as "Brethren." We shall see that this is not just a theory but is something that has been well documented throughout the history of the Brethren movement. In chapter 4 of this book we will see just how many times particular individuals who held onto an idiosyncratic interpretation of Scripture were excommunicated or "put out of fellowship," and left to form their own, new, sectarian Brethren group. Such a new group will be made up of like-minded individuals who hold onto a shared, yet alternative, explanation of Scripture. Similarly, in chapter 7 below we shall see how "Babylon" was used in such situations to vilify those who interpreted Scripture differently to the Brethren from which they seceded.

Iser's Hermeneutical Approach

Wolfgang Iser's phenomenological approach to reading outlined in his book *The Act of Reading* (1978) posits the inseparability of texts and their reception;[37] the interaction between text and reader is the place where meaning is constructed.

Iser's reader-oriented theory is constructed around the concept of what he calls "narrative gaps." These gaps are the missing details, the connections, the areas of vagueness that can be found within any story. He also refers to these gaps as "places of indeterminacy" or "vacancies." The task of the reader is to fill in or take up meaning from his or her own experience and place it within the gaps. He writes,

> What is missing from the apparently trivial scenes, the gaps arising out of the dialogue- this is what stimulates the reader into filling the blanks with projections. He is drawn in to the events and made to supply what is meant from what is not said.[38]

---

37. Davis and Schleifer, *Contemporary Literary Criticism*, 158.

38. Iser, *Act of Reading*, 168.

The structural needs of the text, or indeed of the author, is for the reader to fill these "gaps." Doing this acts as a way of the text completing itself through the reader's own experience and ensuring the reader's existential self is placed in that work. Iser writes: "It is the gaps, the fundamental asymmetry between text and reader, that give rise to communication in the reading process . . . the interaction between persons."[39]

This dialogue, the communication between text and reader, is a symbiotic relationship where both text and reader are in some way reliant on each other, both playing integral parts in the composition of the text. The reader is reliant on the text for narrative, and the text is reliant on the reader to complete it with the missing details. In this way the reader becomes absorbed or assimilated by the text. There is a flow of information from reader to text and text to reader—as Iser notes, "the message is transmitted in two ways, in that the reader 'receives' it by composing it."[40]

There is no story, no matter how realistic, that can provide the number of details that would lead to such gaps disappearing altogether. Although reader and text assume similar conventions from reality, texts leave great portions unexplained to the reader, whether as gaps in the narrative or as structural limits of the text's representation of the world.

Iser states that "one automatically seeks to relate it to contexts that are familiar"[41] and this is certainly true in the area of biblical exegesis, and is particularly true in the interpretation of the Apocalypse. Essentially there are three types of gaps in the book of Revelation. The first is the gap that is created by the author failing to name, or positively identify, any of the specific motifs and symbols found there. For example John mysteriously speaks of a bloodthirsty prostitute riding on a ten-horned beast in Revelation chapter 17. However, he fails specifically to name the identity of this image, thus enticing interpreters to fill in the gaps, becoming part of the text and composing the meaning through suggesting who and what such things must be. The second type of gap found in the Apocalypse is that the author fails to give specific times when things will happen, thus in participating in the composition of the text the medieval interpreter may see the events being fulfilled in his own time and likewise the sixteenth-century interpreter will fill in the gaps and often suggest that the prophecies are being fulfilled in his own time. The final type of gap left in the text of Revelation is a failing to give specific location or place where things will happen. Thus in filling in the gaps an English interpreter will ordinarily see events unfolding in Eng-

39. Ibid., 167.
40. Ibid., 21.
41. Ibid., 22.

land whereas an American interpreter will in general see events unfolding in America.

Iser's hermeneutical approach helps us to realize that understanding Revelation is not like approaching a locked box awaiting the right person to come along with the right key to unlock it and reveal its secrets (as perhaps interpreters in the five above schools of exegesis would suggest). Rather, according to Iser, the process of reading is a fusing together of text and imagination in an experience of continual modification analogous to one's own existential experiences in life. The study of literature, and thus by association the exegesis of Revelation, Iser concludes, tells us perhaps more about ourselves than about the books we read. In reading we discover not only alternate visions to explore, but also our own human thirst for freedom of action, ultimate understanding, and unity of experience. Within the context of this particular book, these insights help us to conclude that the study of the exegesis of the book of Revelation by the Brethren of the nineteenth century may reveal more about the identity of the Brethren themselves than it does about the actual meaning of the Apocalypse.

Holland's Hermeneutical Approach

In his work *Five Readers Reading* (1973), Norman Holland provides another example of literary criticism in which the reader, rather than the author, plays the central role in understanding the text. However, unlike Fish and Iser, Holland begins his work from a more psychological perspective. The "five readers" in Holland's work can be defined as psychological subjects whose unconscious drives may be studied by examining their interpretations of texts for the errors of omission and commission they reveal. The text of the author itself, therefore, is not the most important aspect of the reading experience, but rather the text of the readers' own interpretations of literature is the critic's true "text." These interpretations are read for thematic repetitions of, additions to, or subtractions from, the literary work which reveals the reader's "life themes," personality, and grounding narrative about his or her own existence.

The meaning of a text, according to Holland, does not come from the author, but rather is determined by the type of person the reader is and the stage in life that that reader has attained:

> Typically, the dynamics in any given reader's mind will not coincide with the authors processes, nor will one readers experience

match another's, and even the same reader, we shall see, will respond differently at different times in his life.[42]

Thus Holland recognizes the ability of a reader to misread the text, but treats this as a reader's "symptom" rather than as an erroneous reading.

Holland believed that it was possible to classify every reader into archetypical groups according to their psychological makeup.[43] As a result he created a number of ways to test his students and determine how they responded to texts. A number of psychoanalytical personality tests were carried out on his literature undergraduates including the Rorschach personality test, which involved the interpretation of an inkblot, the Thematic Apperception Test (TAT), in which a person tells a story about a picture, and the COPE test, a questionnaire designed to determine an individual's defense mechanisms. The collection of this data, Holland argued, would lead to determining "feelings about gender and sexuality, attitudes towards aggression, preferred defences, sensory modes, recurring configurations, and imagery of all kinds."[44]

Holland concluded that there are four overarching principles that describe the inner dynamics of reading. Each reader has their own style based on the extent and nature to which these principles are present or absent in their responses. The first principle is that "Style Seeks Itself." What Holland means by this is that if a reader has read a story, enjoyed it, and responded in a positive way to it, then that reader will be able to identify with the work to such a degree that they place themselves in that work. The reader can become so absorbed by the text that he sees dimensions of the text in which

---

42. Holland, *Five Readers Reading*, 13.

43. In *Five Readers Reading*, Holland comes across as somewhat dogmatic and inflexible about the five archetypal readers he identifies. Such rigidity has, of course, come under criticism in, e.g., Bennett, *Readers and Reading*, 44, and Freund, *The Return of the Reader*, 123, 127–28. Both criticize the validity of Holland's empirical research. Holland himself, in later years, was to become more tentative about his conclusions. In his later work, *The I*, 94–106, Holland reinforces the conclusions made in *Five Readers Reading* ten years previously, yet he is more cautious in that he reworks the material without insisting that the readers belong to fixed archetypal groups. Holland acknowledges here that such fixed archetypal groups were, to an extent, a result of his own desire to create a "model that makes the person active [and] allows us to understand reading and listening and speaking more fully" yet continues to "insist on the evidence" (102). As we shall see in ch. 9, when the Brethren authors read Rev 17–18 they reacted to the text in a psychological way which seems to simultaneously transcend two or more of Holland's reading archetypes. While this adds further weight to a more cautious definition of reading archetypes, it in no way undermines the central point being made here: that the meaning of a text is determined, in part, by the reader's psychological make-up.

44. Holland, *Five Readers Reading*, 67.

he can "act out his own lifestyle."[45] Such an insight is easily applied to the text in hand, namely the book of Revelation. A person who reads Revelation and finds it both absorbing and something with which they can identify, in terms of finding themselves in a place of persecution or suffering on account of their religious convictions, will become absorbed by the work to such an extent that they place themselves in the text and act out their own lifestyle according to the text. This response can be seen in the Brethren movement insofar as in seceding and segregating from their original denominations, and in rejecting all associations with the world and its politics, they saw their true citizenship as being in heaven and perceived themselves as discriminated against, as a result of their religious convictions, by those from whom they had seceded. The Brethren became absorbed in apocalyptic texts, such as Revelation, as these presented a picture of a rejected, persecuted and suffering church, for whom the world was just a temporary place of sojourn, until the future day arrives when they would be translated to heaven.

The next principle of literary experience Holland puts forward is that "Defences Must Be Matched." Here Holland suggests that if the reader is to engage with the text fully, the text must itself react or respond to danger or perceived threat in a way that is a reality, at least in parallel form, to the experience of the reader. Holland explains the various defense responses that an individual may use to cope with danger from a psychological stance. The important thing is that different individuals have different defenses and different forms of verbal, physical and intellectual responses in fight or flight situations. Holland writes,

> This re-creating of one's own defences from the materials of the story becomes very delicate and unpredictable . . . for a reader to match his defences by means of elements within the story, he must be able to satisfy his ego with them at all levels . . . perceptions of the texts, even the most subtle and intellectual ones, rest on their need to match defences.[46]

The book of Revelation is full of predictions of danger, whether that is the danger of receiving the mark of the beast, dangers of hail, fire and brimstone, or of having one's blood drunk by the great whore. In Revelation the way that these dangers are averted is through remaining faithful, pure and uncorrupted by the social and religious evils of the world. Those who are to be defended from danger by the Lamb must not bow down and worship the beast or his statue, neither must they receive his mark or fornicate

45. Ibid., 114.
46. Ibid., 117.

with Babylon, the Great City. Their robes must remain white, they must be unpolluted, a spotless virgin bride. As we shall see in chapter 9 below, "flight or fight" responses to reading texts will be shown to be a very important factor in the development of the "Secret Rapture of the Saints" doctrine in the Brethren movement.

In the book of Revelation the Brethren read of a terrifying, seductive prostitute who has become drunk on the blood of the true believers. They read also that the true believers would not be able to fight and overcome her. Applying Holland's views, therefore, they were left with only one psychological response: "flight."

Holland suggests a third overarching principle of literary response, that "Fantasy Projects Fantasies." Once again, this involves the reader strongly identifying with a character in the text. Developing on the ideas of the nineteenth-century German philosopher Ludwig Feuerbach, Holland suggests that for a reader to be fully absorbed by the text he must be able to read out a "wish-fulfilling fantasy characteristic of himself."[47] Rather than seeing a fantasy as trapped or placed in the text by the author, Holland postulates that "fantasy is not 'in' the work but in the reader . . . works do not have fantasies—people do."[48] Each reader will build up a fantasy surrounding the text according to their own specific characteristics and reading styles. In Revelation, a reader who finds himself in a situation similar to that of the people described in the text might project their fantasies into the text in two ways. The first positive fantasy projection would be concerning sections of Revelation which describe the final blessing of the saints of God such as Revelation chapters 7 and 21. Here the reader might project onto the text his or her own fantasies about desiring a better future where things will turn out all right in the end. The second projected fantasy might be a more negative one concerning the punishment and judgment of the reader's enemies, such as Revelation chapters 12, 17–18, 20, etc. Here the reader might project onto the text his or her fantasy to see those who have caused them to suffer eternally punished.

The final principle of literary experience that Holland identifies is termed "Character Transforms Characteristically." The reader will transform what he has read, through identifying himself within the work, identifying the defense mechanisms within the work as being like his own and projecting his own fantasies into the text, into an interpretation that is characteristic of him and pleasing to him. With regards to specific transformation strategies, Holland writes that individual transformation may be

47. Ibid.
48. Ibid.

analogous to sublimation, that is the channeling of an individual's impulses or energies which may be regarded as socially, morally or religiously unacceptable (especially sexual desires) toward activities regarded as more socially acceptable. Perhaps this may include the prolific publication of apologetic material or the formation of a sectarian denomination, as was the case with the Brethren. Alternatively the reader might be transformed as he or she constructs meaning from the content of the text through symbolization whereby the symbols from a highly symbolic text such as Revelation are used to represent something completely abstract in the reader's own life experience in order to give concrete and even divine meaning. In both instances the text has had some kind of transformative effect on the reader.

Some Concluding Remarks on Texts and Meaning

In concluding this chapter on texts and meaning, it can be said here that the book of Revelation is not interpreted or even approached by readers in the same way; each individual reader brings their own unique experience of life to the text and constructs meaning out of the text in union with their life experiences. Readers who have defense mechanisms of "turning-on-the-self" will identify strongly with the Letter to the Churches, in Revelation chapters 2–3, who have been found guilty and await punishment. Readers who have a defense mechanism of "sexualizing" a threat will be absorbed by the image or Babylon in Revelation chapters 17–18; a wrathful, bloodthirsty enemy of the church, is sexualized as a whore, she is filthy and mysterious. A reader whose fantasy is violent, hostile and bloodthirsty will find a fantasy like their own to be transformed by the language of locusts, plagues and beasts. For those who perceive the world as a great mystery, the mysterious images of Revelation such as the mark of the beast, the whore, the rich symbolism and metaphors, will be particularly absorbing.

In the modern, rational, post-enlightenment age, it is impossible to believe that the original intentions and thoughts of the author can be unlocked from a text simply by finding the right key. John of Patmos still speaks, but through the millennia his voice cannot be heard directly, only indirectly insofar as the reader must translate meaning from his words, from the roar of a lion to the language of a twenty-first-century individual.[49] Meaning and interpretation come through belonging to an interpretative community. If one belonged to the early Brethren group and believed that the Babylon of Revelation referred to the kinds of entities which are explored later in this

49. To use Wittgenstein's analogy, "if a Lion could talk, we could not understand him." Wittgenstein, *Philosophical Investigations*, 223.

book, then because this is a common interpretation held by all the community, then for that community it is true. To accept such an interpretation is to place oneself within the Brethren community's conceptual sphere, or list of truth claims, beliefs and worldview. To hold onto divergent interpretations is to place oneself outside the conceptual sphere of that community and thus, for the Brethren community at least, the interpretation is wrong. It is entirely possible that different communities may hold different truth claims and interpretations, however, it is adherence to a certain interpretation that holds an individual within their distinctive community, and difference is maintained. There is a place in interpreting the Apocalypse for an individual to develop their own view, but only insofar as there occurs gaps or areas of vagueness in the text which allow an individual to cocreate meaning with the author. Individuals within communities will identify with specific passages of Revelation to a greater or lesser extent depending on the level to which a specific motif, narrative and/or character absorbs the individual reader. Thus we will see a variety of different interpretations of Revelation chapters 17–18 are held simultaneously by the Brethren community because of the "gaps" John has left in the text. A reader will find texts more absorbing when he can identify with the lifestyle of the character, when the reader's and the text's defense responses to perceived threats are similar, and when the fantasy within the text becomes the fantasy of the reader. In such cases the reader is transformed not only by the experience of the author but existentially through the actions of the character in the text. Thus throughout history Revelation has always been held as an important text by communities on the fringes of society, who perceive or experience persecution. Within mainstream Christian movements however, the Apocalypse often has less importance since they are less able to identify with the suffering church.

3

"Babylon" in the History of Interpretation

In the previous chapter it was shown that although many readers who engage in biblical exegesis, particularly those who adhere to a literalistic understanding of Scripture, believe they can unlock the text and discover a single absolute meaning, it is not quite that simple. The historical and cultural tradition in which we locate ourselves, the community to which we belong, the enticing areas of indeterminacy or vagueness within the text and one's own psychological profile, all mean that it is the reader who determines the perceived meaning of the text and not the author of the text or the text itself.

We turn now to trace and identify the history of the interpretation of Revelation's Babylon motif in particular, and in some detail, in order to provide the broader context within which to see the Brethren writers, whose work forms the heart of this book. As we shall see, the Brethren authors were not the first biblical interpreters to become interested in the "proper" application or "true" meaning of Revelation chapters 17–18. Many other readers of the Apocalypse have, throughout history, tried to understand and make sense of this motif. In this chapter some of those other attempts to identify the Babylon of the Apocalypse are sketched in. The survey is not exhaustive, but it is illustrative and helps us to see the Brethren in context. The survey stretches from the earliest hermeneutical efforts towards the end of the first century Common Era, to the start of the first quarter of the nineteenth century, which is when the Brethren interpreters began their work.

The link between early commentators on the Apocalypse and the Brethren authors may well have been direct. Prominent Brethren authors Darby, Kelly and Newton were all trained in Classics to degree level and excelled in the reading of Latin and Greek.[1] Through them the views of the early church may have been passed to others in the community. This is not to say, of course, that the views of the Fathers were necessarily held in any particular regard. "The tradition" held little sway in this community. Darby's disdain for appealing to the authority of tradition can be seen, for example, when he writes, "Superstition and spiritual ignorance" covered the "Fathers' minds."[2] Yet it is not all-negative criticism from Darby towards the authors of the Patristic era, as he writes that "though they misapplied it [i.e., Scripture] I believe in the substance, Papias, Irenaeus, Justin Martyr and Nepos, and the orthodox of those days, were right."[3] William Kelly was by no means any less aware of the authors of the early church period than was Darby. In his work references to the views of Papias, Eusebius and Polycrates can all be found. In addition Kelly shows an awareness of other authors from the Patristic period including Athanasius, Cerinthus, Eusebius, Papias, Caius the Roman Presbyter, Origen, Dionysius of Alexandria, the Sabellians, Jerome, Augustine, Justin Martyr, Theoderet, Celsus, Porphyry, Basilides, Theophilus of Antioch,[4] and Clement of Alexandria.[5] Clearly, then, the Brethren community did have access to the views of those who had gone before, even if they would have felt under no particular obligation to accept what they there found.

It does not stop here: the same Brethren commentators show an awareness of later exegetical developments. Thus Kelly refers to "the Abbot Joachim," in his *Lecture on the Book of Revelation*,[6] while the Waldensians and Bohemians, two groups for whom the book of Revelation was pivotal, are referred to in key Brethren author Miller's *Church History*.[7] Darby too refers to the Waldensians and the Inquisitor Reinarius Saccho who con-

---

1. See ch. 4 below.

2. Darby, "Miracles and Infidelity," 284.

3. Darby, "Romanism," 76. Darby also mentions, Papias, Irenaeus, Justin Martyr, Nepos, Origen, Dionysius, Victor Bishop of Rome, St. Augustine, Ambrose, Cyprian, Tertullian, Montanus, Praxeas, Pope Gregory the Great, Chrysostom, Jerome, and Pope Leo in this work (66–74). See also Darby, "Evangelical Protestantism," 244, 246; Darby, "Miracles and Infidelity," 275; Darby, "Dialogues," 364, 367, 371, 428, 476, for further negative references to Patristic authors.

4. Kelly, "On the Millennium," 252.

5. Kelly, *Exposition of the Gospel of John*, 482.

6. Kelly, *Lectures on the Book of Revelation*, xii.

7. Miller, *Short Papers*, 2.376–97.

demned them for heresy in *The Vaudois*.[8] Later in this chapter it will also become clear that the Brethren authors were acutely aware of the exegesis carried out in the later Reformation period by both Protestant and Catholic expositors.

EXEGESIS IN THE PERIOD 100–400 CE

In the first epoch of the exegesis of the book of Revelation, ca. 100–400 CE, Babylon appears to be commonly used as a cryptogram both for the city of Rome in particular and the Roman Empire in general. The earliest recorded use of the motif "Babylon" used in this way is attributed to Papias (ca. 60–130 CE), Bishop of Hierapolis. Although Papias' five books of *Interpretation of the Sayings of the Lord* is no longer extant, his views on Babylon were known by Clement (ca. 153–217 CE) who, in the eighth book of his *Hypotyposes*, another lost book, agreed with Papias' exegesis. Although neither of these books now exist, a summary of the lost views of Papias and Clement on the Apocalypse can be found in Eusebius' *Church History* (3rd c. CE). Eusebius himself wrote with regards to the use of the term "Babylon" by the Apostle Peter in 1 Peter 5:13 as a cryptogram for "Rome."[9] This illustrates that the reference to "Babylon" in the Petrine epistle was already understood at that time to be referring to Rome rather than to geographical Babylon. Eusebius wrote,

> Clement in the eighth book of his Hypotyposes gives this account, and with him agrees the bishop of Hierapolis named Papias. And Peter . . . in his first epistle which they say that he wrote in Rome itself . . . calls the city, by a figure, Babylon . . . "The church that is at Babylon, elected together with you, saluteth you."[10]

Eusebius makes a clear reference here to 1 Peter 5:13 and it is highly unlikely that this reference to Babylon implies the actual geographical Mesopotamian city of Babylon.[11]

Along with Papias and Clement the cryptic metaphor of Rome as Babylon was developed also by Irenaeus of Lyons (ca. 120–202 CE), disciple of Polycarp and Bishop of Lyons, in *Against Heresies*. Irenaeus began chapter

---

8. Darby, "Vaudois," 534, 536, 540.

9. The dispute over the authorship of 1–2 Peter is not relevant here. Eusebius takes it as a given that it was by the Apostle, as did the Brethren authors.

10. Eusebius, "Church History," in *NPNF*, 1.116.

11. Cullmann, *Peter*, 86.

26 of this work with the words, "John and Daniel have predicted the dissolution and desolation of the Roman Empire which shall precede the end of the world." He went on to explain how the Roman Empire will befall such a fate by using the language of the Apocalypse to describe the danger the church was experiencing in his own time, using the cryptic title "Babylon" to refer to Rome: "They shall lay Babylon waste, and burn her with fire, and shall give their kingdom to the beast, and put the Church to flight."[12] Thus a link is made between the imperial city of Rome and Babylon the Great of Revelation chapter 17:1—18:24. Irenaeus used the metaphor again, but this time he did not explicitly identify Babylon as Rome but allowed the allusion to remain cryptic describing a city called

> Babylon, haughty in the flower and pride of impiousness, and
> its inhabitants completely given over to sin of every description.
> But he, emerging from the depth, spat out the brine of sins, and
> rejoiced to plunge into the sweet waters of piety.[13]

Thus although Irenaeus did not proclaim outright that the imperial city Rome is the Babylon of Revelation, he clearly understood the plight of the church in his own time as the fulfillment of Revelation chapters 17:1—18:24. It is very probable, given the terrible persecution of the martyrs of Lyons and Vienne[14] under the "good Aurelius,"[15] (177 CE) as he was miscalled, that it is Rome to which Irenaeus referred.

This idea that Irenaeus held, of associating the suffering of the church in his own day and time with those who suffer in Revelation, is not unusual. In fact, as we have seen, the act of placing oneself into the text can be seen throughout the history of the exegesis of this passage.[16] The very text itself invites the reader to do this.[17] And the Christian Brethren movement of the nineteenth century did exactly this, understanding the events of Revelation to be referring to their own *Sitz im Leben*.

Tertullian (160–ca. 225 CE) from Carthage in North Africa was another commentator who described Rome as the Babylon of Revelation chapters 17–18. He wrote: "Babylon, in our own John, is a figure of the city Rome, as being equally great and proud of her sway, and triumphant over the

12. Irenaeus, "Against Heresies," in *ANF*, 1.555.

13. Irenaeus, "Fragments from the Lost Writings of Irenaeus," in *ANF*, 1.578.

14. Coxe, "Introductory Note to Irenaeus," in *ANF*, 1.310. See also Osborn, *Irenaeus of Lyons*, 4.

15. Coxe, "Introductory Note," 310.

16. See ch. 1.

17. See Iser above in ch. 2, "Texts and Meaning."

saints."[18] With regards to the imminent *parousia* expected in the (disputed) Pauline epistle 2 Thessalonians 2:1–2, Tertullian resigned himself to a long continuation of the world before the Lord's arrival, for: "the very end of all things ... is only retarded by the continuing existence of the Roman Empire ... in praying that their [i.e., the 'dreadful woes' of Revelation 9:12] coming may be delayed, we are lending our aid to Rome's duration."[19] Again, in *On the Pallium*, Tertullian spoke of Rome in cryptic terms, using the imagery of the Whore of Babylon in Revelation. So, for example, Tertullian described the Rome of his own day using such language as "Prostitute" (cf. Rev 17:1, 15, 16), dressed in "purple and scarlet and gold and precious stones" (cf. Rev 17:4; 18:18), as presiding over very many waters (cf. Rev 17:1, 15), and as cursed (cf. Rev 16:9; 17:1; 18:8, 10, 20, 21; 19:2).[20] Similarly he carried on the tradition of interpreting the bloodthirsty nature of the whore (cf. Rev 17:6; 18:20, 24; 19:2), and blamed the Babylon of Revelation for the death of the martyrs in his own time.[21]

Thus Tertullian identified Babylon as a cryptogram for Rome in the same way that Papias, Clement, Eusebius and Irenaeus did, and along with Irenaeus he understood the deaths of the martyrs at the hand of Imperial Rome in his own day to be evidence for this. However, Tertullian developed the exegesis of the Apocalyptic Babylon one stage further, using it for the first time in the history of interpretation as a polemic against the world and prevailing society. Tertullian used the Babylon motif in Revelation chapter 18:4 "Come out of her" as a call to the people of his own day to flee from decadent secular Roman society.

> For state reasons, the various orders of the citizens also are crowned with laurel crowns; but the magistrates besides with golden ones, as at Athens, and at Rome ... From so much as a dwelling in that Babylon of John's Revelation we are called away; much more then from its pomp.[22]

The next expositor of the Apocalypse who tried to understand the image of the Whore of Babylon in Revelation was Hippolytus (ca. 170–ca. 230 CE), bishop of Portus, then Rome, and disciple of Irenaeus. In his *Dogmatical and Historical Treatise on Christ and Antichrist*, we read, "Tell me, blessed John ... what didst thou see and hear concerning Babylon? Arise,

---

18. Tertullian, "Writings of Tertullian," in *ANF*, 3.162.

19. Ibid., 3.43.

20. Tertullian, "On the Pallium," in *ANF*, 4.24.

21. Tertullian, "Writings of Tertullian," in *ANF*, 3.332. see also 3.646.

22. Ibid., 3.101.

and speak; for it sent *thee also* into banishment."[23] Hippolytus then went on to quote Revelation chapters 17–18 and John of Patmos' description of the Great Whore. The identity of Babylon can be deduced from the quote above, as "for it" means the one who sent John "into banishment," that is, Rome. Babylon is Rome. It was, according to tradition, under the authority of Rome that the Apostle John was exiled.

Hippolytus also compared the Apocalypse with Old Testament prophecies and alluded to the spiritual connection between the Babylon of the prophet Daniel and the Rome of the Apostle John's day. Hippolytus identified the Rome of which he was bishop not just as the Babylon of Revelation, but also as the beast who represents the fourth and last revived Babylonian kingdom in Daniel 7:7,[24] and urged his reader that, although obliged to discuss "such matters of the times," people should not be hasty and make predictions of when the end will come.

Hippolytus finally identified Babylon as the "world" in a broader, more spiritual sense. This can be seen in his work "On Susannah" where he identified Babylon as the world, stating:

> Susannah prefigured the Church; and Joacim [*sic*], her husband, Christ . . . And Babylon is the world; and the two elders are set forth as a figure of the two peoples that plot against the Church . . . in this world they exercise authority and rule, judging the righteous unrighteously.[25]

This designation of Babylon as a spiritual rather than physical allusion to "the world" can be further seen in *The Refutation of All Heresies*, and although while not referring to Babylon in the Apocalypse, Hippolytus still used the language of Revelation here to speak of the world as a "spiritual Babylon" through evoking such rich Apocalyptic allusions as "mystery," "evil," and "carnal." He writes,

> We, however are spiritual, who, from the life-giving water of Euphrates, which flows through the midst of Babylon, choose our own peculiar quality as we pass through the true gate, which is the blessed Jesus. And of all men, we Christians alone are those who in the third gate celebrate the mystery, and are anointed there with the unspeakable chrism from a horn, as David (was

---

23. Hippolytus, "Extant Works and Fragments," in *ANF*, 5.211, my own italics.

24. Ibid., 5.178–79, 182.

25. Ibid., 5.192.

anointed), not from an earthen vessel, he says, as (was) Saul, who held converse with the evil demon of carnal concupiscence.[26]

Thus for Hippolytus, the emerging tradition of identifying Rome by the cryptogram "Babylon" that began with Papias was continued, but was also broadened out to mean the world in general, a place through which the spiritual are only passing. Rome is indeed seen as a great threat to the church but is not simply identified just as the Apocalyptic Babylon figure, Hippolytus also sees Rome as being like the Danielic "beast"—terrible, powerful, and exceedingly strong, devouring and destroying the church.

As we shall see later in this book, in the nineteenth century the Christian Brethren engage in a form of exegesis that has a number of remarkable similarities with that of Hippolytus. They too identify Babylon in light of Old Testament prophecy; they too understand Babylon as referring to "worldliness"; and they too, at times, undertake both a spiritual and literal or physical exegesis of the Babylon motif.

The final commentator in this first period of exegesis that will be examined is Origen (185–254 CE). The view that Babylon referred in a metaphorical and cryptic way to the city of Rome, rather than being a physical and geographical reference, sits well with the method of exegesis developed by Origen whose hermeneutical framework was based on a spiritual rather than physical interpretation of Scripture. For instance, in Origen's "Homily on Exodus 1," and in his *Scholia*, the "144,000" of Revelation 7:4 spiritually alludes to the "whole church" but in his commentary on the First Epistle of John, the "144,000" has a spiritual interpretation as meaning the first fruits of Jewish and Gentile converts. Thus with regards to the exegesis of the Babylon motif, Origen is able to understand the prophecy concerning Babylon within his more general hermeneutical approach to Revelation as referring to "spiritual Babylonians."

> The prophecies delivered concerning Judea, and Jerusalem, and Judah, and Israel, and Jacob, not being understood by us in a carnal sense, signify certain divine mysteries, it certainly follows that those prophecies also which were delivered either concerning . . . Babylonia and the Babylonians . . . are not to be understood as spoken of that . . . which is situated on the earth, or of the earthly Babylon.[27]

In Origen's exegesis of the Babylon motif a new interpretation developed. In *De Principiis*, above, we find that Babylon is a symbol of confused,

---

26. Ibid., "Refutation of All Heresies," in *ANF*, 5.57–58.
27. Origen, *De Principiis*, in *ANF*, 4.371–72.

troubled and sinful thoughts. This can also be seen in Origen's interpretation of Psalm 137, in the context of which he writes,

> For "the little ones" of Babylon (which signifies confusion) are those troublesome sinful thoughts which arise in the soul and he who subdues them by striking, as it were, their heads against the firm and solid strength of reason and truth, is the man who "dasheth the little ones against the stones."[28]

This suggests that for Origen "Babylon" symbolized a sinful thought process, and that those who are Babylonians are the ones who have not used reason and truth to overcome such sinful thoughts. For him, the correct understanding of what Babylon is can be found in Genesis 11 and the story of the tower of Babel, a place where people became "confused" in their thoughts and speech for the first time.

Origen's understanding of Babylon as confusion of thought is also expressed in the Brethren exegesis of the passage some sixteen hundred years later. This is not necessarily to argue for direct literary dependence on the part of the Brethren on Origen's exegesis, but simply to note what was to become a recurring theme in the exegesis of this passage. We shall see in chapter 7 of this book, that the concept of Babylon as doctrinal confusion became a very important way of interpreting the Babylon motif.

More could be said about this period of exegesis, though this is not necessary since already the main lines of interpretation seem fairly clear. For writers in this period Babylon meant Imperial Rome, and to a lesser extent Babylon referred to worldliness and confusion.[29] As we shall see below, some Brethren writers also identified Babylon in similar ways, although their identification would be understood primarily in religious rather than

---

28. Origen, "Against Celsus," in *ANF*, 4.619–20.

29. See further: Athanasius, "Circular Letter," in *NPNF*, 4.95, 234. The Arian and Meletian "madmen" are "Babylonians" and have drunk from the cup of Babylon. Victorinus, "Commentary on the Blessed John," in *ANF*, 7.352. Babylon is the Roman state responsible for the deaths of the martyrs in his own day. Victorinus, in *ANF*, 7.357–58. Babylon means "confusion" and "names of blasphemy." Methodius, "Banquet of the Ten Virgins," in *ANF*, 6.324. Babylon is voluptuousness, impurity, corruption, sensual, pretentiously distorting and degrading the Scriptures, captivating, enticing and deceiving. Commodianus, "Instructions of Commodianus in Favour of Christian Discipline," in *ANF*, 4.211. Babylon is a cryptogram for Imperial Rome. Theodoret, "Ecclesiastical History of Theodoret," in *NPNF*, 2.3.100–101. The Roman Emperor Julian Valens is identified as a Babylonian King. Addaeus the Apostle, "Memoirs of Edessa," in *ANF*, 8.656. Babylon is the city of Satan. In the *Sibylline Oracles* (ca. 3rd–5th CE), book 2, lines 16–21; book 3, lines 442–45; book 8, lines 48–109, and *Apocalypse of Baruch*, 41, 81. Imperial Rome is Babylon.

political terms.[30] They did, however, identify Babylon as the "world"[31] and "confusion."[32]

EXEGESIS IN THE PERIOD 400–1100 CE

The first major exegete of Revelation in this period is Augustine (354–430 CE) in whose voluminous writings there are to be found a number of attempts to provide an exegesis of the Babylon motif in Revelation. For example, in *Confessions* we read of the author's awareness of Babylon as something unpleasant where he uses the language of John of Patmos to describe her. She is filthy (cf. Rev 17:4), seductive (cf. Rev 18:3, 9), and something from which to flee (cf. Rev 18:4). He writes,

> I walked the streets of Babylon. I wallowed in its mire . . . the unseen enemy trod me underfoot and enticed me to himself because I was an easy prey for his seductions . . . my mother . . . had by now escaped the centre of Babylon.[33]

Further treatment of the motif can be seen in *City of God* where Augustine explores the "city of earth" and links it with Babylon the Great City of Revelation. The first thing that we can ascertain from *City of God* is that the city of the earth is Babylon: a city of confusion.[34] The source of confusion experienced in Babylon is highlighted as the speaking of falsehood mixed with some truth regarding doctrine, which Augustine describes as "contradictory errors," however as of yet Augustine has not given any positive identification as to who Babylon is:

> Even if some true things were said in it, yet falsehoods were uttered with the same license; so that such a city has not amiss received the title of the mystic Babylon. For Babylon means confusion, as we remember we have already explained. Nor does it matter to the devil, its king, how they wrangle among themselves in contradictory errors.[35]

---

30. See ch. 5 below.

31. See ch. 8 below.

32. See ch. 7 below.

33. Augustine, *Thirteen Confessions*, 2.46.

34. Augustine, *City of God*, 368, 370–72, See also, Augustine, *Expositions on the Psalms*, 4.269; and Augustine, *On the Catechising of the Uninstructed*, 3.305.

35. Augustine, *City of God*, 373.

The king of Babylon is identified by Augustine as Satan and sometimes referred to as Lucifer, of whom he writes:

> "How he is fallen from heaven, Lucifer, son of the morning!" and the other statements of the context which, under the figure of the king of Babylon, are made about the same person, are of course to be understood of the devil.[36]

Augustine makes the first direct identification of who Babylon is in chapter 2 of *City of God*. He is quite clear that the Babylon that he has been describing, a place of confusion and lies mixed with half-truths, a place that is ruled by the devil whose inhabitants are the enemy of the church.[37] This Babylon is Rome. In another place we find an apparent reference to Revelation 18:4, "Come out of her," as he writes,

> Men must fly out of the midst of Babylon . . . this prophetic precept is to be understood spiritually in this sense . . . we must flee out of the city of this world, which is altogether a society of ungodly angels and men.[38]

Augustine was not alone in his age. For John Chrysostom (ca. 347–407 CE) the antitypical harlot who seduces the church is not Babylon but Egypt. However, Chrysostom does identify Babylon as the fiery trial that every believer must resist in order to remain chaste and pure before the Lord and something that the believer must, in the language of Revelation 18:4, "come out of" and "flee from."[39] Chrysostom sees the world in which he and the church live as a "spiritual" Babylon and that, whether or not his contemporaries realize it, they are subject to a "spiritual" captivity akin to the captivity that the Jews underwent during their physical captivity in Babylon.[40] Chrysostom stresses the importance of coming out of this Babylon captivity and further reiterates the hidden, mysterious nature of the spiritual captivity that weakens the Christian who is caught unaware. However, the full force of captivity has not yet arrived. It is in someway an eschatological event at the end of this world, yet the nature of this eschatological captivity is not clear. It could be a move from spiritual bondage into physical bondage or

---

36. Augustine, *On Christian Doctrine*, 100; Augustine, *Expositions on the Psalms*, 1.286.

37. Augustine, *City of God*, 372.

38. Ibid., 369. See also, Augustine, *On the Catechising of the Uninstructed*, 3.295; Augustine, "Expositions on the Book of Psalms," in *NPNF*, 8.213.

39. Chrysostom, "Homilies on the Gospel of St. John," in *NPNF*, 1.14.239.

40. Chrysostom, "Homilies on the Epistle to the Hebrews," in *NPNF*, 1.14.485.

simply an increase in the level and intensity of the spiritual captivity, for he writes,

> "Out of weakness were made strong." Here he alludes to what took place at their return from Babylon. For "out of weakness," is out of captivity . . . But to us, some one says, "no such thing has happened." But these are figures of "the things to come."[41]

The Brethren authors from the nineteenth century onward held a similar understanding of what it meant to "come out" of Babylonian captivity. They too, like Chrysostom, believed that such a call to "come out" referred to the church of their own time having nothing to do with the seductions of the world.

Jerome (ca. 340–420 CE), in *Lives of Illustrious Men*, written in Bethlehem towards the end of his life, used Babylon as a cryptogram for Rome. Not only is he aware of this use of Babylon by Clemens and Papias,[42] but he too, like Origen and Augustine, makes reference to Babylon as a symbol of confused doctrine and heretical interpretation of apostolic teaching. In particular the heresy espoused by Rufinus is identified as Babylonian:

> You alone have the privilege of translating the venom of the heretics, and of making all nations drink a draught from the cup of Babylon. You may correct the Latin Scriptures from the Greek and may deliver to the Churches to read something different from what they received from the Apostles.[43]

There a number of letters from Jerome in which he discusses the Babylon of Revelation. For example, in his letter to Asella we read: "Pray for me that, after Babylon, I may see Jerusalem once more."[44] Jerome is probably referring to a "spiritual" Babylon and a "spiritual" Jerusalem here as they have a juxtaposed relationship in Revelation and are seen as antitheses. Although it is possible that he is referring to literal Babylon and literal Jerusalem in this letter, this is unlikely, for the text would refer to him returning to his home in Rome not Jerusalem. In another letter, maintaining the use of Babylon as a cryptogram for the city of Rome, and vilifying the decadence and worldly corruption of that city he writes:

---

41. Ibid., 14.488.

42. Jerome, "Lives of Illustrious Men," in *NPNF*, 2.3.364.

43. Jerome, "Jerome's Apology in Answer to Rufinus," in *NPNF*, 2.3.532. For further examples where Jerome explicitly links Babylon with confusion, see also Jerome, "Principle Works," in *NPNF*, 2.6.266, 274.

44. Ibid., 2.6.60.

Read the apocalypse of John, and consider what is sung therein
of the woman arrayed in purple . . . of Babylon. "Come out of
her, my people" . . . It is true that Rome has a holy church . . .
[and] a true confession of Christ . . . But the display, power, and
size of the city, the seeing and the being seen, the paying and the
receiving of visits, the alternate flattery and detraction, talking
and listening, as well as the necessity of facing so great a throng
even when one is least in the mood to do so—all these things
are alike foreign to the principles and fatal to the repose of the
monastic life.[45]

To "come out" of Babylon is then, for Jerome, only fulfilled when one
takes up the monastic life. Jerome uses the image of Babylon in Revelation
as a warning to women to stay away from worldly and fleshly activities. Thus
for example in his letter to Laeta he sends out the warning:

Prevent her from drinking of the golden cup of Babylon . . . keep
her from going out with Dinah to see the daughters of a strange
land . . . save her from the tripping dance and from the trailing
robe? No one administers drugs till be has rubbed the rim of
the cup with honey; so, the better to deceive us, vice puts on the
mien and the semblance of virtue.[46]

This emphasis on "worldliness" is found also in the Brethren writers as
shall be seen in chapter 8, where the Brethren use the Babylon motif to vilify
the world; the "secular other," in order to define the "self."

Cappadocian Father Gregory of Nyssa (d. ca. 385 CE) built on the concept of Babylon as a metaphor for doctrinal confusion. Those who adhere
to doctrinal heresy are described by Gregory as "carried away captive to
Babylon from Jerusalem that is above,—that is from the Church of God to
this confusion of pernicious doctrines,—for Babylon means 'confusion.'"[47]
Gregory again speaks of heresy by using the image of Babylon, this time
linking the death of Melitius of Antioch, the president of the first council
of Nicea, and his leadership in the war against heretical teaching, with the
loss of the one who will guide the church through the waters of Babylon,
that is, through confused and heretical doctrine.[48] The idea that Babylon
may be a metaphor for heretical teaching was to become a very important
notion in the writings of the Christian Brethren in the nineteenth century.
As is shown in chapter 7 of this book, Darby and the Exclusives developed

45. Ibid., 2.6.64.
46. Ibid., 2.6.194.
47. Gregory of Nyssa, "Against Eunomius," in *NPNF*, 2.5.222–23.
48. Gregory of Nyssa, "Oratorical: On Meletius," in *NPNF*, 2.5.512.

a coherent doctrine based on the contagious or contaminating effect of heretical teaching through a novel application of the Whore of Babylon motif, in order to define who was "in" and who was "out" of the Brethren on an epistemological level.

Gregory Nazianzen (ca. 325–389 CE), another of the Cappadocian Fathers, continues in this vein of using Babylon to describe doctrinal confusion, he writes of

> the Sacred Night, the Anniversary of the confused darkness of the present life, into which the primeval darkness is dissolved, and all things come into life and rank and form, and that which was chaos is reduced to order . . . the children of Babylon dashed against the rocks and destroyed . . . the removal of leaven; that is, of the old and sour wickedness . . . or relic of Pharisaic or ungodly teaching.[49]

Ambrose (b. ca. 340 CE), bishop of Milan, continued the growing hermeneutical tendency to use Babylon as a metaphor for doctrinal confusion and a love for heretical teaching in his own writings, stating of

> the daughter of Babylon . . . "Blessed is he who shall take thy little ones and dash them against the rock." That is to say, shall dash all corrupt and filthy thoughts against Christ . . . if any one is seized by an adulterous love, to extinguish the fire, that he may by his zeal put away the love of a harlot, and deny himself that he may gain Christ.[50]

Yet we also see that Ambrose understood Babylon in the same way as some of his other predecessors as being a symbol of worldliness and lustfulness, thus he writes:

> The snares of Babylon, that is, of the tumult of this world, are to be likened to stories of old-time lust, that seemed upon this life's rocky shores to sing some tuneful song, but deadly withal, to catch the souls of youth.[51]

It would be easy enough to extend this list of interpreters who similarly looked to "Babylon" as an image of all that the true church and Christian should not be. Andreas of Caesarea (fl. 6th c.),[52] the anonymous *Apocalypse*

---

49. Gregory Nazianzen, "Select Orations," in *NPNF*, 2.7.428.

50. Ambrose, "On Repentance," in *NPNF*, 10.358.

51. Ambrose, "On the Christian Faith," in *NPNF*, 10.242–43.

52. Andreas of Caesarea, in Wainwright, 45. Babylon is something worldly.

of Daniel (9th c.),[53] and Remigius, Bishop of Lyons (d. ca. 875 CE)[54] all interpreted Babylon in one way or another in line with the unfolding hermeneutical schema. However, little is perhaps to be gained by extending the list here. Rather, we note the main point that has already been adequately documented in the work of the authors cited above. It is this: that worldliness and confusion are beginning to take over from Imperial Rome as the main interpretations of Babylon in the second period of exegesis here examined. Brethren authors were able to combine all of the above.

EXEGESIS IN THE PERIOD 1100–1800 CE

Much has been written about the specific methods of interpretation the visionary Calabrian monastic Abbot Joachim of Fiore (1135–1202 CE) used to read the book of Revelation.[55] Here we are concerned only with his understanding of Revelation's "Babylon." Joachim's unique contribution to the history of the exegesis of the Babylon motif was through his juxtaposing of two different Babylons to fit in with his proto-dispensational recapitulatory method of interpreting Scripture. According to Joachim, in the second dispensation or status, from the time of king Josiah through to Christ, there was an entity known as "Old Babylon," the historical enemy of God's people, yet in the present status, the third dispensation, which began with Saint Benedict and will continue till the end of the world, there will arise a "New Babylon," who will be the persecutor of the monastic order and the faithful.[56]

In the *Liber Figurarum*, a series of Apocalyptic diagrams drawn by Joachim ca. 1202 CE, we see Babylon portrayed in both these ways. The "Earlier Table of Concords" (Old Testament Half),[57] in which a stylized diagram of a tree is used to show seven subjects that are represented in both Old and New Testaments, we see, on the left, the "striking of the first

53. "Apocalypse of Daniel," in *Old Testament Pseudepigrapha*, 764–66, 3.13, 6.2, 6.10, the Empress Irene is the whore, Constantine V is the fornicating king.

54. Remigius, *Libellus de tribus epistolis*, in *Early Medieval Theology*, 4.175. Remgius identifies Babylon as "the whole city of the world."

55. See the numerous works on Joachim by Marjorie Reeves and in particular her classic study, now reissued as *The Influence of Prophecy in the Later Middle Ages: A Study in Joachimism*. In addition the work of McGinn, *Calabrian Abbott* and bibliography, is important here.

56. Reeves and Hirsch-Reich, *Figurae*, 142–52; Reeves, 1, 14, 23; Kovacs and Rowland, *Revelation*, 192.

57. Joachim, *Earlier Table of Concords (Old Testament Half)*, from the *Liber Figurarum*, in Reeves and Hirsch-Reich, *Figurae*, plate 10.

Babylon." On the right of the illumination, the "Later Tables of Concords" (New Testament Half),[58] we see the "striking of the new Babylon." This image describes the two parallel destructions of Babylon, one, occurring in the sixth division of the first age when the Jews returned from the literal Babylon upon Malachi's death, the other, with the sixth seal of Revelation in the third age, which in Joachim's own day referred to the "striking" of the "New Babylon."[59]

Continuing with the *Liber Figurarum*, we see another diagram of a tree which Reeves and Hirsch-Reid title *Babylon/Rome Figure (Old Dispensation).*[60] Here Joachim shows Babylon as "the Mother of fornication" and links her with Adam, perhaps in order to contrast the original or first sin, with the final or last form of sin. The next tree *figurae*, titled *Babylon/Rome Figure (New Dispensation),*[61] was created to warn against "trusting in earthly apotheosis" (i.e., human achievement as the highest point of society) yet also to give comfort to those who "had descended into Babylon."[62] Of this New Babylon Joachim writes that in the future a *Novus Rex Babilonis* (a new king of Babylon) will arise to persecute the church and lead the last great pope, *summus pontifex*, along with the church, into captivity.[63]

Although it may be said of Joachim in general terms that Babylon represents any force "in opposition to the Church of St. Peter,"[64] this opposition takes two main forms. The first form of Babylonian opposition to the church that Joachim identifies is that of the worldly or "reprobate" Christians of Rome,[65] that is, those who comprise the carnal church in contrast to the spiritual church. The true church, the *sacrum ecclesia sancte mysterium*[66] or *the sancte miris ecclesia*, is juxtaposed against the Great Whore Babylon, the

58. Joachim, *Later Table of Concords (New Testament Half)*, from the *Liber Figurarum*, in Reeves and Hirsch-Reich, *Figurae*, plate 11.

59. Reeves and Hirsch-Reich, *Figurae*, 134.

60. Joachim, *Babylon/Rome figure (Old Dispensation)*, from the *Liber Figurarum*, in Reeves and Hirsch-Reich, *Figurae*, plate 23.

61. Joachim, *Babylon/Rome figure (New Dispensation)*, from the *Liber Figurarum*, in Reeves and Hirsch-Reich, *Figurae*, plate 25.

62. Reeves and Hirsch-Reich, *Figurae*, 191.

63. Ibid., 295. Joachim consistently identified the Roman Empire with Old Babylon, the persecutor of the Church, and simultaneously expected a New Rome symbolized by a New Babylon to arise during the opening of the sixth seal to persecute the church. For further examples, see Reeves and Hirsch-Reich, 114–16, 184–91; McGinn, 67. Reeves, 14. West and Zimdars-Swartz, 22–24; Froom, *Prophetic Faith*, 1.701–2.

64. West and Zimdars-Swartz, 24.

65. Joachim, *Expositio in Apocalypsim*, fols. 194r., 195r., 198r.

66. Reeves and Hirsch-Reich, *Figurae*, 251.

novus dux de babylone,[67] that which Joachim describes as being made up of
the *ecclesia cum generali multitudine reproborum*,[68] or the evil members of
the church. It is to warn the faithful of such evil members of Babylon within
the church that Joachim writes a *Letter to the Faithful*, in which we read that
the apostate children have not remained faithful to the church and have
abandoned "the bosom of the Chaste Mother . . . and preferred the Whore
who rules over the kings of the earth . . . the kings of the earth will assemble
against you, daughter of Babylon."[69]

The other main form of opposition to the church that Joachim identifies as Babylonian is that of the German Empire. It is in Henry VI of
the *Hohenstaufen* dynasty, King of Germany and Holy Roman Emperor
(1190–1197 CE), that we find Joachim's final identification of Babylon,[70]
for he writes *Lucifur rexit Rex alius in babylone . . . Henrici . . . intracitis
questionibus angustatur ecclesia.*[71]

Joachim's dispensational worldview can be seen in the apocalyptic diagram of the Seven Headed Dragon. He annotated the diagram: "Just as the
old Babylon was struck under the sixth seal, so the new one will be pierced
under the present sixth opening."[72] McGinn suggests that this refers to the
abbot's parallel or recapitulatory understanding of "the victory of Cyrus
over Babylon in the sixth age of the Old Testament with the coming defeat
of the German empire at the hand of the revived sixth head allied with the
seventh."[73] Just as Old Testament prophecy foretold the coming of Cyrus,
the Messiah,[74] to destroy the Babylonian kingdom Joachim believed that
New Testament prophecy foretold that Henry VI and his Babylonian German kingdom would be destroyed in the present dispensation.[75]

---

67. Joachim, *Liber Concordia Novi et Veteris Testamenti*, 56. See also Joachim,
Expositio in Apocalypsim, fols. 189 vb., and 193r.–194r., in McGinn, 152, for Joachim's
remarks about evil simoniacal bishops and unholy clergy and monks.

68. Reeves and Hirsch-Reich, *Figurae*, 149.

69. Joachim, "Letter to the Faithful," in McGinn, 114–15.

70. Joachim, *Liber Concordia Novi et Veteris Testamenti*, 52. See also McGinn,
152. Reeves, 23.

71. Joachim, *Liber Concordia Novi et Veteris Testamenti*, 56. "The Devil directs the
King, the one in the midst of Babylon . . . Henry . . . provokes complaining and choking
inside the church."

72. Joachim, *Liber Figurarum*, "Fourteenth Table, Seven-Headed Dragon," in Mc-
Ginn, *Apocalyptic Spirituality*, 138.

73. Joachim, *Liber Figurarum* in McGinn, 295n16.

74. See Isa 44:28; 45; 46:11.

75. On this point history proved Joachim to be wrong. Henry VI died in the height
of his power in 1197. While Germany was divided by rival kings, Henry's son Frederick II, made Sicily and southern Italy (which included Calabria, Joachim's place of

The Christian Brethren, who began writing some six hundred years after Joachim, interpreted Babylon in a number of ways that had a remarkable similarity to the Calabrian Abbot showing again the enduring yet flexible afterlife of this biblical image. The Christian Brethren, like Joachim, found in the motif of Babylon a symbol of worldliness within the church.[76] Some Brethren authors, like Joachim, identified Babylon as secular ungodly authority (albeit British and European rather than specifically German). However, unlike Joachim, the Brethren saw little or no godliness within the Roman church and little or no chance for the system itself to "come out of her," only for individuals to leave her captivity.

Joachim was not the only person who began to interpret the Whore of Babylon motif in this time period, as not referring only to Imperial or Pagan Rome, but as referring to Papal, Catholic Rome. The Waldensians, a movement that began towards the end of the twelfth century in Lyons and spread rapidly through the Languedoc and Piedmont into Central and Eastern Europe, identified the pope as the Whore and the Church of Rome as the Beast on which the Whore rides.[77] One indication of this is found in the work of Dominican Inquisitor Rainier Sacchoni, the author of "Treatise on the Cathars and Waldensians" (1250), in which he published a catalogue of the doctrinal errors held by the Poor Men of Lyons, as the Waldensians were frequently called at the time.[78] The treatise reveals that the Waldensians identified the Catholic Church as the Whore of Babylon: "They say that the Roman Church is a church of evil, the beast and the harlot which are found in the book of Revelations."[79]

The Albigensians, also known as the Cathars, were a heretical sect that flourished in southern France in the twelfth and thirteenth centuries, which adhered to a number of dualistic Gnostic and Manichaean beliefs.[80] They too identified the Catholic Church in light of their exegesis of Revelation chapters 17–18, understanding that church to be "a den of thieves and the harlot spoken of in the book of Revelation,"[81] and stating that the "Roman church is the Devil's church and her doctrines are those of the demons, she is the Babylon whom St. John called the mother of fornication."[82]

domicile), the seat of his power.

76. See chs. 5–9 below.
77. Froom, *Prophetic Faith*, 1.877–79.
78. Audisio, *Waldensian Dissent*, 10.
79. Sacchoni, "Treatise on the Cathars and Waldensians," 145.
80. See Sibly and Sibly, *History of the Albigensian Crusade*, xxxiii.
81. Peter of les Vaux-de-Cernay, *Historia Albigensis*, 12.
82. Strayer, *Albigensian Crusades*, 22. See also Madaule, *Albigensian Crusade*, 31;

It is clear enough, then, that in the work both of Joachim, Waldensians and the Albigensians that the symbol of Babylon was now being applied very directly to refer to the Church of Rome rather than just Imperial Rome. The change in interpretation reflected the change in the *Sitz im Leben* of the interpreter. Imperial Rome had now long gone, and since her fall in 476 CE, Papal Rome had become not only a powerful religious force, but also a formidable political power. While successive popes had crowned successive kings as Holy Roman Emperor from 800–1806 CE in return for their protection, the European Renaissance of the fourteenth to sixteenth centuries sought to revive and imitate the Classical era, of which Imperial Rome was the culmination. It was perhaps inevitable that the symbol of Babylon which, as we have already seen had begun to be applied to the Roman Church in particular, should prove a particularly effective weapon in the arsenal of the emerging Protestant movement.

Perhaps the most famous character from this period is that of Martin Luther (1583–1546 CE). Luther's treatise on the *Babylonian Captivity of the Church* (1520) was a sustained attack on the bondage in which the church had been held by Catholicism. In making this attack Luther used the image of Babylon as the enemy and captor of the true church.[83]

Surprisingly, in *A Treatise on Goods Works* (1520) Luther extols his reader to pray and offer intercession for those who have ecclesiastical authority in the Catholic Church. In the treatise he draws an analogy from Jeremiah's exhortation to pray for the king of Babylon, and thus again makes a link between Babylon and the Roman Catholic Church. Luther writes, "Those who belong to the parish or bishopric . . . pray for the city and land of Babylon, because in the peace thereof they should have peace."[84] Likewise, Luther urges his reader to pray for the government, temporal power and authority. Such authority should not be lied to, neither should it be cursed, for no matter how unjust the secular authority appears, its power is only temporal and cannot destroy the eternal soul. In this way, Luther suggests that the injustice of the governmental authority of his own day is like the injustice the people of Israel suffered at the hands of the King of Babylon: "Even if the government does injustice, as the King of Babylon did to the people of Israel, yet God would have it obeyed, without treachery and deception."[85]

Continuing with *A Treatise on Goods Works*, Luther explains, in line with the tradition of interpretation that began with Augustine (which is

and de Sismondi, *History of the Crusades against the Albigenses*, 7.

83. Luther, "Babylonian Captivity of the Church," 3–126.

84. Luther, "Treatise on Goods Works," 64–65.

85. Ibid.

hardly surprising given that Luther was himself an Augustinian), that the image of "the little ones of Babylon" (Ps 137) symbolically referred to evil lust, thoughts and adultery. These sinful compulsions can be "dashed on the rock" which is Christ, and overcome through prayer and God's mercy. He does not however link these "little ones of Babylon" with confused heretical doctrine as Augustine does. He writes:

> When evil lust stirs let a man flee to prayer, call upon God's mer-
> cy and help, read and meditate on the Gospel, and in it consider
> Christ's sufferings. Thus says Psalm 137 . . . "taketh and dasheth
> the little ones of Babylon against the rock," that is, if the heart
> runs to the Lord Christ with its evil thoughts while they are yet
> young and just beginning; for Christ is a Rock, on which they
> are ground to powder and come to naught.[86]

Although Protestant Reformer John Calvin (1509–1564) did not write a commentary on Revelation he was, however, an important and influential person in the Reformation. His *Institutes of the Christian Religion* (1536) were widely distributed and read throughout Europe, and he too, like his contemporary Luther and their protesting predecessors of the thirteenth century, identified the Roman Catholic Church rather than the Roman Imperial Empire as the Apocalyptic whore. He writes of Papal Rome:

> What is it at the present day that the world venerates in its
> horned bishops unless that it imagines those who are seen pre-
> siding over celebrated cities to be holy prelates of religion? . . .
> God alone knows who are his . . . his own people were dispersed
> and concealed amidst errors and darkness, he saved them from
> destruction. No wonder; for he knew how to preserve them
> even in the confusion of Babylon.[87]

In his *Institutes of the Christian Religion* Calvin uses language reminiscent of Luther's description of the captivity of the true church in *Babylonian Captivity of the Church* through employing a comparison between the Reformers and ancient Israel, both of which were subjugated at the hand of Babylon: "God the Redeemer, who was not only to bring back the people from Babylonish captivity, but restore the Church, and make her completely perfect."[88]

Calvin specifically identifies the pope as Babylon, a wicked and abominable character, profane, cruel, evil and poisonous. We read of the "Roman

---

86. Ibid., 44.105.

87. Calvin, *Institutes of the Christian Religion*, 1.19–20.

88. Ibid., 1.180.

Pontiff" and his "wicked and abominable kingdom" full of "evil and deadly doctrines like poisoned potions" a place which presents "the appearance of Babylon rather than the holy city of God."[89] For Calvin the Catholic Church as a system is only a pseudo-church, a pretend temple of God, devoid of the truth of God. It is for this reason that Calvin suggests,

> In this way the Romanists assail us in the present day, and terrify the unskilful with the name of Church while they are the deadly adversaries of Christ. Therefore, although they exhibit a temple, a priesthood, and other similar masks, the empty glare by which they dazzle the eyes of the simple should not move us in the least to admit that there is a Church where the word of God appears not . . . Nay, Jerusalem is to be distinguished from Babylon, the Church of Christ from a conspiracy of Satan, by the discriminating test which our Saviour has applied to them.[90]

Many other authors and artists interpreted the Whore of Babylon motif found in Revelation chapters 17–18 during the Reformation period as either the pope, individually or as Roman Catholicism, corporately. Thus Boxall refers to an "Anti-Papal Tradition" developing in this time period as part of his work on the *Wirkungsgeschichte* of this passage.[91] Froom lists many other authors in the Reformation period who identified Papal Rome as the Great Whore, including, Melancthon, Lucas Cranach, Osiander, Funck, Flaciu. He writes that "the Christian Church . . . this unchaste, figurative woman was guilty of spiritual adultery with her lovers . . . she was denominated a 'harlot' or 'whore.' These terms were frequently employed."[92]

The Christian Brethren were well aware of the Protestant Reformers and their methods of biblical exegesis. Darby states in a very complimentary manner:

> I see in Luther an energy of faith for which millions of souls ought to be thankful to God, and I can certainly say I am. I may see a clearness and recognition of the authority of scripture in Calvin, which delivered him and those he taught (yet more than Luther) from the corruptions and superstitions which had overwhelmed Christendom.[93]

89. Calvin, 3.55.
90. Ibid., 3.48.
91. Boxall, "Many Faces of Babylon," 63.
92. Froom, *Prophetic Faith*, 2.241–64.
93. Darby, "Sufferings of Christ," 205.

In like manner, Kelly informs us that Luther was "a man known for the wonderful work God gave him to do."[94] Brethren author Edward Dennett observed in the Reforming work of Luther an anti-papal purpose: "God, in His sovereign grace, used Luther to recover, in measure, this precious truth from the corruptions of Popery."[95] Brethren author T. B. Baines, speaking specifically in the language of Revelation 18:4, writes of Luther: "The horrible mass of corruption in the professing Church in the days of Luther compelled him and all who cared for God's glory to come out."[96]

Clearly the Brethren authors were aware not only of what these Protestant Reformers had achieved on a historical level, but also their methods of biblical exegesis and hermeneutics and the way that they interpreted the Babylon motif.

Moving onward into the eighteenth century, the religious identification of Babylon has moved from being understood as the religion of Pagan Rome, to being understood as Papal Rome, and then for the first time as referring to all forms of corrupt, violent and worldly Christianity.

John Wesley (1703–1791 CE), an important figure in the eighteenth-century Evangelical revival and the primary founder of Methodism, saw the figure of the Apocalyptic Babylon all around him in the form of Christians who act in a violent persecuting manner towards other Christians:

> See how *these Christians* love one another! These Christian kingdoms, that are tearing out each other's bowels, desolating one another with fire and sword . . . that bear the name of Christ . . . and wage continual war with each other! that convert sinners by burning them alive! that are "drunk with the blood of the saints!" Does this praise belong only to "Babylon the Great, the mother of harlots . . . ?" Nay, verily; but Reformed Churches (so called) have fairly learned to tread in her steps. Protestant Churches too know to persecute, when they have power in their hands, even unto blood.[97]

---

94. Kelly, "Jonah," in *Lectures Introductory . . . Minor Prophets*, 206. See also Wigram, *Letter Dated March 8th*, 3; and Trotter, "Millennial Reign of Christ," 114–15.

95. Dennett, *Recovered Truths*, 8. N.B., Darby mentions specific individual Reformers in thirty-six further publications. Kelly names the major Reformers in a further forty-five publications. Wigram in a further seven publications, and Dennett in a further seven publications. Clearly they were acutely aware of Reformation hermeneutics in general, and thus also aware of the developing paradigm of exegesis pertaining to the identification of Babylon.

96. Baines, "Church of God," 394.

97. Wesley, *Works*, 507–8.

Wesley speaks of Babylon as symbolic of the type of idolatry experienced by the Protestant Church and also links Babylonian idolatry with Roman Catholic idolatry; the worship of created things of gold and silver, however, he does not see this kind of idolatry as the primary threat to the dissenting church of his time. The main type of idolatry is quite simply in not giving one's heart to God. The "gross Idolatry" that "entangled" the Israelites during their Babylonish captivity is likened to the "idols that are now worshipped in the Church of Rome," and Wesley concludes that "whatever takes our heart from him, or shares it with him, is an idol; or, in other words, whatever we seek happiness in independent of God."[98]

EXEGESIS AT THE START OF THE NINETEENTH CENTURY

The survey presented above is indicative rather than exhaustive but it does give a sense at least of the very broad tradition that the Brethren writers inherited (and it is worth noting again that the Brethren writers with which we are here concerned were well-read in much of the literature that has been cited).

As we arrive at the start of the nineteenth century, less than thirty years away from the formation of the Brethren movement, we find that the interpretation of Revelation chapters 17–18 was still an important concern for those engaged in biblical exegesis. On the one hand the historical-critical school which developed in Tübingen Germany began to interpret the text in light of its original *Sitz im Leben*, whereas on the other hand, popular exegesis grew exponentially with Prophetic Schools meeting to discuss the meaning of Revelation, such as the Powerscourt and Albury conferences, the London Missionary Society, and the Society for the Investigation of Prophecy.[99] All provided opportunities for the popular discussion of all kinds of Apocalyptic symbolism. Something in the region of one hundred important books appeared on the premillennial advent and the interpretation of prophecy in the first four decades of the nineteenth century.[100]

Thus, in light of such increased study and discussion on all things prophetic at this time, it is indeed fair to see the start of the nineteenth century as a time of significant increase in the study of apocalyptic scriptures. Froom suggests this rise in popularity developed from a "definite conviction that mankind has entered a new epoch—the era of the last things, the time

98. Ibid., 1.103–4.

99. See, e.g., Gribben and Stunt, *Prisoners of Hope?*

100. Froom, *Prophetic Faith*, 3.266.

of the end."[101] Weber on the other hand takes a more sociological approach listing sightings of comets, erupting volcanoes, the Great Reform Act of 1832 and the production of penny handbills and broadsheets as reasons for such an increase in things prophetic.[102]

Perhaps this increase in apocalyptic interest was due in part to the French Revolution, an event which "encouraged English evangelicals to study the signs of the times, and Catholic emancipation stirred again the Apocalyptic mysteries."[103] Thus, in reaction to this event, in 1795 Richard Brothers wrote that the revolution was a sign from God of imminent judgment. He states, "The British government's support of the French monarchy made London a latter-day Babylon."[104]

Such increase in prophetic study was also due in part to the cholera epidemic which reached England from the continent in 1831 killing some estimated fifty thousand people. Many saw this disease as a judgment of God upon the nation in an evil hour. Chadwick notes: "There were cries to close theatres and ballrooms, to destroy card tables, to remedy breaches in keeping the Sabbath."[105] It was not only religious fanatics that looked for such "signs of the times," but many educated, wealthy and political men, too. For example, writing during a time of European cholera infection, Lord George Montague Mandeville, during the 1829 Albury Prophetic conference, continued in the anti-papal tradition when he "declared the Papacy to be the Apocalyptic Babylon from which the Continental Society urged Europeans to depart,"[106] and William Wilberforce (1759–1833), campaigner against slavery, held a "literal belief in the prophecies concerning the premillennial return of Christ to usher in the millennium in a darkening world" and a "fierce hatred of Roman Catholicism and of the papacy as the Beast and Scarlet Woman of the Book of Revelation."[107]

For Edward Irving, founder of the Catholic Apostolic Church, in this time of pestilence and plague, all of Christendom had failed to maintain faithfulness to God, every denomination was guilty of the sins of Babylon. God was in the process, through Irving's charismatic movement of "redeeming his church out of the captivity of Babylon."[108] Whereas Scottish

---

101. Ibid., 3.263.

102. Weber, *Apocalypses*, 119–21.

103. Chadwick, *Victorian Church*, 36.

104. Brothers, *Revealed Knowledge of the Prophecies and Times*, 27–31.

105. Chadwick, *Victorian Church*, 36.

106. Montague, in Gribben and Stunt, *Prisoners of Hope?*, 28.

107. Norman, "Church and State Since 1800," 296.

108. Irving, "Interpretation of the Fourteenth Chapter," 284.

Presbyterian Andrew Bonar writing in 1839, uniquely identified Paris as "the streets of that Great city," her sin was a political one, being subject to Roman Catholic authority.[109]

Thus we have arrived at the time of the formation of the Brethren movement with some 1,700 years of exegesis of the Whore of Babylon motif to hand. The next chapter of this book will examine the formation of the Brethren movement before we go on to the archival section of the book which will examine specific Brethren exegesis of the Whore of Babylon motif.

109. Bonar and McCheyne, *Narrative of a Mission*, 47–48, 293. See also Bonar, *Development of Antichrist*, 71.

4

History of the Christian
Brethren Movement

After tracing the history of the interpretation of the Babylon motif, from the first century and through to the early nineteenth century, we arrive at the place in history in which the Christian Brethren interpreters began their work, that is, the first quarter of the nineteenth century. In this chapter the *Sitz im Leben* of the Christian Brethren is determined through an examination of the history of the movement, and a discussion of its principle ideas and doctrines (in particular ecclesiology and eschatology). This will enable us to find the place in which the new movement stands within the stream of interpretation that went before them.

Such a historical overview of the movement will facilitate both an understanding of the history of the movement generally and the unique stories of the individual authors specifically, thus enabling us to understand why and how their biblical exegesis developed according to the social and historical factors they experienced. Biblical exegesis does not arise simply out of the interplay between text and reader in a vacuous and closed environment, but is informed and influenced by every social, cultural, historical, emotional and religious experience that the reader has had. Identifying such sociological factors will shed light on how, and perhaps more importantly why, individual Brethren authors interpret texts the way they do. Given these sociological and historical considerations, Revelation 18:4 ("Come out of her") became highly important to Brethren interpreters.

FOUNDING FATHERS

The history of the Christian Brethren movement is the history of a group that began with the aim of seeking unity, commonality and inclusiveness—a pan-denominational "pure" church within the broader Christian tradition. It ended with separation, exclusivity and sectarian division. In 1829 in a room at nine Fitzwilliam Square, Dublin, Ireland, five young men disillusioned with the distance to which their own denominations had diverged from the simplicity of the New Testament early church model, shared Holy Communion.[1] Their desire was to find a way in which they could come together in a simple act of worship and communion regardless of individual denominational affiliation or tradition. They came from the established Protestant and Catholic Churches as well as from the Non-conformist groups and Dissenters. Some were members of the clergy others the laity. All were educated and wealthy upper-class Victorians.[2] The group desired to be ecumenical, nondenominational and inclusive of all who called themselves Christian in their sharing of the Lord's Supper, an act of devotion that they believed could transcend the fractured and fragmented churches of their day and bring true Christian unity. It was to this shared sentiment of unity that this group opened the invitation to "break bread" to all who would come rather than to those who held adherence to any particular creed or doctrinal belief.

Within only one year, the group had grown in number, attracting other small groups who, in like manner, were meeting in other homes throughout Dublin, and as they grew, they began to meet in a public hall in Aungier Street, Dublin. Just one year later, in 1831, Providence chapel was founded in Plymouth, England,[3] and during the next ten years (1832–42) the movement spread geographically out from England's West Country into London, the North of England, and even into parts of Europe. Churches were opened in Bristol, Torquay, Bath, Salcombe, Islington, Tottenham, Hereford, Stafford, Kendal, Hull, Geneva, Vaud and Stuttgart.

The movement continued to grow and by the time of the Religious Census of 1851 we find that on Sunday 30th March 1851 there were in England and Wales 7,272 Christian Brethren attending chapel services. Although this seems an insignificant figure when compared to a population of

---

1. Hutchinson, Bellett, Darby, Brooke and Cronin (a Roman Catholic convert) joined forces with another small house group which included William Stokes and Lord Congleton (J. V. Parnell) in 1830 shortly before moving to the larger public premises in Augnier Street. See Coad, *History of the Brethren Movement*, 29–30.

2. Ibid., 84.

3. Ibid., 308.

27,533,755, it can be put in perspective when one considers that Anglican Church attendance on that day came to 5,292,551 combined for morning, afternoon and evening services,[4] merely 20 percent of the English and Welsh population, and that the census also revealed that 5,500,000, people attended no church service at all![5] Brethren attendance at the time of the census was over twice the number of Irving's Catholic Apostolic Church, which numbered 3,077 people on that Sunday and was founded in 1831, roughly the same time as the Brethren Movement, and around half the amount (14,363) of the Quaker "Society of Friends" founded in 1660, nearly two hundred years earlier.[6] One does need to take into account, however, with such statistics the specific problem of the Brethren not wishing to be labelled as a denomination or church per se, as well as the more general and well-known problems of the census.[7] Social-religious historians Embley and Wilson accept these statistics as more or less accurate, believing the morning attendances recorded on the Census Returns to give a fair guide of the actual membership of Brethren meetings.[8] By 1880, just over fifty years on from those first house meetings in Dublin, there were believed to be some 750 congregations established in the United Kingdom, 101 in Canada, 91 in the USA, 189 in Germany, 146 in France, and scattered congregations throughout some twenty-two other countries. Brethren publishers in London printed some eleven monthly journals with an estimate readership of 40–50,000 people.[9]

4. Flindall, *Church of England 1815–1948*, 131.

5. Ibid., 124.

6. Chadwick, *Victorian Church*, 36, 430.

7. Thompson, *Religious Census of 1851*, 247–49. Thompson notes that the main problem with the religious census relates to the incompleteness of the returns. Because enumerators were asked to seek out every place of worship in their district it seems likely that some smaller places of worship (such as meeting rooms) would have been missed. Moreover, many forms were only partially completed and thus out of 34,467 completed forms, 2,524 contained no information about sittings and 1,394 contained no information about attendance. However, in compiling the published tables the census authorities attempted to overcome this problem by estimating both the total attendance and the number of sittings. See also Embley, "Origins and Early Development," 11, who states that "the Returns of the 1851 Census of Religious Worship in England and Wales are essential sources for estimating the distribution and numerical strength of Brethren meetings shortly after the schism of 1848 . . . Those who completed the Returns on behalf of the meetings only rarely described the congregations as 'Plymouth Brethren,' and often felt obliged to register a special protest in the 'Remarks' column against accepting any denominational title."

8. See also Embley, "Early Development of the Plymouth Brethren," 213.

9. Miller, *Brethren*, 163.

There were a number of important factors for this rapid growth and proliferation, the first and most important being the influence of leading figures involved in doctrinal teaching and leadership. Although the community to this day strongly reject any formal ministry or clergy, it is clear that there have always been a number of dominant personalities in the movement who have been influential. These characters were able to impress their insights upon the ordinary members who looked to them as spiritual guides through their "sheer personal charisma" and this was, according to Embley, the most important factor for the growth and spread of the Brethren Movement.[10] It is somewhat paradoxical that the publication of Henry Pickering's *Chief among Brethren* (1931), a comprehensive list of the prominent men who joined and had an influence on the formation of the movement in its early years, places the words "Chief" and "Brethren" next to each other in the title. This publication illustrates that although ideologically the Brethren rejected formal authority, which led to a clergy-laity divide, in practice and reality human ambition is the arch foe of egalitarian brotherhood and theistic government, thus the individual chapels and congregations increasingly looked to their charismatic founders to provide authoritative church government and leadership.

It is important to mention at this stage, before any examination of individual Brethren authors is undertaken, something about the potential for "use" of Scripture within such a sociologically sectarian group. As will become clear throughout their history the Brethren became increasingly exclusive and more sectarian concerning who was "in" and who was "out" of the community. Such a factor promoted an increasingly sectarian use of Scripture as the group sought to give divine authority and credence to their numerous excommunications, schisms and segregations. The Whore of Babylon was a text that was used by the Brethren to define the "self" by vilifying the "other." As we shall see in what follows, the Brethren authors leveled the accusation of being "Babylon" upon all those from who they wished to distinguish themselves, on a religious, epistemological and secular level.

It is something of a tradition within Brethren historical writings to begin with John Nelson Darby. Darby, the godson of Lord Nelson, was educated at Trinity College Dublin where he read law, and later became an Anglican curate in county Wicklow, Ireland. He was one of the original five that met at nine Fitzwilliam Square. Darby began tirelessly to spread his message first of all throughout the UK, then into Europe. He was involved in the foundation of the first Dublin congregation, the Raleigh Street chapel in Plymouth, and congregations in Geneva and Vaud in Switzerland.

---

10. Embley, "Origins and Early Development," 217.

His untiring and energetic itinerant preaching tours led to a geographical spread of the movement.

Darby was a prolific writer and had an essential role in developing doctrine through his many publications. The antiestablishment polemical tone of his first publication *On the Nature and Unity of the Church* (1829) was to flavor the tenor of all his subsequent writings. In particular, from quite an early time, Darby began to develop a "doctrine of contamination," a belief that doctrinal heresy could be transmitted from one believer to another through fellowship (if the heretical member was not put out of fellowship the purity of the whole community would suffer), which became a fundamental factor in the Exclusive split and the movement towards sectarianism that followed it. Again the image of "Babylon" was a useful motif on which to draw in this context.

Darby's influence was fundamental and lasting to the extent that in effect he became the leader of a movement that denied it had a leader, for: "The real authority lay in effect with Darby."[11] His influence on the movement was so significant that it lasted far beyond his years or his own Exclusive Brethren community: "Without understanding the driving forces of Darby's personality we cannot understand, even today, the nature of many of the currents which run beneath the surface of the diverse expressions of the movement."[12] Such a charismatic individual, it will be seen, was able to exert a tremendously strong influence over the identity, beliefs and practices of the nascent Brethren movement. His exegesis of Revelation chapter 17–18 played a fundamental role in not only defining the movement but also influencing the exegesis of the next generation of Brethren authors.

Benjamin Wills Newton (1807–1899), the next Brethren author to which the attention of this book is turned, met Darby in Oxford 1830. A Fellow of Exeter college and a gifted academic, Newton was born into the Quaker tradition but had become a practicing Anglican by the time of his early adulthood. A dissenting fire was lit in Newton after hearing his friend and mentor Henry Bulteel preach a radical sermon at the University Church on the 6th February 1831. During this sermon Bulteel rejected the authority of the Established churches and resigned from his curacy to begin a career preaching in the Non-conformist congregations. However, Newton became repelled by the accompanying practice of charismatic gifts such as *glossolalia* and healings, which he associated with the Irvingite movement. Thus Newton returned with Darby to his hometown of Plymouth in 1831,

11. Ibid., 242.

12. Coad, *History of the Brethren Movement*, 109. N.B. The various subsects of the Brethren movement will be discussed below in the remainder of this chapter.

leaving Oxford, academia, and his affiliation to the Church of England behind. Newton was the first leader of Providence chapel in Plymouth, which was one of the most flourishing Brethren chapels at that time, a testimony and demonstration of his skills of leadership and persuasive manner. As far as his influence on doctrinal development is concerned Newton was "more of an intellectual than almost anyone among the Brethren."[13] Even after his excommunication his influence remained in part through his so-called "theological censorship" of the *Christian Witness Journal*.[14] Newton was indeed one of the movements most brilliant teachers[15] as well as a prolific writer, and his many publications still exert an enduring influence to this day over students of millennialist prophecy through the reprinting and dissemination efforts of Sovereign Grace Advent Testimony publishers.

Newton's exegesis of the Babylon motif differed vastly from that of Darby. These two early driving forces in the Brethren community differed significantly in their exegesis of Babylon on two levels. First, for Darby Babylon was predominantly a spiritual entity, whereas for Newton she was predominantly a physical entity.[16] Second, for Darby Babylon's destruction would occur after the church had been "raptured," whereas for Newton her destruction would occur before the *parousia* and the rapture of the church.[17] The difference in emphasis continued into Darby and Newton's Christological disagreements. Newton placed more of an emphasis on Christ's humanity and less emphasis on the supernaturally divine dimension of Christ's existence, suggesting that throughout the whole thirty-three years of Christ's life he had experienced real physical human suffering as a consequence of being born both fully human and a Jew.[18] He did not deny that Christ was divine, but merely emphasized his humanity and suffering,[19] and that as Christ was born a Jew, a descendant of Adam, although sinless, was accredited with vicarious guilt or Adam's guilt.[20] Darby responded by emphasizing the sinless divine nature of Christ, suggesting that if Christ had

---

13. Embley, "Early Development of the Plymouth Brethren," 228.

14. Ibid., 229.

15. Coad, *History of the Brethren Movement*, 153.

16. See ch. 8 below.

17. See ch. 9 below. For a detailed analysis of Darby and Newton's disagreement on the timing of the rapture see Burnham, *Story of Conflict*, 155–57.

18. Harris, *Sufferings of Christ*, 6–10, 24–37.

19. Newton, *Observation on a Tract*, 11–12, 20–21, 49–50.

20. Newton, *Doctrines of the Church*, 112.

been in such a position that he himself would be classed a sinner in need of salvation.[21]

The same difference occurred in the ecclesiology of the two early Brethren leaders. Newton's ecclesiological approach to the Plymouth Ebrington Street chapel, which had grown to some eight hundred members under his leadership, was one that, although rejecting formal ordination, required a formal organized structure of ruling elders, prearranged primary teachers preaching on a platform and a strict order imposed on worship.[22] Darby's ecclesiology was, in contrast, much more impulsive, supernatural, spiritual and divinely led. For Darby the church's hopes and promises were spiritual and heavenly, not earthly and human. This led him to develop an impulsive theory of ministry, whereby the service was led entirely by the Holy Spirit rather than by pastors or elders; the earthly church was far too corrupt to be led by men.[23]

William Kelly (1821–1906), the next author relevant to this current work, was, like Darby, a graduate of Trinity College Dublin where he read Classics.[24] He first met Darby in 1845, only a year before the damaging schisms of the 1846 Exclusive/Open break and the 1848 Bethesda division, and thus Kelly remained untainted by the painful events of earlier years. His skill as a church leader was immense. Within the Exclusive movement he was renowned as a "prominent leader"[25] and the most "erudite" of Darby's followers.[26] His theological and doctrinal influence was vast, and as a man of "deep learning" he became the "chief interpreter of Darby's theology."[27] His publications included *The Prospect* 1849–1850, *The Bible Treasury* 1856–1906, *The Christian Annotator* and he collated and edited *The Collected Works of Darby*. He penned some three hundred commentaries on every book of the Bible along with numerous other books, pamphlets and tracts, and translated the New Testament from Greek into English.

Of these publications nearly one hundred contain comments on "Babylon." As we shall see later, Kelly did not interpret Babylon simply in just one way. He held a multilevel and layered understanding of the text. This

21. Darby, "Observations on a Tract," 63.

22. See Newton, *Answers to Questions*, 10–14. Also Darby, "Narrative of the Facts," 32–34, 20, 23, 29. Darby notes that Newton stopped public prayers, impulsive hymn singing and prayer and that a discourse was prepared prior to the service.

23. Ibid., 24. Regarding "ministry" Darby writes, "I trust Brethren will seek nothing but the guidance of God's blessed Spirit."

24. Cross, *Irish Saint and Scholar*, 14.

25. Coad, *History of the Brethren Movement*, 74.

26. Ibid., 162.

27. Ibid., 210.

enabled him to understand Babylon on a religious level as Roman Catholicism and all of the major denominations of Christendom, on an epistemological level as the source of heretical doctrine and confusion, on a secular
level as worldly behavior and on an eschatological level as the event which
immediately follows the rapture of the saints.

Kelly led the 1881 schismatic Exclusive Kelly division, which was the
opposing faction to Darby's Exclusive division, thus becoming the leader
of his own Brethren sect bearing his name. In the following chapters it will
become clear that Kelly "used" the Babylon motif to give a scriptural basis
to his increasingly sectarian tendencies.

It is often quoted that Spurgeon remarked that Kelly had "a mind made
for the universe, but narrowed by Darbyism,"[28] yet Kelly was of the opinion
that Darby's exegetical foundations were certainly worthy of building on,
and thus he disseminated and popularized "Darbyite" doctrine to a wide audience through his vast publication record of his own work and through his
compilation of Darby's *Collected Works*. In this way Kelly helped maintain
and strengthen Darbyite Exclusive Brethrenism into the twentieth century.
It is little wonder then that with such an illustrious track record, Kelly has
been labelled "the greatest of all the Exclusives"[29] and that he was regarded
as "second only to Mr. Darby in knowledge of the Truth, and first in ability
to state it clearly."[30]

FINANCIAL FACTORS

The second significant reason for the rapid growth of the movement was
through the financial giving of wealthy members who, whether through
business or birth, were rich enough to pay for the construction of churches
and chapels. The nineteenth century ushered in a time of financial prosperity in England with agricultural and industrial accomplishments, both at
home and throughout the colonial empire, enriching trade with Europe and
the United States of America. It was a time when "Victorian Middle class
philanthropy, munificence of the nouveau riche, and the moral earnestness
of the aristocracy provided the capital to erect churches."[31] Many wealthy
Victorians, already attracted to numerous nineteenth-century evangelical
awakenings, became members of the Brethren movement and gave their

28. Cross, *Irish Saint and Scholar*, 7.
29. Coad, *History of the Brethren Movement*, 210.
30. Cross, *Irish Saint and Scholar*, 12.
31. Flindall, *Church of England: 1815–1948*, 4.

financial backing to the building and purchase of the movement's own places of worship.

It must be stressed at this juncture that the Brethren, like many sectarian groups with a high interest in apocalyptic sections of Scripture during that time period, originated as much from within intellectual circles as they did from more humble origins. Garrett has convincingly demonstrated that the end of the eighteenth and start of the nineteenth century was a time when discussion regarding the identity of the Beast and the Whore was a "respectable" pursuit of the wealthy, titled and privileged classes.[32] Such an interest in the prophetic was not merely the pursuit of the uneducated, poor and underprivileged people, whose desire for a better world to come was fuelled by hardship in this one, but was a particular preoccupation of the intelligentsia and wealthy people throughout Europe. It will become clear that many of the key figures in the Brethren movement were educated to a very high standard, and many seceded to the movement from a place of financial security. The Brethren did not offer a Christianity based on mere "wish-fulfillment" of a better world to come for those who could find no amelioration in this life, but offered an internally cohesive and intelligent, albeit uncritical, hermeneutical alternative to that which the Established churches offered.

The first character that played an important role in the development of the movement during its early years through finance was Henry Drummond: banker, wealthy Tory MP and "generous supporter of evangelical enterprise."[33] He was not a Brethren member but a member of the Catholic Apostolic Church led by Irving. However, his conferences of 1826–1830, which were convened annually for the study of biblical prophecy, became an excellent opportunity for the early Brethren members to meet like-minded individuals, often clergy, who were attracted to Prophetic study and ready to secede from the Established churches. These conferences were held at Albury Park, Drummond's countryseat six miles east of Guildford, and nearly half of the forty evangelicals who attended the first of them were clergymen of the Established church. Drummond became known as "the Banker of the New Doctrine,"[34] and while the Irvingite and Darbyite followers viewed each other at best with suspicion, he was responsible for the dissemination of Brethren ideals in an age without internet, television and telephones through facilitating this melting pot of dissenting minds.

---

32. Garrett, *Respectable Folly*, 6–9, 225.
33. Coad, *History of the Brethren Movement*, 71.
34. Ibid., 86.

While the Exclusive Brethren such as Kelly, Wigram and Mackin-tosh would come to identify the Irvingites to which Drummond belong as "Babylon,"[35] Drummond's influence on the formation of the very group that came to deride him as "Babylonian" cannot be dismissed as his home provided the fertile soil in which some peculiarly Brethren doctrines would grow into internally coherent doctrinal systems.[36]

Lady Theodosia Powerscourt (1800–1836) was not a member of the new Brethren movement, although she had attended some of those earli-est meetings in Augnier Street, Dublin, and even contemplated marriage to Darby. Her untimely death occurred before Brethren ideology had coalesced into a solid well-defined movement. However, after attending Drummond's Albury Conferences on prophecy, she opened her Irish mansion, Power-scourt House, near Bray, for a series of Prophetic Truth Conferences which ran from 1830–1833.[37] Lady Powerscourt had been overwhelmed by the sense that Christ was soon to return, thus, she invited the group to her family mansion to discuss unfulfilled prophecy and the signs of the times. Subjects like the meaning of 1260 days of Daniel 12:11 and Revelation 11:3 and 12:6, and the question of whether the saints are to suffer in the last days were discussed at her home. Discussion also was centered on dis-senting themes, such as, "Is it the present duty to resist or endure corrupt Institutions?"[38] These conferences were immensely popular and it has been noted that they were attended by significant numbers of interdenomina-tional participants.[39] Indeed, it was here that Darby met Groves and Parnell (Lord Congleton), thus providing a platform for the earliest members to meet likeminded, influential people and thereby facilitate the growth of the movement. Darby, Bellett, Craik, Newton, Müller, Wigram all attended these conferences, as did Irving and the radical evangelical rector Daly.[40]

Lady Powerscourt was clearly intrigued by prophetic scriptures, not only insofar as she opened her home for the discussion of such theories, but in that she discusses prophecy in a number of her personal letters, and

35. See ch. 6 below.

36. The role of Albury Park in the formation of the Secret Rapture of the Church doctrine will be discussed in more detail in ch. 9 below.

37. Froom, *Prophetic Faith*, 4.422, suggests 1830, others sources suggest 1831, e.g., Rowdon, *Origins of the Brethren, 1825–1850*, 88.

38. Rowdon, *Origins*, 88. The relevance of this theme will become clear in ch. 8 below.

39. Sandeen, *Roots of Fundamentalism*, 18–22.

40. Ibid., 34–36, 61–62. See also, Dunton, *Millennial Hopes and Fears*, 181–210.

indeed mentions Babylon in a number of them,[41] the exegesis of which will be discussed in the following chapters.

George Vicesmus Wigram (1805–1879), another key figure in this present book, was a close friend of Newton at Oxford, and he too decided to secede from the Established Church after hearing Bulteel's fiery sermon of 1831.[42] He was an eccentric character who was prodigal with his wealth, using his financial resources to purchase a disused chapel on Providence Road, Plymouth,[43] which was to become the flagship Brethren congregation of the mid- to late nineteenth century. The movement in London was started in the early 1830s largely through the philanthropic activity of Wigram who "was active in the initiation of a like testimony in London, where by the year 1838 a considerable number of gatherings were formed on the model of that at Plymouth."[44] In his later life Wigram was able to devote his whole time to religious pursuits, writing, and preaching throughout the Brethren movement. The Exclusive community after 1848 was on the whole a wealthy one, in part through the generosity of Wigram, who after his death made bequests totaling £36,000 in his Will to the movement, and through this financial support he proved to be influential in promoting the rise of Darby as the single most respected and authoritative leader among Brethren. Like Darby and Kelly, fellow Exclusive Wigram had a multivalent interpretation of Babylon and his views on the exegesis of Revelation chapters 17–18 will be seen in all but one of the following chapters.[45]

PROLIFIC PUBLICATION

The final significant reason for growth came through prolific publication and the use and distribution of pamphlets and journals. (This was to some extent linked into wealth and charismatic teachers: the wealthy were able to pay for print runs and fund writers who had a great deal to write about.) Darby, Newton and Kelly were prolific writers, not only of books but also of journal articles, with wide readerships and large publication numbers, as well as pamphlets that could be distributed quickly, easily and cheaply, thus

41. Powerscourt, *Letter and Papers*, letters 18, 23, 46, 57, 60, 78, and "Paper on Genesis 22," written between 1828 and 1836 contain references to Babylon.

42. Rowdon, *Origins*, 75.

43. Ibid., 76.

44. Coad, *History of the Brethren Movement*, 76.

45. In the following chapters of this book the only identification of Babylon that Wigram does not make is that of Roman Catholicism. He does, however, identify Catholicism as part of the "professing church" thus we may conclude that he indirectly identifies Catholicism as Babylon. See ch. 6.

promoting the Brethren movement and encouraging likeminded Christians to secede from their traditions and join the movement. Evidence of the above can be seen in the very formation of the Christian Brethren archive.[46] During the first century of the Brethren movement there was an overwhelming number of authors contributing to the dissemination of Brethren doctrine and theology.

Scotsman Andrew Miller (1810–1883), a wealthy business man in London and voluntary Baptist pastor, seceded to the Brethren movement after an invitation to attend a Brethren Bible study. He is mentioned as a prominent member of the Brethren movement in Pickering's *Chief Men among the Brethren*.[47] His publication *Plymouthism and the Modern Churches* (1900) is cited in E. E. Whitfield, "Plymouth Brethren," in *New Schaff-Herzog Encyclopaedia of Religious Knowledge*, P-R, 9.98. His highly regarded and extensively comprehensive *Papers on Church History*, 3 vols. (1873–1878), and *The History of the Brethren (commonly so-called) A Brief Sketch of their Origin, Progress and Testimony* (1879) are among the most well known of his publications, and the latter was considered such valuable source within Brethren circles that W. R. Dronsfield would write a sequel to it a century later entitled *The Brethren Since 1870* (ca. 1966). Miller's exegesis of the Babylon motif will be seen in all but two of the following chapters[48] suggesting that, for Miller, defining the Brethren on a religious level over and against other Christian denominations and on a secular level as in contrast to the world, was of more importance than defining the Brethren movement on an epistemological level or eschatological level.

Irish Brethren member Charles Henry Mackintosh (1820–1896) converted to Brethrenism after the prayerful reading of Darby's *Operations of the Spirit of God* (1865). He was a prolific author, but perhaps his most well-known publications are his massive *Notes* on the five books of the Pentateuch and the frequently reprinted *Miscellaneous Writings* (ca. 1880) consisting of seven volumes, totaling over 2500 pages. His importance as a Brethren author cannot be underestimated. It has been correctly noted that it was Mackintosh who both popularized and disseminated Darby's ideas throughout North America. Furthermore in Mackintosh's exegesis we find the starting point for the trajectory of Brethren doctrine and practices from England to America at the end of the nineteenth century. Like Miller's, Mackintosh's exegesis of the Babylon motif will be explored in detail in

---

46. The archive is found in the John Rylands University Library, University of Manchester, UK.

47. Pickering, *Chief among Brethren*, 74.

48. See chs. 7 and 9 below.

chapters 5, 6, and 8. He is notable by his absence from chapters 7 and 9. This is because Mackintosh, unlike many Brethren writers, did not make a link between Babylon and doctrinal confusion and Babylon and the secret rapture.

Edward Dennett (1831–1914) was originally an Anglican who, after studies at London University, became a minister of a Baptist Chapel in Greenwich from which he seceded to the Brethren movement after attending a Brethren breaking of bread service during a period of illness at Veytaux, Switzerland.[49] He published a number of books and papers and preached widely throughout England, Ireland, and Scotland, and paid visits to Norway, Sweden, and America. Dennett's exegesis of the Babylon motif will be seen in all of the following archival chapters with the exception of chapter 7, "Babylon Is Doctrinal Confusion," and as such this suggests that in the general terms of using Babylon as a means of defining the "self" by vilifying the "other," Dennett places a greater emphasis on the religious, secular and eschatological boundaries of the movement than the epistemological or doctrinal boundary.

James G. Bellett (1795–1864) was one of the original five brethren who began to meet in Fitzwilliam Square, Dublin, in 1829.[50] Among his best known books are *The Patriarchs* (ca. 1875), *The Evangelists* (1889), *The Son of God* (ca. 1870), and the *Moral Glory of the Lord Jesus* (1865). Bellett's interpretation of the Babylon of Revelation chapters 17–18 will be examined in all of the following archival chapters, demonstrating a highly complex and multifarious exegesis of the text, which Bellett uses as a tool to distinguish between those who are "in" and those who are "out" of the community. Bellett's most intriguing hermeneutical offering will be viewed in chapter 8, where, in an unusual and imaginative application of the biblical text he identified the Great Exhibition of 1851 as the Apocalyptic Whore.

W. T. P. Wolston (1840–1917)[51] was trained as a lawyer and a doctor when he experienced conversion at the age of twenty years. For forty-five years he was editor of the magazine *God's Glad Tidings* later known as *The Gospel Messenger*, and composed a hymnbook which was reprinted at least seven times and reached at least eight-eight thousand copies by 1933. He penned nine volumes on spiritual subjects, on the subjects of *Behold the Bridegroom* (1891), *Forty Days of Scripture* (1904), and *The Church: What Is It?* (1945). Wolston has a complex compound understanding of Babylon

49. Pickering, *Chief among Brethren*, 156.

50. Ibid., 10–11.

51. Ibid., 141.

which will be seen in all but one of the following archival chapters.[52] Clearly Wolston, as an early member of the Exclusive sect of the Brethren community, is intent on defining strict boundaries between "insider" and "outsider," and by using the Whore of Babylon as a designation for those who are "outside" of the Exclusive group, finds a useful scriptural designation for vilifying the "other."

Little biographical information is known Of Thomas B. Baines (dates unknown) and he is not mentioned in Pickering's *Chief among Brethren*. His publications include *The Lord's Coming, Israel, and the Church* (1876), a series of three papers on the eschatological hope of the church and of Israel, and *The Revelation of Jesus Christ* (1879) a series of three lectures by Baines based on an inaugurated futuristic reading of Revelation which will be examined in detail below. Baines is noted as taking part in the burial service of Wigram at Paddington Cemetery in 1879 along with Kelly and other noted Exclusive Brethren.[53] His exegesis of the Babylon texts is found in all but the final chapter of the archival section, chapter 9, "Babylon and the Secret Rapture of the Church," which demonstrates that for Baines, the interpretation of Babylon was an important activity in defining the enemy and the outsider and reinforcing the boundaries of the movement. Babylon represents the religious outsider, the epistemological outsider and the secular outsider. Although Baines does promote a typically Brethren two-stage rapture hypothesis,[54] he does not use Babylon as either the reason for leaving the earth, nor does he connect the judgment of Babylon with the first stage of events on the world after the true saints have left.

Yorkshire man William Trotter (1818–1865)[55] was ordained as a Methodist minister at the age of nineteen, but by 1844 he had seceded and begun to attend regularly a Brethren congregation in Halifax. His *Plain Papers on Prophetic and Other Subjects* (1854) was a series of twenty essays on apocalyptic subjects, whereas his *Eight Lectures on Prophecy* (1852) was a series of papers predominantly concerned with the role of the church and the Jews in the last days. His work was often included in Kelly's magazine *The Prospect*, and Edwin Cross, Kelly's biographer, identifies him as one of the

---

52. Wolston is not mentioned in ch. 5, "Babylon Is Papal Rome," but in ch. 6, "Babylon Is All of Corrupt Christendom," he does identify Catholicism as the Thyatiran Church (Rev 2), in whom Jezebel is to be found, and then, later, connects Jezebel with Babylon.

53. Cross, *Irish Saint and Scholar*, 132.

54. Baines, "Glorious Coming and Kingdom," 252–63. N.B., Baines remains silent as to the possibility of a "rapture" but stresses the second stage: "the coming of Christ back to the earth with His saints."

55. Pickering, *Chief among Brethren*, 31.

"notable prophetic authors of the day."[56] The interpretation of the Babylon motif by Trotter will be seen in all but the first of the archival chapters below. He is absent from chapter 5, "Babylon Is Papal Rome," although even here the situation is not completely clear since he does, by virtue of identifying Catholicism as the nominal Christianity of the Church in Thyatira (Rev 2:18–27), which develops chronologically, or "ripens," into the Church of Laodicea (Rev 3), include Catholicism in the Apocalyptic judgments which are to come on Babylon. Clearly for Trotter, the strong supporter of Darby and early follower of the Exclusive schism of the Brethren, the question of who was in the group and who was out was of utmost importance. It will be seen in what follows that Trotter uses the Babylon motif to denigrate those who belong to other Christian denominations, believe other doctrines and enjoy "worldly" pastimes. Such people, he says, will be left behind on the earth when the true church is secretly "raptured," and according to Trotter's reading of Revelation chapters 17–18, the unrighteous remnant will then be destroyed.

Frederick W. Grant (1834–1902) was born in London and ordained within the Church of England in Canada from which he seceded after reading Brethren literature.[57] In the Christian Brethren Archive there are a number of his publications but perhaps of most interest to this book are *A Divine Movement and Our Path with God Today* (1973) and the last part of the *Open Letter to Mr. F. E. Raven* (ca. 1899) written by Grant on the 28th September 1897 concerning his exclusion in 1885 from the Exclusive Kelly faction for entertaining Open and Ravenite influences,[58] even though only less than two decades previously Kelly had commended his exegesis as "luminous."[59] Yet it is also to be noted that he was originally one of the thirty or forty that in 1847 had "protested in vain [and] withdrew from fellowship with those meeting at Bethesda"[60] along with Darby, Wigram and Trotter. Thus Grant had experience of both excluding and being excluded on account of doctrinal differences. Once again experience can be seen to lead to exegesis, since Grant's sectarian tendencies are apparent in the way he interpreted the Babylon motif, and, as will become clear in four of the five following chapters, he identified Babylon in such a way as to give scriptural authority to his efforts to exclude those who differed to him on a denominational, doctrinal and moral (i.e., "worldly") level. His exegesis of the Babylon motif will not

56. Cross, *Irish Saint and Scholar*, 29.
57. Pickering, *Chief among Brethren*, 100–101.
58. Ibid., 67, 83n86.
59. Kelly, *Lectures on the Gospel of Matthew*, 295.
60. Smith, *Open Brethren*, 5.

be seen in chapter 9, "'Babylon' and the Secret Rapture of the Church," since although he does follow a two-stage rapture hypothesis, he does not use the Babylon motif in working through this conclusion. Rather Grant uses the image of the Church in Philadelphia (Rev 2–3), of which the Brethren are part, to argue for this doctrine.[61]

Thomas Newberry (1811–1901)[62] was involved in the so-called "Sufferings of Christ" controversy of ca. 1866 during which Darby had been accused of Christological errors identical to Newton's error some twenty years earlier. This controversy led to Newberry along with W. H. Dorman, Captain Percy Hall and Joseph Stancomb seceding from the Exclusive Darbyite group. Newberry was well known in Brethren circles for editing the Newberry Reference Bible which used a system of symbols to explain verb tenses. He, as an expert on biblical Hebrew and Greek, wrote many books on the typology of the Old Testament tabernacle, temple and offerings, and a popular short publication titled *Brief Outline of the Book of the Revelation* (ca. 1891) which will be examined below. Newberry's exegesis of Babylon contributes to chapters 6 to 9 of this book, and although he does not mention explicitly that Babylon is Roman Catholicism, and is hence not found in chapter 5 of the archival examination, he does identify Babylon, in religious terms, as superficial and external Christianity, and by virtue of this identifies all of the denominations of Christendom as Babylon. Newberry's highly schismatic tendencies, to secede from the Establishment to the Brethren movement, then to secede again to join Darby in the Exclusive Brethren schism, and then to secede yet again from the Exclusives in response to perceived doctrinal confusion in Darby's teaching, was fuelled to a certain extent by his exegesis of the Babylon motif. As will become clear in chapter 7 below the doctrinal principle established during the first major schism in the Brethren community was that of a "Doctrine of Contamination" whereby heresy could be transmitted like an infectious disease. Such a view was worked out exegetically in the context of Revelation chapters 17–18.[63] It could be argued then, that Newberry, Dorman, Hall and Stancomb, in seceding from the Darbyite Exclusives, were simply "following the logic" of the principle of excommunication first established at Bethesda,[64] to "come out" of doctrinal confusion, so as not to "receive Babylon's plagues" (Rev

---

61. Grant, *Divine Movement*, 5–10. Proof that "the Lord takes us to be with Himself above" is found in the Letters to the Churches (Rev 2–3).

62. Pickering, *Chief among Brethren*, 80.

63. See ch. 7 below.

64. Coad, *History of the Brethren Movement*, 162.

18:4). What is certain, is that for these Brethren, engaging with the text in the light of personal experience was central.

Brethren author F. C. Bland (1826–1894) was noted for his *Twenty One Prophetic Subjects* and was known as "one of the ablest ministers of the word which Ireland has supplied."[65] He was converted to the Brethren by Mackintosh and promptly moved from Dublin to Plymouth.[66] He had a friendly connection with Sir Robert Anderson, Chief of Scotland Yard in London, and it was through this friendship that Anderson was influenced to some extent by Bland's Brethren premillennial dispensational futurism, which Anderson picked up on when he wrote the famously influential book *The Coming Prince: or, The Seventy Weeks of Daniel, with an Answer to Higher Criticism* (1895). As shall be seen in chapter 5 below, Bland identifies Babylon as the Roman Catholic Church, yet he does not identify Babylon as any of the other denominations of Christianity, which suggests that he was not overly concerned with using the Babylon motif to define his own religious boundaries within the Brethren movement against the Babylonian outsider. This is surprising given that Pickering describes him as "naturally haughty, intolerant of opposition, and quick to resent an injury or slight."[67] In the context of this book, Bland's significant contribution to this book comes in chapter 7, "Babylon Is Worldliness." Here it will be seen that he takes a highly literalistic exegesis of the text and concludes that there will be a literal and physical rebuilding of the ancient kingdom of Babylon somewhere in modern day Iran. Bland also uses the Babylon motif to argue for a physical rapture of the saints in order for them to be spared the tribulational dangers, of which the destruction of Babylon is the first. This will be seen in chapter 9.[68]

65. Pickering, *Chief among Brethren*, 89.

66. Ibid., 90–91.

67. Ibid., 92.

68. It is believed that the survey of brethren writers listed above, which is based upon extensive use of archival material not heretofore examined in detail, is substantially comprehensive. Some very minor figures have been excluded as they add little to what has already been said. Such figures include Rossier (1835–1928), who argued, among other things, that in the last days a new physical kingdom of Babylon would literally reappear. See *Le Livre du Prophete Habakuk*, and *Meditations sur le Seconde Livre de Chroniques*. Also a small number of anonymous authors who wrote in such periodicals as the *Bible Treasury*, the *Northern Witness*, and the *Christian Witness* have been omitted as they add nothing new to the book.

THEOLOGICAL THEMES

The theology of the Christian Brethren movement is, in very general terms, that of the Reformed Protestant tradition, with prime importance placed upon the supreme authority and adequacy of Holy Scripture. The Brethren are moderate Calvinists, acknowledging the irresistible prevenient grace of God. They place utmost importance upon the personal justification of the individual believer and the total atonement of those who have been saved, an event followed by believers' baptism. Those from Established Catholic or Anglican traditions are re-baptized after their secessions. An ensuing life of purity and holiness must follow baptism. With regard to many doctrines the group have much in common with Dissenting and Non-conformist groups of the eighteenth and nineteenth century, for example the Wesleyan Methodists, the General Baptists, the Particular Baptists and the remnants of the Presbyterians and Independents. However, the Church of England and Roman Catholicism are generally regarded as corrupt forms of Christendom by the group. In particular the tendency to gloss over any distinction between true believers and unbelievers, through the indiscriminate use of rites and ceremonies, was seen to remove the need for personal salvation, by grace and through faith. This is reflected in the Brethren's polemical style of writing regarding the doctrines of such Established Churches. It will become clear in chapters 5 and 6, however, that regardless of what doctrines may or may not be shared in common with the above denominations, the Brethren still managed to identify all Christian groups around them as Babylon.

The two areas of doctrine where the Brethren movement can be seen to diverge most obviously from their Reformed Protestant, moderate Calvinistic and Puritan heritage are in the areas of ecclesiology and eschatology. Brethren ecclesiology is based on the single underlying principle of the complete rejection of formal ministry. Such ecclesiology could be described as an extreme democracy whereby anyone may preach and no one should lead the meeting, except the Holy Spirit. Thus the meetings would be free from any type of formal authority which might lead to any clergy-laity divide. Instead the Brethren would look only to Christ as their head and the Holy Spirit as their guide. They rejected the idea of a clerical order believing in the Lutheran ideal of the priesthood of all believers which was combined with an underlying sense that the Established laity had become corrupt and complacent.

The early Brethren developed this democratic, free ecclesiology into a coherent doctrinal system often referred to as the "Impulsive Theory of Ministry" whereby the "Head of the Church," i.e., Christ, exercises authority over the church through the "direct impulsive movement of the Spirit on the members of the Churches"[69] rather than through authority delegated to human clergy. Thus Darby writes that the church is to be a place where God might "lead believers to more explicit reliance on the operations of the divine Spirit."[70] The church should be a place where "men have their place . . . by virtue, not of their official situations, but of the gifts which God has given them" and the competency of the individuals to minister should be judged only by "the gifts of God's Spirit which they may have."[71] Indeed Darby was of the opinion that such beliefs gave the Brethren an ecclesiastical superiority over the Established Protestant churches and he did not hesitate to use the image of Babylon to argue this point.[72]

The ecclesiastical "doctrine of separation" is undoubtedly the single most important doctrine that has defined the movement in the eyes of other Christians over the course of their history. In essence it is a sectarian doctrine that postulates that the true believer must be separate from the world and all its impurity, this is so since the Brethren believe that evil has a contaminating effect, sticking like dirt to the believer's soul. Their sectarian approach could be seen through the mission of the Brethren leaders in "calling out Christians from the world and from churches that were under imminent judgment."[73]

This kind of sectarian teaching is common within all sectarian groups but is taken to an extreme in Brethren circles through the suggestion that even impure doctrine or teaching has some kind of contaminating effect and can defile the true believer. Darby developed what would become known as a "doctrine of contamination" whereby evil is transferred contagiously as miasma from assembly to assembly. This development was, in part, a reaction to what he deemed as heretical teaching, and the doctrine would play a part in the Open/Exclusive division of 1846 and the Bethesda Schism of 1848, the language of Babylon giving divine credence to the theory. The Open Brethren did not develop such a sectarian dogma, but rather it was primarily Darby, as leader of the Exclusive sect, who was responsible for this increasing movement to separation according to pioneer missionary and early Brethren member A. N. Groves. In his letter of 1836, Groves wrote to Darby to tell him that he had perceived a change in emphasis from inclusiveness and commonality of spirit to an emphasis on error in church order and of separating oneself from error. He warned Darby: "You will be known

69. Coad, *History of the Brethren Movement*, 270.

70. Darby, "Considerations on the Nature and Unity of the Church," 31.

71. Darby, "Thoughts on the Present Position," 81.

72. Ibid., 78–102.

73. Coad, *History of the Brethren Movement*, 67.

more by what you witness *against* than what you witness for, and practically this will prove that you witness against all but yourselves."[74] However, as the rift began to open between the moderately conservative Open Brethren movement and Darby's more extreme and fundamental Exclusive Brethren movement "Darby became increasingly suspicious of all outside his own circle, and [became] morbidly preoccupied with the 'evil' and 'worldliness' around him."[75] As we shall see in the remainder of this book, such doctrines informed Brethren readings of much of Scripture and Revelation chapters 17–18 appealed greatly to them in particular in this context.

Much of Darby's ecclesiastical writings focused on a call to become separate from the world and to be pure from contamination. Purity was not only sought through adopting an *extra muros* stance with regard to the world, but care must be taken even *intra muros vis-à-vis* the broad Brethren movement not to be contaminated by heretical doctrine from within.

The excommunication program began when Newton's teaching in the Plymouth assembly was perceived as heretical in the area of Christological doctrine. He was excommunicated in 1847 for doctrinal errors,[76] an event which set a precedent: from that point onward any individual perceived to adhere to non-brethren doctrine would be put out of fellowship. Moreover any congregation receiving the excommunicated Brethren was seen as becoming miasmatically contaminated by their toxic and contagious teaching. For example, Brethren historian Coad has noted the presumed corrupting effects of "wrong" understanding in Darby's ecclesiology:

> Darby early developed a theory of the workings of heresy which
> coloured his actions for the whole of his life. Heresy was to him
> a real and evil thing, working secretly and deviously beneath the
> surface, until it broke out in its full development, to the ruin of
> churches . . . a subtle, hidden evil.[77]

Whole fellowships could be excommunicated. Darby began increasingly to insist that new members adhered to a strict set of doctrinal statements as a prerequisite to admission into the fellowships. Kelly also maintained this dual concept of both separation from the dangers of the world without and separation from the dangers of doctrinal untruth and heresy within. Using the language of Revelation chapters 17–18 he wrote concerning the need for separation from both moral and worldly evil in

---

74. Groves, *Letter from A. N. Groves to J. N. Darby*, March 10th, 1836.

75. Coad, *History of the Brethren Movement*, 211.

76. See ch. 7 below.

77. Coad, *History of the Brethren Movement*, 112.

the same paragraph as he talked about mental "delusion" regarding the "full pure truth" of doctrine.[78]

Separation from evil began to take on a new dimension within the Brethren movement that had been missing from other sectarian movements. Not only was a general separation from the unbelieving evil world required but also a separation from the believing yet deluded brother whose heresy could contaminate the believer, as well as separation from the Established, yet corrupt, Churches whose influence could lead to impurity.[79] Inevitably this doctrinal stance was worked into the movement's understanding of the biblical text.

Turning now to the other highly distinctive area of Brethren doctrine, eschatology, it is important to note that the Brethren have always been highly interested in the study of prophecy and of apocalyptic scripture. The group are generally Futurists[80] in their reading of prophetic texts, however, this is expressed as an inaugurated (already begun to take place) and partially realized Futurism rather than merely projecting the text into some remote age to come.

In the early nineteenth century the Futurist hermeneutic was a radical methodological stance to take. The accepted Protestant interpretive norm for reading prophetic scripture was to take a Historicist stance[81] as Futurist readings of Revelation were generally associated with the Catholic Jesuit Counter-Reformation approach of Ribera in the sixteenth century, and the counter-historicist approach of Cardinal Walmsley in the eighteenth century. The Tractarian movement in the early nineteenth century rejected Historicism in favor of Futurism as part of their Romanizing trend, partly in order to disassociate the pope from identification with the Antichrist. Thus the Brethren, as Reformed Protestants who rejected the authority of Rome, were taking a brave step in accepting the Futurist hermeneutic.

The Brethren were also a pre-millennial group believing in a literal personal reign of Jesus, with his advent before its commencement. However the Brethren developed a novel form of millennial eschatology insofar as it was they who were responsible for, if not inventing at least for massively popularizing, what is now commonly known as the "secret rapture of the saints" doctrine,[82] whereby the true believers leave the earth before the so-

78. Kelly, *Lectures on the Book of Revelation*, 355.

79. See ch. 7 below.

80. See ch. 1 above.

81. See ch. 1 above.

82. Coad, *History of the Brethren Movement*, 130. The influences on the Brethren development of the Secret Rapture of the Church theory will be studied further in ch. 9 below.

called tribulational events described between Revelation chapters 4–19 and then return with Christ to inaugurate his millennial kingdom.

With the meeting together of people with a common interest in prophecy at Albury Park and Powerscourt Estate this apparently previously unknown doctrine began to be formulated. Newton suggested in the Fry MSS[83] that this theory was first introduced to the delegates by Irving, and was undoubtedly discussed among those there to study prophecy.[84] This doctrine postulates that the Second Advent will take place in two stages, the first being a "rapture" of the church and the first resurrection at Christ's *parousia*. Of this event Darby writes, "I believe firmly that all true Christians will be preserved and caught up to heaven."[85] This will happen before the Great Tribulation. The true believers leave the earth and are engaged in post-rapture events in heaven, before any of the terrible apocalyptic post-rapture judgments occur on earth. This rapture will be in secret and the world will not be aware of it. The true believers will remain in the sky or in heaven for a period of time during Antichrist's reign. The second stage sees the visible return of Christ, or *epiphaneia*, with the saints after either three and a half or perhaps seven years to destroy Antichrist and set up the millennial kingdom on earth. Darby writes that the "things which are" (Rev 1:19) show the churches in their moral character on earth, but of the "things which shall be hereafter" (Rev 4:1), he writes, "We are necessarily caught up to the throne"[86] at which point the tribulational period begins: "The world, meanwhile, not the church, is the subject of the statements contained in these portions . . . the church is looked at, I apprehend, as in the heavens from the end of chapter 3."[87] Then the millennial kingdom will be established, the post-millennial events described in Revelation chapters 19–22 will take place, and the Brethren will enter the promised eternal state of bliss.[88]

83. The Fry MSS here refers to the collection of handwritten letters and papers from early Brethren members such as Darby and Newton contained in the JRULM archives.

84. Coad, *Prophetic Developments*, 22. The theoretical antecedents to the secret rapture doctrine will be explored fully in ch. 9.

85. Darby, "What Is the Church," 131.

86. Darby, "Notes on the Revelation," 262.

87. Ibid., 280–82n.

88. The view was quite widely accepted throughout the Exclusive Brethren movement and although rejected by the more moderate Open Brethren, had a lasting and enduring effect on the popular study of prophecy. It will be examined in more detail in ch. 9 below.

This doctrine is fundamental to contemporary North American rapture culture, as seen for example in the *Left Behind* series of novels written by LaHaye and Jenkins. Its popularity in recent years can traced directly back to the early Brethren movement. Kelly, it is noted, met the American dispensationalist Gaebelein in 1897 at the Brethren Blackheath assembly, and this meeting provided the earliest point of trajectory of Brethren dispensational two-stage "secret rapture" eschatology over the Atlantic to America. Gaebelein is of course widely accepted as being an early and enthusiastic proponent of this doctrine.[89] The itinerant preaching of many of the early Brethren leaders resulted in frequent tours of North America which further spread Brethren eschatology. Darby frequently travelled to North America where his teachings on premillennial dispensationalism gained great influence. The *Scofield Study Bible* (1917) was absolutely central to this development. This is so since Scofield added here for the first time a futuristic, premillennial commentary alongside the biblical text.[90] His commentary did much to popularize "rapture theory" in terms of Darby's hermeneutical schema throughout the Western world. Scofield's work had an enormous influence in shaping modern American prophetic beliefs and the influence that Darby had on him cannot be easily dismissed.

Probably the most lasting and enduring legacy of Darby's biblical exegesis of eschatological scripture is his propagation and popularization of the Dispensational theory, the broad outline of which can be traced back to Joachim of Fiore in the twelfth century. Darby, like Joachim, suggested that the history of the world is divided into different dispensations or epochs of time, yet Darby went further implying that as each epoch progresses mankind become increasingly sinful and the world slowly decays until a cataclysmic or apocalyptical event destroys the old world order and a new world order is established.

For Darby the key to understanding all of Scripture, and indeed the key to understanding the whole world around him, was to be found in dividing correctly the history of the world up into the Jewish dispensation and the Gentile dispensation and appropriately assigning the promises and hopes of Scripture to either epoch. It cannot be claimed that the dispensational worldview began with the Brethren movement, however up until the time of the Brethren this doctrine only existed on the fringes of the Christian community and was not widely known or accepted. For instance, in 1812 the Chilean Jesuit Manuel Lacunza secretly published *The Coming*

89. Boyer, *When Time Shall Be No More*, 92. He notes that Gaebelein's *Our Hope* "spread the millennial word far and wide."

90. Ibid., 97. Boyer describes Scofield as "a towering figure in twentieth century premillennialism."

of Messiah in Glory and Majesty in which he hinted at a dispensational division of world history. Edward Irving, founder of the Irvingite or Catholic Apostolic Church, translated Lacunza's work into English and added a significant "preliminary discourse" by way of introduction. This sensational book, with its radical "futurist" exegesis of the Apocalypse, found its way into Brethren hands. Irving regularly attended the Albury Park Conferences as well as the Powerscourt Conferences and it is entirely possible that at one of these events he met Darby and/or his translation of Lacunza's book reached Darby's hand. The *Left Behind* series is again significant here, since in addition to the doctrine of the secret rapture already noted above the series makes use of Darby's dispensationalist legacy. Boyer notes:

> Darby taught that God has dealt with mankind in a series of epochs, or dispensations—in each of which the means of salvation differed. While Bible prophecy reveals much about past and future dispensations it is silent on the present one, the Church Age. . . . Darby's system contained nothing new . . . but Darby wove these strands into a tight and cohesive system that he buttressed at every point by copious biblical proof texts, then tirelessly promoted through his writing and preaching tours.[91]

The reason Boyer gives for the widespread growth and popularity of Brethren eschatology is primarily political. He writes, "No doubt the anti-institutional bias of the Plymouth Brethren, a major theme in Darby's prophecy writings, found fertile soil in nineteenth-century America, where laissez-faire ideology abounded."[92] Yet it must be the sum total of the new Brethren package, which included copious publication of coherent Brethren eschatological doctrine combined with the tireless preaching tours of America, in combination with a political and sociological climate ready to hear such an anti-establishment impulsive ecclesiology, that would prove to be the catalyst for what would become the predominant view of North American Christians in the twenty-first century.

SCHISM AND DIVISION

Unfortunately no history of the Brethren church would be complete without a section on the divisions and schism that has plagued the unity of the movement. Indeed a number of publications get so bogged down in these matters and the nuances of doctrinal differences that they inform the reader

91. Ibid., 87–88.
92. Ibid., 88.

of little else. Brethren history simply becomes caricatured as a list of different schisms and divergences.[93] It cannot be denied however that the history of the movement has been marred by heated division over a number of doctrinal issues. The first and most well known division was in Plymouth, 1846. Next came the 1848 division between so-called "Open" and "Exclusive" Brethren, in which Newton taught that Christ took on sinful flesh and Christ could have sinned. Brethren were divided as to whether to receive a member who came from Newton's gatherings. The schism began a famously antagonistic relationship between Newton and Darby. Darby here began on a path of increasingly moving towards separation.[94] Darby, the leading influential charismatic "founder" of the Exclusives, along with those Brethren loyal to him, became obsessed with separation: the logical outworking of such sectarian doctrine.

With the Plymouth and Bethesda schisms there began a long chain of division and segregation as time and time again individuals and congregations so obsessed with the corruptive danger of doctrinal untruth sought to separate themselves from the slightest hint of heresy. Numerous other divisions occurred which, when relevant, will be discussed below. It will be seen that at times the image of Babylon was used to further such sectarianism as the more Exclusive Brethren saw in that image a picture of their own enemies.

SOME CONCLUDING REMARKS ON THE HISTORY OF THE CHRISTIAN BRETHREN MOVEMENT

The movement began as a nondenominational and fully inclusive group who accepted all to share the Lord's Supper regardless of adherence to any particular creed or doctrine. They grew both numerically and geographically through the tireless endeavors of charismatic and persuasive leaders who were energetic in their itinerant preaching and prolific in their publication. The movement's growth was also to a lesser extent a result of a number of wealthy and eminent individuals who gave of their finances into building and buying chapels, and who put their well-respected names behind the movement thereby increasing social acceptance.

Between 1830 and 1846 the movement began to crystallize into a distinct evangelical movement. The number of Brethren chapels were growing,

93. Coad, *History of the Brethren Movement*, 312. Coad describes Noel's *History of the Brethren* as a "grossly misnamed" book "largely an almost incoherent account of exclusive quarrels."

94. Embley, "Early Development of the Plymouth Brethren," 223–24, 226.

as those who generally attended the breaking of bread service seceded from their denominational affiliations and the Brethren meetings became full time places of worship in their own right. Through the work of Groves, a missionary movement was born and through the work of Müller, a social enterprise scheme of orphanages was born. In those earliest years the movement was nonsectarian, yet after the first two schisms in the movement (1846 and 1848), and as the movement entered the twentieth century, it had become highly fragmented in nature. Brethrenism was a highly distinctive, exclusive and sectarian entity with well-defined boundaries between insider and outsider. It was comprised of some ten subsects each of which placed a fundamental stress on the importance of doctrinal purity yet were unable to agree on the exact details of those doctrines. Excluding and putting out of fellowship all who did not adhere became a frequent occurrence, a far cry from those early meetings in Augnier Street which were open to all who would come regardless of doctrine or denomination. As we arrive at 1900, the *terminus ad quem* of this book, Brethren historian Neatby's views sum up the place the Brethren had arrived at well: they "began with the principle of universal communion, but ended with universal excommunication."[95] As we shall see in the remainder of this book, these historical and sociological developments gave rise to varied and imaginative exegetical strategies.

---

95. Neatby, *History of the Plymouth Brethren*, 59.

5

"Babylon" Is Papal Rome

The preceding chapters of this book have been essential in setting the context for what is to follow. We turn now to examine the specific ways in which the Brethren movement has understood, used, and been influenced by the image of the Whore of Babylon found in Revelation chapters 17–18. From this point on this book is based almost exclusively upon archival material which has not to this point been extensively researched in the particular context of the history of biblical interpretation. Following an exhaustive and detailed analysis of the Christian Brethren Archive it is possible to extrapolate a number of ways that the text has been received and used by the group. This chapter is devoted to the first explanation of the text that the archive yields, namely, that the Whore of Babylon in the Christian Brethren movement is understood as a religious entity. As we shall in this chapter, that religious entity is specifically identified as the Roman Catholic Church.

For any new religious tradition it is important to define one's own identity over and against the identity of those from whom one has broken away or seceded. This was true for the earliest Christians. Jews themselves originally, they could have been seen as simply just one more "Palestinian Jewish Sectarian group."[1] They eventually came to separate from their religious parents, however, and form an autonomous and independent "new" religion. The same sectarian pattern can be seen in the time of the Reformation when the Reformers such as Luther, Calvin and Zwingli, who were

1. Macrae, "Messiah and Gospel," 169.

themselves originally Catholic, came to separate from Rome and form their own autonomous Christian communities.

When examining the concept of sectarian religion both the notion of *secare*, to cut off, and of *religare*, to bind together, are of equal importance. For a new religious tradition to be "successful" one must both cut off any external ties to that from which one used to belong and also bind fast together and solidify internally the beliefs and practices of the new community. For nascent sectarian religious communities that hold the prophetic and apocalyptic in high esteem the wild and dangerous images in the book of Revelation prove to be ready tools to use in both defining one's own "religious" identity and the identity of the outsider.[2] For the Christian Brethren, to which we now turn, the image of the Whore of Babylon was a useful device in both the acts of *secare*, cutting off from the groups from which they seceded, and *religare*, or binding together like-minded religious dissidents.

ANTI-PAPAL OR ANTI-POPE INTERPRETATIONS

It may be said at this juncture that the first identification of Babylon as Papal Rome is somewhat unimaginative and unoriginal, and to an extent this may be the case. It has been noted above that this passage has always been associated with "Rome" in some way and the normative Protestant exegesis of the passage since the time of Luther in the sixteenth century has been to identify this passage as referring to the pope. Of course the antecedents of this anti-papal and developing anti-pope[3] interpretative tradition, it has been noted above, had begun forming in the work of Joachim in the thirteenth century.

What will become clear is that the Brethren exegesis of this passage is truly anti-papal, unlike many of the interpreters before them who had a much narrower "anti-pope" explanation.[4] That is, the Brethren authors

2. Collins, "Vilification and Self-Definition," 308–20.

3. It is important to distinguish here between "anti-papal" interpreters who identified Babylon quite broadly as a papal "system," and interpreters who were specifically "anti-pope" in their understanding of Babylon as an "individual" pope. This difference has not been stressed before in the secondary literature with authors using the phrase "anti-papal" as a very broad brushstroke to identify the exegesis of Babylon (see, e.g., Boxall, "Many Faces of Babylon"). The reasons for making such a distinction are explained below. Please note my usage of the term "anti-pope," although linguistically similar to "antipope," is not used here in the same way. "Antipope" is used by Catholic theologians to specifically refer to a false claimant to the Holy See.

4. This is, to a certain extent, only to be expected. It has been demonstrated above that the predominant Protestant hermeneutical approach from 1550–1800 was the historicist method which sought to identify specific individuals at specific periods of

identified the Whore as the whole system of Roman Catholicism through-out time rather than as a specific pope confined to a specific period. Some reasons for this are suggested here.

It is possible, through an insufficient reading of those prophetic inter-preters that have been engaged in the act of biblical exegesis of Revelation chapters 17–18, to assume that those who identified Babylon as in some way pertaining to the Catholic Church were anti-papal in their exegesis. For example, Froom notes that Nicholas Bernard (d. 1661), chaplain to Oliver Cromwell, "summons the testimony of the English Bishops Jewel, Abbot, Whitgift and Andrewes to testify of Papal Rome as Babylon . . . [as] a suc-cessive dynasty not an individual pope."[5] Whereas Boxall (2001) uses the term "Anti-Papal Tradition" to refer to the "clear identification of the Bishop of Rome, and the papacy as an institution"[6] as the standard Reformation exegesis of Revelation chapters 17–18, but then goes on to state that Olivi, Joachim and Fulke specifically identify the Bishop of Rome as the Anti-christ with the Roman Church being the Whore.[7] While such statements are arguably true, many interpreters, exercising a predominantly Historicist hermeneutical framework, actually identified Babylon as a specific pope, a specifically "individual" interpretation of the motif, in order to best fit into their diachronic reading.

Although most Protestant Reformers were indeed anti-papal, insofar as they rejected, even abhorred, the whole system of Catholicism, for many their exegesis of the Whore of Babylon was not anti-papal but anti-pope. Their exegesis of the scarlet colored beast (Rev 17:3) upon which the indi-vidual pope rides should be, more correctly, termed "anti-papal."[8] Alter-natively, when the Whore of Babylon is described as a woman (Rev 17) this is understood by some to refer to an individual pope and is thus an "anti-pope" interpretation, whereas when the Whore of Babylon is described as a city (Rev 18), this is understood to refer to the whole papal system[9] and is

time as the fulfillment of specific images in the Apocalypse. A [modified] Futurist her-meneutic, like that held by Brethren authors, is not predisposed to identifying specific individuals as being the actual fulfillment of Revelation's motifs.

5. Froom, *Prophetic Faith*, 2.562.

6. Boxall, "Many Faces of Babylon," 63.

7. Ibid.

8. In the Reformation Era, Nicholas Ridley, John Hooper, Thomas Cranmer, John Bale, John Jewel and John Foxe all specifically identified the Scarlet Beast (Rev 17:3) as referring to the papal system; see Froom, *Prophetic Faith*, 2.530–31.

9. A very common interpretation in the Reformation era, e.g., Luther, Melanch-thon, Osiander, Bullinger, Funck, Tyndale, Ridley, Hooper, Cranmer, Bale, Jewel, Foxe and Napier, who were all "anti-papal" in their exegesis of the city of Babylon in Rev 18, i.e., Babylon as a "system" rather than as an "individual." See Froom, *Prophetic Faith*,

thus anti-papal. Thus at this stage we must differentiate between such individual and corporate identifications of Babylon.

The first author that identifies the Whore not just as a papal system but also as an individual pope (a "pseudo-pope" or "anti-pope" exegesis) is the Calabrian Abbott Joachim of Fiore who, believing the rule of St. Francis to be divinely inerrant, suggested that any pontiff who tried to change it must be a pseudo-pope or "anti-pope" riding on the carnal church of Babylon.[10] For Joachim the "scarlet multitude" of Rome represented the beast of Revelation 17:3[11] and the pseudo-pope represented the Whore. However at the time of Joachim's writing, because of the future prophetic nature of this identification, Joachim refrained from identifying Babylon as a specific, real, historical pope. Nevertheless, for Joachim the Whore was, on this level at least, an individual and not a system.

Only a century after Joachim the identification of the Whore of Babylon, not so much with the papal system but with more specifically an individual pope, in this case Pope Clement V (1305–1314), was made by the renowned prophetess Bridget of Sweden (1303–1373). Bridget wrote a letter to Pope Clement V urging him to break the bonds of the Babylonian captivity in which he held the church. In this letter she explicitly identifies Clement V as the Great Whore: "Now I wail over you, head of my church, who sits on my throne . . . you who should release the souls and present them to me, you are in reality a murderer of souls."[12] Writing around about the same time as Bridget, Gerard of Borgo San Domino, professor of theology at the University of Paris, in *Introduction to the Eternal Gospel*, predicted a simoniacal pope shortly to come but, unlike Joachim, who believed that this pope would be the Whore, Gerard suggested that he would be the Abomination of Desolation.[13] The Minorite poet Jacopone da Todi in the thirteenth century CE commented on the appearance of "a new Lucifer in the papal chair."[14] These writers, although not identifying a specific pope as Babylon, used individualistic language. Such personal language would pave the way for other expositors to identify individual popes as the Great Whore.

In 1513, immediately before the major events of the Reformation, Leo X began his papal reign. He had engraved on the marble portico entrance to

2.530–31.

10. Reeves, *Influence of Prophecy*, 72–73.

11. Joachim, *De articulis fidei*, n.pg.

12. Bridget of Sweden, *Leben und Offenbarungen der heiligen Brigitta*, 239–30.

13. Gerard of Borgo San Donnino, *Liber Introductorius in Evangelium Aeternum*, 49–98.

14. Froom, *Prophetic Faith*, 2.74.

his Bishopric: "Holy Lateran Church, the mother and head of all the churches of the city [Rome] and of the world." It was noted that his inaugural pro-
cession involved "the pope riding on a white horse and wearing a tiara . . .
Various paintings adorned the scene. One showed kings kneeling before
the pope." Such events were highly reminiscent of the Whore of Babylon to
those versed in the language of the Revelation, and as Froom notes, these
scenes were "powerfully used" by the coming Reformers.[15] Only a matter
of months before Luther nailed his famous decree at Wittenberg, Leo X effectively silenced the Piedmontese, Waldensians and Bohemian Hussites
(all of whom as has been noted above found in Revelation a picture of Papal
Rome). This event caused Antonius Puccius to confess to Leo X: "Now all
Christendom sees that it is subjected to one head, that is to thee." Such a
confession was understood by many at the time as being the fulfillment of
Revelation 18:7, with Pope Leo X speaking the words of the Whore: "I sit
a queen . . . and shall see no sorrow."[16] The bloodshed of those so-called
heretics by Leo X inspired John Milton (1608–1674) to write *On the Late
Massacre in Piedmont* in which he identified the Piedmontese as "slaugh-
tered saints." Their "martyred blood" at the hand of the "Triple Tyrant" was
a "Babylonian Woe."[17] Protestants were not only identifying Babylon as the
papal system but some were, it is clear, identifying an individual, Pope Leo
X, as the Whore. This placing of oneself within the context of history is a
noticeable characteristic of the historicist method of exegesis. The Brethren,
however, as futurists, did not engage in it but found other ways of identifying themselves with the biblical text.

Thomas Cranmer (1489–1556), Archbishop of Canterbury, writing in
the mid-sixteenth century identified the Whore of Babylon as an individual
pope. He writes, "In the seventeenth chapter he [John] lively setteth forth
the pope in his own colours, under the person of the whore of Babylon
being drunken with the blood of saints."[18] Such individualized and per-
sonalized language was perhaps referring to Paul III (1534–1549), Julius III
(1550–1555), Marcellus II (1555) or Paul IV (1555–1559), all of whom sat
on the papal throne during Cranmer's lifetime. Of the details one cannot be
certain, but it is clear that here Cranmer identified an individual pope as the
Whore rather than the whole system of Catholicism.

The individualistic anti-pope exegesis can also be seen in the writings
of John Calvin (1509–1564), Cranmer's French contemporary, who stated of

15. Ibid., 179.

16. "Oratio Antonii Puccii," in Mansi, 32.892.

17. Milton, Sonnet XV, "On the Late Massacre in Piemont," in *Poems*, 411–12.

18. Cranmer, *Writings and Disputations*, 18, 376.

the individual pontiff reigning as he wrote: "We regard the Roman Pontiff as the leader and standard-bearer of that wicked and abominable kingdom."[19] Such language was clearly pertaining to an individual pope rather than Catholicism as a system.

A diplomat of the French Huguenots and follower of Calvin called Philippe de Mornay (1549–1623) placed all prophetic negative epithets on Rome and as such can be defined as an "anti-papal" interpreter. In particular, however, de Mornay suggested that the individual Pope Paul V was personally fulfilling these motifs.[20] In England, at a similar time, the Parliamentarian Sir Edwin Sandys (1561–1629) noted that the Protestant cry was quite individualistic in character: "The Lord of Rome was none other than that imperious bewitching Lady of Babylon."[21] As to which "Lord of Rome" Sandys was referring we cannot be certain; Clement VIII (1592–1605), Leo XI (1605), Paul V (1605–21), Gregory XV (1621–23), Urban VIII (1623–44), would all have been "Lords of Rome" during Sandys' lifetime. The exegesis of Andreas Prolaeus was clearer on this matter. In a lecture on July 10th 1631 titled *30 Lectures on Babylon in Revelation 17, 18 and 19*, Prolaeus referred to Scandinavian King Gustav Adolf's distaste for Pope Urban VIII: "Your majesty, being from such a noble pope-hating house . . . you do not only hate the whore, but even much more love the lamb."[22] Again an individual rather than corporate exegesis is taking place.

Perhaps the most significant identification of an individual pope as the Apocalyptic Whore occurred in 1798 just two years before the birth of arguably the most famous of the Brethren authors, Darby. According to Richard Duppa (1770–1831) the events of 1798, during which Bonaparte and his army of French Revolutionaries in their attempts to bring democracy and nationalism to the Italian people removed Pius VI (1755–1798) from the papal throne, were understood by many onlookers to be the literal fulfillment of Revelation chapters 17–18:

> Napoleon . . . on his way to overthrow the pope . . . the hour of vengeance had struck. [Napoleon] routed the papal army, and made new overtures to the pope [Pius VI] . . . the mob proceeded to make public harangues, and pretended to shew clearly, by several texts of scripture, that the time was at hand to overthrow the existing government.[23]

19. Calvin, *Institutes*, 3.55.

20. Froom, *Prophetic Faith*, 2.635.

21. Sandys, *Europae Speculum*, 164.

22. Prolaeus, in Froom, *Prophetic Faith*, 2.602.

23. Duppa, *Brief Account of the Subversion of the Papal Government*, 11.

It was not simply those in "the mob" who understood Pius VI's demise to be the literal fulfillment of the Whore's fall. The leader of the revolutionary army General Haller understood his own role to be one of fulfilling Revelation 18:2:

> February 15th 1798 . . . Pius VI repaired to the Sistine Chapel . . . when in the midst of the ceremony, shouts penetrated the conclave, intermingled with the strokes of axes at the doors. Soon General Haller, a Swiss Calvinist, with a band of soldiers broke into the chapel and declared that the Pope's reign was at an end . . . the glory, honour and power had vanished.[24]

Among the contemporary authors that believed that the removal of Pius VI from Rome was the fulfillment of the destruction of the Whore was Edward King (1735–1807) who in *Remarks on the Signs of the Times* (1800) suggested, "Is not the Papal power, at Rome, which was once so terrible, and so domineering, at an end? . . . If these things are so:—then truly that Great City Babylon is fallen."[25] These very lines were quoted in the Millerite periodical *Signs of the Times and Expositor of Prophecy*[26] as evidence for the fulfillment of Revelation 18:2. The removal of Pius VI from the papal throne was also interpreted as the fulfillment of the fall of Babylon by Richard Valpy (1754–1836),[27] Francis Wrangham (1769–1842),[28] Charles Daubney (1745–1827),[29] and C. G. Thube (fl. 1796).[30]

Thus, we may conclude already that although Boxall has noted there was developing from the time of the Reformation onward a strong "anti-papal" tradition in the interpretation of the Whore of Babylon, that there was also simultaneously developing a strong "anti-pope" tradition. Clement V, Leo X, Paul V, Paul III, Julius III, Marcellus II or Paul IV, and most notably Pius VI, whose "fall" would have been fresh in the memory of many of the early Brethren, were all specifically identified in some pre-Brethren sources as being the Great Whore of the Apocalypse. Nevertheless, as will become apparent, Brethren writers themselves did not adopt such an interpretation. It is argued here that the reason for this is that in Brethren exegesis a more open-ended futurism has replaced a more finely focused historicist reading of the text.

24. Duppa, "Anecdotes Respecting Pius VI."

25. King, *Remarks on the Signs of the Times*, 18–21.

26. Hale, "Letter to Dr. Pond," 42.

27. Valpy, *Sermons Preached on Public Occasions*, 57–59.

28. Wrangham, "Rome Is Fallen," 247–48.

29. Daubney, *Fall of Papal Rome*.

30. Thube, *Ueber die nächstkommenden vierrzig Jahre*.

DARBY

It may be suggested then that the Christian Brethren exegesis of the Whore of Babylon motif as "Papal Rome" is neither new nor original (though as will be seen in later chapters of this book there are aspects of Brethren interpretation which concerning such suggestions of a lack of exegetical imagination could not be made). However, even in the context of the "Papal Rome" interpretation of the Whore motif, it is not the case that the Brethren were simply caught up in the flow or going along with the historicist crowd. It is true that this group did have a standard Protestant understanding of this text; such an understanding was important and enabled them to iden-tify with the broader Protestant interpretive community's normative her-meneutical schema. It will be shown, however, that a particularly nuanced variation of this form of interpretation developed.

It has been noted above that Fish's social reader-response theory has identified that readers belong to "Interpretive Communities." As such this "anti-papal" interpretation, although not original, is still important as such an interpretation holds and binds the Brethren into the Protestant herme-neutical circle. When the group began meeting together in 1829 and began interpreting religious texts, the reader's membership of this particular new "Protestant" religious institution called the Brethren and, perhaps more im-portantly, the reader's rejection of membership of the alternative religious institutions from which that they have seceded, became essential in deter-mining how they understood texts. Such social affiliation predisposes the reader to a shared interpretation rather than facilitating the imposition of an individual subjective and idiosyncratic reading of the text. The Brethren read not only as part of the Brethren interpretive community but also as part of the wider Non-conformist, Dissenting, Protestant interpretive com-munity. Thus, turning now to the exegesis of this passage in the work of Darby, and beginning with his previously un-transcribed and unpublished handwritten notes on this passage from his personal commentary on the Greek New Testament we find his understanding of Babylon as follows:

> The Romano-Christian body . . . The Pope [crossed out by Darby's own hand and replaced with] Papal . . . Satan's usurped religious authority in the world . . . Babylon seems to be the Roman Church ["as a body political" is crossed out by Darby's own hand and replaced with] as a religiopolitical body—Roman Christendom.[31]

31. Darby, *Commentary on Greek New Testament*, 4.532–603. The pages of *Novum Testamentum Graece* are interleaved with pages containing pages with copious hand-written notes on the text.

Thus it is clear from these handwritten notes that Darby placed himself within the normative Protestant hermeneutic circle in his identification
of Babylon as Papal Rome. This exegesis continued into his other published
works and letters. There are altogether fifty-three of Darby's publications
where he makes a link between Babylon and the Papacy. In particular, Roman Catholicism as an institution or system of Babylon features heavily in
Darby's exegesis of Revelation chapters 17–18, for example: "How different
the spirit of Popery! It was glad to get the world's capital for its own. But it
is a city of confusion; Rome is Babylon thus viewed."[32] Also Darby writes, "I
believe what you call the Catholic Church to be Babylon,"[33] and, "Corrupt
Rome, Babylon, the idolatrous harlot."[34] Darby also describes Babylon as
a "system . . . of Papal Idolatry."[35] Thus it is very clear that Darby identifies
the Great Whore of Revelation as the Roman Catholic system and not as an
individual pope.

There are just two occasions when Darby uses the word "pope" in a
singular individualistic way, when interpreting Revelation chapters 17–18,
to refer to a specific pope. The first is when he comments upon Babylon's
fornication with the "kings of the earth" (Rev 17:2), which he interprets in
light of the events of 1798: "This in a hidden way we may find going on now.
The departure of the pope from Rome was the beginning of it. The kings of
the earth are allying with the pope in order to keep down radicalism, which
is an enemy to him."[36] The only other occasion that we read of Darby identifying Babylon as an individual pope and not as the papal system reads as
follows: "I find rather the majority of Christians condemning your sect, and
the pope's claims as corrupt, false and unfounded, and by a vast majority of
Christians held to be the corrupt Babylon of Scripture."[37] It is important
to note here that the pope is referred to individually as the one with whom
fornication is committed and thus is personally identified as Babylon, not

32. Darby, "Sketch of Joshua," 512.

33. Darby, "Romanism," 49, 92.

34. Darby, *Letters of J.N.D.*, 1.427.

35. Darby, "Fragmentary Thoughts," 328, also, 340–41, 348, 352. See also Darby,
"Progress of Democratic Power," 510; "Brief Outline," 78; "Outline of the Revelation,"
384; "Readings on the Seven Churches," in *NJ*, 367; "Considerations on the Nature and
Unity of the Church," 33; "Presbyterianism," 509; "Analysis of Dr. Newman's, 'Apologia,'" 156; "Second Address," 22; "Further Notes on the Revelation," in *NJ*, 135–57; "Edinburgh Meeting: Address, Titus 2:11–15," in *NJ*, 69–70; "Reading on 1 Peter," 238–55;
"Notes of a Lecture," 264; *Letters of J.N.D.*, 1.191–95. All link the Church in Thyatira
with Popery, which is in turn identified as Babylon in Darby, *Letters of J.N.D.*, 3.79–80,
211.

36. Darby, "Fragmentary Thoughts," 342.

37. Darby, "Familiar Conversations," 272.

just corporately, the second is that Darby sees the verse being fulfilled "now," that is, in his own time.

There are in addition to the two publications above, where a personal identification of Babylon is made with an individual pope, three occasions where a specific "Catholic" movement is identified as being the Apocalyptic Whore. The publication of these three pamphlets reflects particular circumstances in which Darby found himself challenged by the immediate "threat" of increasing Catholicism. The Oxford Movement, a nineteenth-century movement within the Church of England seeking to move back towards a more Roman or Catholic form of worship, led by Pusey and Newman, is singled out specifically as being Babylonian in character. Darby writes with regards to the angelic call of separation to "come out" (Rev 18:4) of Puseyism and Popery, for to be found there is to be found in Babylon: "Come out . . . Puseyism is heathenism . . . Popery slurs over sin; no matter how they sin, an indulgence will atone for it. It is a shame for His people to be there, but still He remembers them."[38]

Thus predominantly we can conclude that Darby, standing in the stream of tradition of Protestant exegesis, did identify the Roman Catholic Church as the Whore of Babylon; however this was overwhelmingly a corporate, denominational identification of the whole system and not specifically referring to an individual pope at a particular time. Babylon, in Darby's exegesis, refers to a false and evil papal system not specifically a particular discrete individual pope. In the handwritten commentary quoted above, Darby originally writes, "The Pope," which he subsequently deletes and replaces with the non-individual word "papal." There are two reasons for this phenomenon. First, the normative Protestant identification of Babylon as a pope fits well with the normative Protestant Historicist or "Church Historical" timescale. This approach (explained above) suggests that specific passages of the Revelation act as historical signposts or identifiers helping the reader ascertain where they stand diachronically in the history of the church. The Brethren hermeneutical approach, as identified in chapters 1 and 4 above, is best described as Futurist, albeit an inaugurated or partially realized futurism. Such an approach of projecting a passage like Revelation chapters 17–18 into the future presents a problem in identifying the apocalyptic motif in the present. If Babylon's arrival is future (and according to the majority of Brethren authors it is) then Babylon cannot refer to the "current" pope, whoever that might be. If the identification of Babylon is bound in time to the rule of a specific pope then when that pope dies and his

---

38. Darby, "Fragmentary Thoughts," 347–48. For further identifications of Puseyism as Babylon, see also Darby, "Claims of the Church," 314; and as the mystery of iniquity in Darby, "Analysis of Dr. Newman's 'Apologia,'" 136.

authority is passed on with the events of Revelation chapters 17–18 still unfulfilled then the interpreter is left with the problem of unfulfilled prophecy.
If, on the other hand, the interpreter identifies Babylon as something that
is in a sense timeless, or at least has been around and will be around longer
than that interpreter, then the problem of unfulfilled prophecy is removed.
Thus Darby writes,

> We may discern the elements of all that evil which will hereafter
> be ripened—the principles now, but not the accomplishment
> till by-and-by. The spirit of Babylon is in Popery: but Popery
> exclusively is not Babylon.[39]

There is for Darby a distinction between different forms of Babylon in
different dispensations or epochs of the history of the world. For example,
Darby differentiates between "Babylon in its mystical character at the end"
and "Babylon proper in Isaiah,"[40] presumably differentiating between the
Apocalyptic Whore and the geographical historical nation and city in Meso-
potamia. He also draws a distinction between the "Babylonish captivity . . .
in our present condition"[41] and the future "fall of Babylon . . . announced
as the day of Jehovah . . . all the world has to look for . . . plainly here a
question of God's ways in times to come . . . the last days,"[42] which suggests
a distinguishing between the Roman Catholic Church in Darby's own time
and the Roman Catholic Church in the future.

Second, Darby had begun to take a much more sectarian and exclusive
approach to interpreting the passage than the Protestant Reformers before
him. As shall be seen below Darby placed quite an emphasis on Babylon as
the "mother" of harlots and deduced from this that being a mother must
mean she had "her daughters." If the interpreter identifies Babylon simply
on an institutional level as the group which he himself has "come out of"
then it is unproblematic enough, through an application of Revelation chapters 17–18 to one's own *Sitz im Leben*, for the interpreter to understand that
group as Babylon. But, if the interpreter belongs to a group like the Brethren

---

39. Darby, "Fragmentary Thoughts," 304. For further similar religious identifications of Babylon, see also Darby, "Irrationalism of Infidelity," 109–10, 334–36, 382–84;
Darby, "Scriptural Criticisms," 18, 20; Darby, "Ryde Address," 59; Darby, "Reading on
the Fifth Book of Psalms," 203–4; Darby, "The Psalms," 130–31; Darby, "Further Note
on Isaiah," 83–84; Darby, "Some Further Development," 272–73; Darby, "What Has
Been Acknowledged," 452; Darby, "Counsel of Peace," 308–9; Darby, "Reply to an Article," 28, 20–21, 25–26; Darby, "Introduction to the Bible," 36; Darby, "Thoughts on
Isaiah," 296–99, 308–10, 339–40, 356–57.

40. Darby, "Further Note on Isaiah," 83.

41. Darby, "What Has Been Acknowledged," 452.

42. Darby, "Thoughts on Isaiah," 297.

that has "come out of" a number of different denominations, then every group that the new sect has "come out of" must be identified as Babylon. Darby writes: "What is Babylon? Popery. But it may have daughters. As a Romish priest once answered one who told him Rome was Babylon, 'But who are her daughters, then?'"[43] The answer is found clearly in another publication where we read, "Would you say that Babylon is confined to Rome? She has her daughters; strictly speaking, it is Rome, she is mother of them all."[44] Thus the "daughters of Babylon" concept became a useful terminology for Darby to identify all of corrupt Christendom as being included "in" the Great Whore. This then represents a new development and a paradigmatic movement away from the standard Protestant understanding of the text and will be examined more fully towards the end of this chapter. Not only is the Whore of Babylon the whole religious system of Papal Rome but, by using this "mother-daughter" idiom, the Brethren authors were able to increase their exclusivity and sectarianism by identifying many other denominations as Babylonian.

Thus while Darby and the Brethren more generally did not identify the Whore of Babylon as a particular pope, and hence one would think were less able to precisely identify themselves within the details of the text, this was not the case, for although they did not have chronological precision in their exegesis, they did have a very clear sense of their ecclesiological status. This is reflected in their reading of Revelation chapters 17–18.

Although highlighting that Babylon is referred to as a mother in the Apocalypse and then deducing that this means she must have children was not completely new before the time Darby was writing it was by no means common. The maternal dimension of Babylon's nature was an area of exegesis that was somewhat under explored. Perhaps the earliest example of exegesis which uses the maternal aspect of Babylon to postulate that she must have ecclesial progeny is to be found in the exegesis of Martin Luther who used the image of Babylon as a mother with daughters to suggest that the Mother referred to literal and historical Babylon who gave birth to a daughter; Pagan Rome:

> The second Babylon is similar to the first, and what the mother has done, that is also practiced by the daughter. The first Babylon defended her faith by fire and burnt the ancestors of Christ. See Genesis 11:9. This Babylon, in Rome, burns the children of Christ.[45]

43. Darby, "Further Notes on Revelation," 152.
44. Darby, "Readings on the Seven Churches," 362.
45. Luther, in Froom, *Prophetic Faith*, 2.277.

Papal Rome at the time of Luther had not, according to contemporary exegesis, given birth to Babylonian progeny or, to push the "mother-daughter" idiom further, to Pagan Rome's "grandchildren."

A remarkably similar method of exegesis is to be found in the futurist counter-reformation exegesis of the sixteenth-century Jesuit author Ribera mentioned above. Like Luther, Ribera understood that Babylon was Rome. Rome pagan in the past was the mother but she had not given birth to her daughter yet. In the present experience of Ribera she was still only pregnant. Rome apostate in the future will be the daughter. The daughter of Babylon will be born only after she has fallen away from the pope's authority and rule. The Rome of Ribera's own day had no part in Babylon, rather, she was "the mother of piety" and the "mistress of sanctity."[46]

Towards the end of the sixteenth century, writing at a similar time to Ribera, English clergyman Robert Browne (1550–1631), leader of a Separatist movement known as the Brownists and regarded as the founder of Congregationalism, seceded from the Anglican Church through a principle of separation which identified Roman Catholicism as the Mother of Harlots. Browne identified Anglicanism along with any Christians who were such in name only and who did not live Christian lives as the daughters of Babylon.[47] Thus he continued the distinction between Babylon as "Mother" and Babylon as "Daughter." However, it is here for the first time that Papal Rome has given birth, as for Luther historical Babylon was the mother of Pagan Rome and for Ribera the pregnancy had not yet reached its full term.

Browne's separatist views were carried across the Atlantic, via Holland, to North America in the first quarter of the seventeenth century by the Pilgrim Fathers where the American Congregationalist Increase Mather (1639–1723), who, like a number of the Brethren authors who were to appear on the scene over a century after him, graduated from Trinity College Dublin. Increase wrote comprehensively on the subject of eschatology. In *Ichabod, or . . . the Glory of the Lord, Is Departing from New England* (1702), he continued the "mother-daughter" exegesis of the Babylon motif, identifying the Church of Rome as the mother of harlots and the churches of New England, like the churches of Africa and Europe centuries before that had once been glorious but in submitting to Rome had lost their glory, as the harlot daughters of Babylon.[48] Thus it appears that on this level at least Mather understood the relationship between Papal Rome and the Congregational churches of New England as a "mother-daughter" relationship.

46. Ribera, *In sacrum Beati Ioannis Apostoli*, 282–83.

47. Burrage, *True Story of Robert Browne*, 11–25, 32–35, 46–47.

48. Mather, *Ichabod*, 65–66.

Likewise, New England preacher Jonathan Mayhew (1720–1766) used the Lisbon earthquake in 1755 as an occasion to deliver a sermon entitled *Discourse . . . Occasioned by the Earthquakes in November 1755* during which he referred to the earthquake as a portent of God's judgment on Papal Rome as "Babylon the Great, Mother of Harlots." He urged his listeners to "refrain from all conformity with the corruptions of Babylon" lest they should be found guilty of being her children by association.[49] Some ten years later, without explicitly using the mother-daughter idiom, Mayhew, in a lecture entitled *Popish Idolatry*, used Revelation chapter 18 as a call for his listeners to "come out of a church, whether Rome or any other, to which the characters of Babylon actually agree" and thus identified Babylon's daughters as any church who conforms to papal doctrine or practice.[50]

At approximately the same time as Mayhew, fellow Congregationalist Isaac Backus (1724–1806) developed the Babylonian "mother-daughter" idiom further in his publication *The Infinite Importance of the Obedience of Faith, and of Separation from the World.* Here he expressed the notion that any church which loved worldly or secular pursuits was to be identified as Babylonian Rome's progeny. He wrote of the Papal Church: "She is the mother of harlots, and all churches who go after any lovers but Christ, for a temporal living, are guilty of playing the harlot."[51]

However, in Darby's time and in Darby's country although a number of authors were simultaneously beginning to use this "mother-daughter" idiom more frequently, such as Charlotte Elizabeth Tonna editor of the *Protestant Magazine* during the mid-nineteenth century, few were to develop this interpretation as fully as the Brethren authors would.

The closest a non-Brethren author got to using the Babylonian progeny motif in anywhere near the way that the seventeenth- and eighteenth-century American Congregationalists did was from an anonymous writer who, upon reading about the Oxford Movements efforts to re-Catholicize the Protestant church and their belief that those who seceded from Rome "are prodigal sons who have left the Father's house," responded by using the "mother-daughter" idiom. The writer suggests that any movement of Anglicanism back to Rome was a movement back to a Babylonian mother and that the true believers should, in the words of Revelation 18:4, "come out and be separate."[52] It is entirely possible however that in 1842 a Brethren

49. Mayhew, *Discourse Occasioned by the Earthquakes*, 46.

50. Mayhew, *Popish Idolatry*, 47.

51. Backus, *Infinite Importance of the Obedience of Faith*, 16.

52. Philos [pseud.], "The Catholic Church," 198–99.

author could have been the anonymous source of the submission to the *Christian Observer*.

KELLY

The next Brethren author to which we turn our attention is William Kelly. Kelly clearly stands within the same interpretive tradition as Darby and the Protestant Reformers before him in that he makes a link between Babylon and the papacy in sixty-five of his publications. The most obvious place to begin is with his publication *Babylon and the Beast* (1872). In this work Kelly predominantly and overwhelmingly identifies Babylon as Roman Catholicism. He writes in no uncertain terms that "Rome and no other is the city aimed at by the woman Babylon in Revelation 17."[53] Yet to make sure that his reader is left with no uncertainty he reiterates this view with the qualifier that he is not just simply speaking about Rome Pagan, Imperial or geographical but that Babylon is "Rome not pagan but ecclesiastical, on Rome professedly Christian."[54]

The evidence he uses to come to this conclusion involves an examination of the word "mystery" that appears in Revelation 17:5 and 17:7. He writes that the inscription "Mystery . . . well suits Rome nominally Christian."[55] Kelly then examines the geographical location of Babylon in Revelation 17:9, concluding,

> Who in the world could doubt where the seven-hilled city is? Still less could it have been doubted in the time of St. John. There was but one such city, and that one rose up before every person's mind instinctively. It was Rome, and none other.[56]

---

53. Kelly, *Babylon and the Beast*, 7.

54. Ibid., 8. See also, Kelly, "Revelation 14:19," 51; Kelly, "Daniel 7," 335; Kelly, "Matthew 16:28," 337; Kelly, "Amos," in *Minor Prophets*, 127–28; Kelly, "Obadiah," in *Lectures on the Minor Prophets*, 189; Kelly, "Micah," in *Minor Prophets*, 257; Kelly, *Lectures on . . . Ephesians*, 116; Kelly, *Unity of the Spirit*," 6–7; Kelly, "Philadelphia and Laodicea," 286; Kelly, *Purpose of God*, 15–16; Kelly, *Righteousness of God*, 46; Kelly, "Scripture of Truth," 6; Kelly, *Lectures on the Church of God*, 73; Kelly, *Letter on the Church of the Scriptures*, 7–8; Kelly, *Eleven Lectures on the Book of Job*, 63; Kelly, *Two Lectures on the Song of Solomon*, 52; Kelly, *Lectures on Ezra and Nehemiah*, 22; Kelly, *Notes on Ezekiel*, 56–57.

55. Kelly, *Babylon and the Beast*, 4.

56. Ibid., 7.

Then Kelly looks at Revelation 17:10 which informs that the Great Whore ruled over the kings of the earth. He takes this as further evidence of Babylon being Papal Rome:

> There was only one city which had reigned over kings. There can be no question therefore that Rome exclusively is the city intended here . . . This is so true that a great many learned persons of the Roman Catholic communion have acknowledged the fact . . . Bishop of Meaux, J. B. Bossuet, Baronius and Bellarmin. These officials, of high distinction in the Romish system, acknowledge Rome to be intended.[57]

Thus, not only using the text as evidence but also, in a traditional Catholic hermeneutical style, Kelly uses the authority of tradition as evidence to identify Babylon as the papal system.

The first twelve pages of this above quoted publication make the point over and over again. For Kelly Babylon is clearly and irrefutably Papal Rome. However, Kelly, like Darby, because of his futuristic hermeneutical approach to the timescale of the Apocalypse, does not identify Babylon as an individual pope, but as the papal system of Roman Catholicism. Thus he writes of "the Pope of Rome. Although we regard his system as a frightful delusion, even Babylon, how can people believe that 'the Apostasy' has arrived yet?"[58] It is important to note here that if, like Kelly, one adheres to a futurist hermeneutic then it is too problematic to identify Babylon as a specific pope at a specific time in history. Rather all that remains possible is to identify Babylon as the papal or Roman Catholic system. For this reason Kelly writes,

> I have no doubt . . . it is Rome that is the peculiar object of God's judgment. Not that Rome is all that is meant by Babylon, but that Rome is at the centre of it . . . Not Rome in the pagan form; not merely Rome in our own days, bad as it is, and becoming increasingly wicked. But I think that the Babylon of the Apocalypse is not merely that system which is now opposed to Christianity, but Babylon when it will have opposed the last testimony that God will send.[59]

The inaugurated nature of this futurism can be seen in the following passage in which Kelly states that the Rome of the past and present can be identified as Babylon, but that it is only in the future that Papal Rome will

57. Ibid.
58. Kelly, "The Coming and the Day of the Lord," 48.
59. Kelly, *Lectures on the Book of Revelation*, 61.

be fully Babylonian. We read: "God has hedged his own draft of Babylon so as to make it quite clear that Rome, city and system, figures in the scene . . . Though the full result will not be until the end of the age."[60] Thus, for Kelly, Babylon cannot be an individual pope, as the time is not right for the final fulfillment of Revelation chapters 17–18. Their fulfillment will be in the future and any identification of Babylon in the Papacy or in Roman Catholicism in the past or present is only an antecedent, a precursor, of what will come.

Kelly, like Darby, was originally a Church of England man. The original sixteenth-century Reformers sought both to define themselves through seceding from the "Babylonian" Catholic Church, and through internally reinforcing the boundaries between insider and outsider. They did this through using the Babylon motif to vilify the "other" in order to define the "self." Kelly agreed wholeheartedly with their use of vituperative rhetoric and their identification of the Church in Rome as the Great Whore.[61] Yet he had "come out" of Rome already, in that the tradition to which he had original adhered had originally protested against her. Thus the problem arose that if Catholicism alone was the Apocalyptic Whore, how could he "come out" of a group that had already once "come out" of Babylon? The answer becomes clear as he writes,

> Nor would one question that God honoured the German re-former's testimony against Babylon, founded on a later portion of Revelation. Does this prove that Luther knew, or that he ought not to learn, a fuller development of the great whore, for which no room is left in the ordinary interpretation?[62]

This belief that Kelly held, of coming out of that which had already come out of Babylon, led him, in agreement with Darby, to emphasize the idea of Babylon as having many daughters, that is, of Roman Catholicism

60. Ibid., 48. For further examples of the future arrival and judgment of Babylon in Kelly's work, see Kelly, "Answers to Questions," BT 18, 286; Kelly, "Answers to Questions," BT, N1, 288; Kelly, CA, 4.187; Kelly, CA, 5.342; Kelly, God's Inspiration of the Scriptures, 250–51, 261; Kelly, "Zechariah," in Lectures Introductory . . . Minor Prophets, 443; Kelly, "Second Advent Before, Not After," 4, 9; Kelly, "Christian Hope," 2; Kelly, "Early Chapters of Genesis," BT, N1–2.192; Kelly, Known Isaiah, 7; Kelly, Hope of Christ, 11; Kelly, Lectures on the Second Coming, 242–43; Kelly, Exposition of the Acts of the Apostles, 647–48; Kelly, Offerings of Leviticus, 82–83; Kelly, Notes on the Book of Daniel, xxvii; Kelly, Exposition of the Book of Isaiah, 31, 49–50, 75.

61. Kelly, "Nebuchadnezzar's Dream," 7. See also Kelly, "The Coming," in Three Prophetic Gems, 425. "Neither he [Calvin] nor any of the Reformers had any real understanding of the book as a whole, though they were not wrong in applying Babylon to Rome."

62. Kelly, "Elements of Prophecy: Answers to Historicism," BT, 11.72.

giving birth to the Church of England and then the Church of England giving birth to a third generation of Babylon, the Nonconformists and Dissenters. Kelly informs us that Babylon is

> a corrupt system, which plainly has its centre in Rome, though taking a larger compass, so as to embrace every religious institution . . . Babylon is not only herself "the great harlot," but "the mother of the harlots and the abominations of the earth." There are more of kindred corruptions in religion, though Rome is pre-eminent.[63]

Kelly goes on to make a distinction between Babylon in the "High" churches and Babylon in the "Low" churches. Such a distinction may perhaps be a differentiation between the Established and un-established churches, or between High and Low forms of Anglicanism, or between Catholicism and Protestant traditions. Regardless of exactly to whom he was referring, Kelly informs that both high and low churches are still Babylonian:

> Babylon is . . . accompanied by the greatest unholiness and the greatest laxity of doctrine when pretending to be the orthodox, the holy Catholic, Apostolic, and I know not what else. Well, that is Babylon, but that is only high Babylon; there is low Babylon too; and all Babylon, no matter whether high or low—all will be the greatest object of God's fury.[64]

Thus Kelly, along with Darby, begins to use the phrase "daughters of Babylon" to refer to the corrupt nature of the whole of Christendom and the Babylonian character of all denominations except their own. Here, for the first time, a new uniquely Brethren "community interpretation" (to use the words of Fish) of Revelation chapters 17–18 has developed, rather than just a continuation of a general Protestant community interpretation, which is becoming increasingly sectarian and exclusive as to who is in and who is out of Babylon. Both Kelly and Darby have used Babylon as a tool to define the "extreme outsider," that is Papal Rome, just as the earliest Christians used the same text to define the "extreme outsider," in their case the Roman Empire.[65] We shall see Kelly's understanding of Babylon as being found in all churches, as he uses the same text to vilify the "nearest outsiders"[66] below.

---

63. Kelly, *Lectures on the Book of Revelation*, 387. See also, Kelly, "The Coming," in *Three Prophetic Gems*, 48–49.

64. Kelly, *Eleven Lectures on the Book of Job*, 63.

65. Collins, "Insiders and Outsiders," 204, 216.

66. Ibid., 204.

DENNETT

Turning now to the writings of Edward Dennett, who identifies Babylon as Papal Rome in two of his publications, it becomes apparent that other Brethren authors continued in the hermeneutical tradition of the Protestant interpretive community. Dennett writes that "Babylon represents the religious corruptress of the earth—[she] is in fact what Rome has ever been and what Babylon will yet more manifestly be."[67] To make sure that no mistake is made, that it is Rome Papal and religious to which he refers not simply Rome pagan, imperial or geographical he writes of the woman shown in Revelation chapters 17–18: "The Romish system, what we understand by the Papal religion—is presented under the form of this woman."[68]

Dennett, like Kelly, appeals to the past interpretation of this passage by the Protestant Reformers as authority for his own identification of the Roman Catholic Church as being the Great Whore:

> It would be a waste of time to show, what has been indisputably proved a thousand times, that Rome was ever known as the seven-hilled city . . . claiming to be Christ's vicegerents on earth, the popes always avowed their title to sovereignty over the kingdoms of the world.[69]

Babylon is not a specific pope in Dennett's exegesis but rather the whole system of Catholicism. Thus, Dennett is continuing in the unfolding hermeneutical tradition of the Brethren interpretive community as identifying the "extreme outsider" as the wider papal system. He writes of the Great Whore that "a woman is a well known symbol in scripture for the expression of a system . . . as for example . . . the daughter of Babylon . . . in the Apocalypse, setting forth a religious organization."[70] This is because Dennett believes that her arrival has not fully occurred yet, it is still a future event, and thus to identify Babylon as a specific individual pope would be to limit the interpretation of the passage to the present. Thus he writes of the future events of Revelation 17:3: "She is seen 'sitting upon' the beast; that is, what the woman represents, Popery in its full-blown form *after* the rapture of the saints, is allied with and upheld by the world-power."[71]

---

67. Dennett, *Visions of John in Patmos*, 201.

68. Dennett, *Zechariah the Prophet*, 54.

69. Dennett, *Visions of John in Patmos*, 222–23.

70. Dennett, *Zechariah the Prophet*, 53–54. See also Dennett, *Visions of John in Patmos*, 226. Here Babylon is "identified with the system, "woman" is used . . . all other systems that derive their parentage from her."

71. Dennett, *Visions of John of Patmos*, 225, my own italics. See also Dennett,

Dennett continues in the interpretive tradition of Darby and Kelly by drawing attention to the fact that Babylon is called a "mother" and therefore must have children. For Dennett the "mother" may be a distant threat, since he himself is distanced from the Church of Rome, but the harlots children, the "nearest outsider," are potentially much closer to home. Thus he writes,

> This wicked "woman" is also a mother, a mother of other systems, as false to Christ as herself. It is thus not only Popery, but all other systems that derive their parentage from her and partake of her character. Are there not such already in existence?[72]

Dennett develops this idea of Babylonian Catholicism giving birth to daughters in quite an interesting way when he suggests that the Apocalyptic Harlot has at least two daughters who are two united but distinct systems, both birthed by the wicked woman. We read:

> And what are these? . . . little doubt that they are twin sisters, superstition and infidelity . . . they are conjoined in their baleful work at this moment in the professing church, and nowhere more apparently than in Romanism.[73]

It will become clear, in what follows, that Dennett used this concept of the "daughters" of Babylon as a way of identifying all of the groups and denominations of Christendom as being Babylonian. He thereby used the text as a vituperative tool to enable the Brethren community to become more sectarian and exclusive on an ecclesiological level by accusing both the "extreme outsider," Papal Rome, and the "nearest outsider," that is Protestantism and of her offshoots, as being Babylon.

BAINES

The next Brethren author to which this book turns is T. B. Baines. Just like his companions, Baines identifies Babylon as Rome papal. He writes: "Babylon the great . . . has not her seat at Jerusalem, but at Rome; is not a Jewish but a Christian apostacy."[74] Here he links Babylon with Rome Christian but further on he makes the link between Babylon and Rome specifically Catholic. Of the relationship between Babylon and the kings of the earth (Rev 18:9–10) Baines comments: "A corrupt alliance with the secular power,

---

House of God, 37.

72. Dennett, *Visions of John of Patmos*, 226.

73. Dennett, *Zechariah the Prophet*, 56.

74. Baines, "Glorious Coming and Kingdom of Christ," 226.

which she upheld as a tool of her own ambition, has always been a favourite policy of the Roman See."[75] Thus it becomes clear that Baines is located within the hermeneutic circle of the Protestant interpretive community in his understanding of Babylon.

Baines does not identify the Whore of Babylon as a specific pope riding on the beast of Catholicism like some of the Reformers and Protestors before him, neither does he distinguish between the Woman of Revelation 17 as an individual pope with the City of Revelation 18 as the Papal Vatican city and system, but rather, he identifies Babylon as a system or institution. In this way he avoids the problem of unfulfilled prophecy that occurs in the identification of an individual pope as Babylon. When that individual pope dies and is replaced by another pope with the prophecies of Revelation chapters 17–18 still unfulfilled, the exegesis has to be modified as it has failed. If, however, the fulfillment of the prophecy is both future and institutional not present and individual, then the prophecy cannot be proven to be unfulfilled. As such Babylon is, for Baines, clearly a "system" and not an individual.[76] Such a view contrasts strongly with the exegesis occurring less than a century earlier, of Pius VI as religious leader, a corrupt individual who was being judged in 1798.

Baines continues in the new Brethren community interpretation which projects the final and complete fulfillment of Babylon's arrival and destruction into the future. He makes a clear distinction between Babylon as Roman Catholicism in the past and present and, in language reminiscent of Ribera and Joachim, Babylon as the Roman Catholicism of the future:

> Is it, then, Romanism in the past and present or Romanism in the future, that is here portrayed? The scene itself is, of course, future . . . But much of the description given is true of the past and present, belonging to the system itself. . . . She has had time given her to repent, and has not repented . . . There is grace for individuals connected with her if they repent, but none for the system itself, which has refused repentance.[77]

Thus the key, for Baines, as to when Babylon will fully arrive on the scene and be judged and destroyed is that it is a future event. He informs his brethren that for as long as the Holy Spirit is active on the earth Catholicism is in some way held back or prevented from becoming fully Babylonian in nature, however, in the coming dispensation during which the Holy Spirit leaves the earth, Catholicism and indeed all who are Christian in name

75. Ibid., 235.
76. Ibid., 221, 225, 233.
77. Ibid., 226–27.

only and not in practice, will, in the future, become part of the Apocalyptic Whore.[78]

Baines also takes the references to Babylon being a "mother" to mean that she must have "daughters" and uses this concept of the Babylonian "mother-daughter" idiom to suggest that Catholicism has given "birth" to denominational daughters. By doing so he is able to develop a more sectarian and exclusive community interpretation of the text than would be possible if only Rome papal was understood as being Babylon, extending the vituperative rhetoric not only to the distant outsider but also to the near outsider.

Baines writes of Roman Catholicism "giving birth" with such language as "for not merely is she an idolatrous system herself, but she has given birth to other idolatrous systems scattered over the world."[79] He then goes on to identify to whom the mother, namely Roman Catholicism, has given birth. Papal Rome's daughters, as in the exegesis of Browne some two-and-a-half centuries earlier, are all of those Christians who are worldly and idolatrous:

> As "the mother of harlots," she may have children walking in her own evil ways, not directly connected with Rome. The principles of idolatry, and of worldly traffic unbecoming the bride of Christ, have eaten into a large portion of Christendom that is not professedly Romanist. But the harlot herself is the religious corruption that has its seat in the seven-hilled city.[80]

Thus we can see already that the Brethren are using the Babylon motif to define themselves on a religious level by vilifying the "other," that is primarily Catholicism, as being Babylon. A distinctive and nuanced version of the established Protestant understanding of the text is emerging from within the Brethren community, as the biblical text is once again read in the light of new experience. Babylon is, in the anti-papal tradition that developed in the sixteenth century, Rome ecclesiastical. As such this movement stands within the Reformation stream of tradition and is located firmly within the Protestant interpretive community. However, the Brethren authors are quite careful to not associate the exegesis of the text with a particular individual pope bound to a particular period of time. To do so would involve the risk of unfulfilled prophecy. Instead Babylon is interpreted as a system or institution rather than an individual pope and the fulfillment of this text is projected into the future.

---

78. Ibid., 221–41.

79. Ibid., 225.

80. Ibid., 226.

MILLER

Andrew Miller, in his three-volume publication *Short Papers on Church History* traces the development of the Roman Catholic Church and the reign of individual popes throughout history. He is absolutely clear in his identification of Babylon as ecclesiastical Rome:

> There can be no question, we think, as to what is meant by the symbol used here. Not only a woman, but a licentious woman, and enthroned amidst the corruptions of the seven hilled city . . . here we have a material point—that which has always characterized Rome . . . Rome is clearly indicated, and her religious corruptions are symbolized by "the mother of harlots."[81]

He makes the identification of Babylon as Rome, not just geographical but distinctly papal, clearer as he writes, "These points being fairly disposed of, and Rome being fully identified, we accept Revelation 17 and 18 as descriptive of the papacy."[82] The text is used once again to castigate the distant outsider.

Yet Miller too understands Babylon as referring to the papal system, rather than an individual pope, and this binds his exegesis firmly into the conceptual sphere of the Brethren community interpretation of the text. He refers to Rome ecclesiastical with such non-individualistic language as "this false woman, or the corrupt religious system of Rome"[83] further reinforcing his anti-papal and not anti-pope exegesis.

He understands the word "fornication," used to describe Babylon's sexual relations with the kings of the world, as a way of describing Rome as a religious system. Rome uses her power to seduce believers away from a true love of Christ. He writes that such fornication "we have no doubt means the seducing power of the Romish system in drawing affections away from Christ."[84] Thus he reiterates the views of Darby, Kelly, Dennett and Baines in identifying the woman, not as an individual pope but rather as a "strange sight—a woman—a religious community, professing to be the true spouse of Christ."[85]

Miller continues in the Brethren tradition of identifying Babylon as a "mother," one who gives birth to daughters, as a tool for identifying other denominations as being Babylonian. He does this in order to develop

---

81. Miller, *Short Papers on Church History*, 2.190–91.

82. Ibid., 2.191.

83. Ibid.

84. Ibid., 2.192.

85. Ibid., 2.194.

a more sectarian and exclusive understanding of the text than is possible by simply suggesting that Babylon is Papal Rome. He continues with the Brethren community exegesis as he writes,

> She is a mother—the mother of harlots, she has many daughters. Every religious system in Christendom, that tends in any measure to lead souls away from Christ, to engage their affections with objects that come between the heart and the Man in the glory, is related to this great parent of spiritual iniquity.[86]

Miller does not specifically link Babylon's arrival and destruction with a specific period of time in any of his publications, unlike the above authors who clearly project her fulfillment, judgment and destruction into the future, rather, he traces the whole history of the Catholic Church in a historicist way through Revelation chapters 17–18, thereby linking the whole of Catholicism historically with Babylon.

In his publication on the history of the Brethren movement Miller clearly rejects all Catholic doctrines concluding that even the "most important doctrines of the word of God . . . the vital truth of salvation through faith in the sacrifice of Christ, without the merit of good works" came as "startling" and "overwhelming" surprises to those who had been "educated in the superstitions of Romanism."[87] As an official chronicler of Brethren history[88] it is reasonable to postulate that, although Miller remains silent regarding a possible future arrival, reign and eventual destruction of Babylon, he stands so clearly within the Brethren interpretive community that he would understand the text as being fulfilled according to the same time scale as others in the movement such as Darby, Kelly, Dennett and Baines.

BELLETT

Turning now to the work of Brethren author Bellett it may be noted that although he does not specifically refer to Babylon as "Rome" either papal or pagan, on a number of occasions he does refer to Babylon as "the eternal city." Such a term would have been well known by all his readers as referring to the seat of the Papacy in Rome. He writes an entry in the magazine *The Christian Friend* in which he states: "This boast of being the 'eternal city' so far identifies her with the Babylon that says 'I sit a queen, and am no

---

86. Ibid.

87. Miller, *Brethren*, 1.

88. Ibid.

widow."'[89] In another entry to *The Christian Friend*, Bellett uses the same language: "We live in a moment when Babylon is filling itself afresh with this boast . . . The boast of 'the eternal city' only the more distinctly marks it for the judgment of God."[90] Thus while not as explicit in his exegesis of Revelation chapters 17–18 as Darby, Kelly and Dennett, the connection between Papal Rome (as a city and not an individual) and Babylon, is still made. Bellett does not develop the above authors' concept of Babylon as Rome papal being a mother with daughters, but he does, along with Darby, Kelly, Dennett and Baines, understand the passage to be fully fulfilled only in the future.

In *The Potter's Broken Vessel* (1880), Bellett highlights Babylon's future judgment, an event that although is being prepared in the present has not yet happened. In like manner, in *A Letter—Jeremiah* (1887), the "doom" and destruction of Babylon is spoken of in the future tense rather than the present.[91] This can be seen in further writings from Bellett—for example, he writes, "The woman, mystically Babylon, is removed by the ten kings . . . this is the closing crowning feature in the picture of the world's apostasy. But we have not reached it yet."[92]

The three key dimensions of the developing Brethren hermeneutic, of the use of the Babylon motif to define the self by identifying Catholicism, the "extreme outsider" as Babylon, of refraining from identifying Babylon as a specific pope but rather projecting the fulfillment of the text into the future, and of using a "mother-daughter" idiom to apply the designation of Babylon in a more sectarian way to the "nearer outsider" can be seen in many other Brethren publications of nineteenth century.[93]

SOME CONCLUDING REMARKS ON "BABYLON" AS PAPAL ROME

In this chapter significant attention has been given to Brethren archival material which has heretofore received only slight attention, at least from a

89. Bellett, "Potter's Broken Vessel," 32.

90. Bellett, "A Letter," 29.

91. Ibid., 14.29.

92. Bellett, "Babylon," 26. For further example of the future application of the Babylon motif in Bellett's writings, see also, Bellett, "Obadiah," 34–35; Bellett, "Ruth," 117–18.

93. See, e.g., Bland, *Babylon, Past and Future*, 6–7; Harris, "On the Increase in Popery," 1–16; Bergin, "Babylon to Be Rebuilt and Destroyed," in *Watching and Waiting*, 10.209.163; Grant, *Divine Movement*, 6–7.

biblical interpretation perspective. Throughout, it has been shown that the
Brethren authors were using the Whore of Babylon motif to achieve two
ends: to define the self on a religious level, and to vilify the religious "other,"
in this case Roman Catholicism. The Brethren use of the text is in no way
different to the original use of the text by the earliest Christians for whom
the text was written. They too, more than seventeen hundred years before
the Brethren, used the text to define themselves and determine boundaries
between the self and other social groups.[94] For both Brethren and early
Christians the text of Revelation expressed a struggle over values, for: "the
supporters of Rome saw the emperor as the primary link between the divine
and human, whereas the Christians viewed Jesus Christ in that role,"[95] and
as such they launched a vituperative attack on Rome. The Brethren believed
that the pope had merely taken over from the emperor as *pontifex maximus*
and found themselves in an analogous struggle against idolatrous worship
in which the same vituperative rhetoric could easily be applied, this time to
Papal Rome.

The Brethren authors are clearly aware of the stream of exegesis that
had gone on before them, in particular the specifically "anti-pope" individualistic interpretation of the Whore of Babylon over and against the "anti-
papal" system interpretation of the scarlet colored beast on which the whore
rides. Specifically individualistic language of Babylon as "a pope" or "the
pope" riding on the back of the Catholic system, the beast of Revelation
17:3, is rejected, in favor of identifying the Woman as the Roman Catholic
system. By depersonalizing the identity of the whore in conjunction with
a rejection of the Historicist framework and a development of the Futurist framework, which enables them to project Babylon's arrival, reign and
judgment into the future, the community are protected from the danger of
unfulfilled prophecy.

The Brethren community, as a result of seceding from many different
denominations, unlike the Protestant Reformers before them who seceded
from only the one Catholic Church, make the interpretation of the text
more exclusive and sectarian by applying it to denominations beyond the
Catholic Church. The danger is both distant, in the case of Rome, and near,
in the case of other denominations. They do this by using the angelic call
"come out of her my people" (Rev 18:4) as a way of giving scriptural authority to their sectarianism and exclusivity, and by suggesting that because
Babylon is designated "Mother of harlots" then she must, by inference, have
daughters who are harlots. These daughters are all the churches that the

94. Collins, "Vilification and Self-Definition," 310.

95. Ibid., 315.

Brethren themselves have "come out of," and will be examined in the following chapter.

In the broader context of biblical hermeneutics it may be noted that once again the reading of a biblical text, in this case Revelation chapters 17–18, is largely parasitic upon the perspective of the one who reads it, in this case the Brethren community. The Brethren authors, to a certain extent, take it for granted that Babylon is Papal Rome. They do not, however, remain with such an identification for long but rather they use this as a springboard to make other, more individualistic interpretations. They are hence both inheritors of a hermeneutical tradition and cocreators of it. This will become apparent in the remainder of this book.

6

"Babylon" Is All of
Corrupt Christendom

As has been shown in chapter 5, a number of Brethren authors identify Babylon as a religious entity. While, like the sixteenth-century Reformers before them, these authors began this identification with Papal Rome (albeit as a system not as an individual pope) the paradigm quickly developed, through the use of the "mother-daughter" idiom, to suggest that as Babylon is the Mother of Harlots she must by virtue of this have her daughters. According to the Brethren writers, Papal Rome too had "daughters."

In the present chapter this investigation is taken further and seeks to address the question of the perceived identity of these so-called "daughters of Babylon." Who, for the Brethren writers, are they and where can they be found? The answer to this question will enable a better understanding of how the Brethren perceived themselves as a religious community as the identification of the Whore of Babylon as Papal Rome and then as every denomination of Christendom is used as a form of vituperative rhetoric: to vilify the "religious other" in order to define the "self."

During and before the time of the Reformation, specifically religious interpretations of the Whore of Babylon motif were severely limited through the obvious lack of denominational variety. This was seen in the previous chapter and also in chapter 3, both of which demonstrated that the primary religious identification of Babylon was that of Papal Rome.[1] There was little

---

1. I stress "religious" here because, as ch. 3 has shown, there has been a variety of nonreligious identifications of Babylon throughout the history of the Christian church.

variation on this theme among Protestant writers. So, for example, Froom identifies some thirty-seven major biblical expositors of this epoch who all identified either the pope individually, or Roman Catholicism corporately, as the Great Whore.[2] The lack of variety in the identification of "Babylon" among Protestant interpreters during the period ca. 1600–1798 is a little surprising given the variety of religious traditions that emerged during this period. Whereas the previous chapter has shown that the Brethren authors are located within the Protestant community paradigm (albeit with some distinctive elements) the present chapter shows that the Brethren had something substantially new, at least within the English tradition, to add to the exegesis of the Babylon motif.

Brethren historian Andrew Miller for example, quite clearly identified Babylon as Papal Rome, yet he would not limit his exegesis to such a narrow interpretation as that held by the Reformers before him. Rather Miller used the "mother-daughter" motif from Revelation 17:5 to suggest that Papal Rome had given birth to Babylonian daughters. Miller, however, refrained from specifically identifying exactly who these daughters were other than in vague terms.[3] A number of other Brethren authors, however, were much more definite about the identity of the daughters of Babylon and rather than using such broad-brush strokes as Miller, they positively leveled the charge of being a "daughter of Babylon" at a number of Protestant, Dissenting and Non-conformist groups. This significant development shows once again how the text of the book of Revelation, replete as it is with its images, may be used by new interpreters who are working in new contexts. The *Sitz im Leben* of the Brethren was in some ways similar but in some ways different to that of those who had gone before them thus the exegesis changes to suit the new situation.

DENNETT

It was noted in the previous chapter that Dennett used the Babylonian "mother-daughter" idiom on a number of occasions in his exegesis of Revelation chapters 17–18 where he identifies the daughters of Babylon very vaguely as "systems false to Christ." This is in part 2 of his work *The Visions*

2. Froom, *Prophetic Faith*, 2.528–31. It has been noted in ch. 3 that Froom has an obvious bias to such interpretations due to his Adventist beliefs, however, his rigorous and exhaustive research cannot be dismissed and is, on the whole reliable. He includes James I of England (1566–1625), Joseph Mede (1586–1638), Daniel Whitby (1638–1726), Sir Isaac Newton (1642–1727), John Gill (1697–1771), Joseph Priestly (1733–1804), and Joseph Galloway (ca. 1730–1803) among the many.

3. See Miller in ch. 5 above.

of John in Patmos: Being Notes on the Apocalypse (1892). In his other work, Zechariah the Prophet: Being an Exposition (1888), Dennett uses terms such as "twin sisters of superstition and infidelity" in relation to the image of Babylon and her daughters. However, Dennett, like Miller, remains quite indistinct about who such daughters actually are and fails positively to identify the "daughters of Babylon" as any particular Christian denominations. The closest he gets to doing this is in part 2 of The Visions of John in Patmos: Being Notes on the Apocalypse (1892). Here he identifies the principles of Babylon as being found in "all State Churches . . . the professing church on earth."[4] This is an interesting development, for Dennett here identifies Babylon as those churches sanctioned and supported by civil, political and monarchical institutions. The most notable example at the time Dennett was writing was the Church of England, which after 1534 identified the monarch as the supreme governor of the church. The state and the church have a relationship in which the state identifies and supports a role for the Church of England to perform on a civil, legal and social level. The term "all State Churches" in this context may also have included for Dennett the Church of Scotland as Dennett was writing some twenty-nine years before the Church of Scotland Act of 1921 when the Scottish Church was given freedom from Parliamentary interference in spiritual matters. Additionally he included Catholicism in this designation as full civic rights in England had been restored to the Catholic Church by the parliamentary act of 1829 some sixty-three years before Dennett was writing. Historically, Catholics perceived the pope to be not only the head of the church, but since the time of Innocent III and his decree Sicut universitatis conditor (1198),[5] as having political authority even over kings. For Dennett such churches were merely "professing" churches not "true" churches, responsible for "keeping the word of Christ ecclesiastically, and at the same time refusing it in walk and conversation."[6] Christ was not the head of these churches but man was.

In part 3 of the same publication on the Apocalypse (an interpretation of Revelation chs. 18–22) Dennett goes back to a more vague identification of who Babylon's daughters are, suggesting that they are the true saints who remain in spiritual Babylon and are "mixed up" in that system. Babylon's corruptions were to be found the "length and breadth of Christendom" and

---

4. Dennett, Visions of John in Patmos, 224.

5. Innocent III, Sicut universitatis conditor (1198). N.B., "the power of the king derives from the authority of the pope."

6. Dennett, "Expository Jottings," 205.

Dennett believed that the call to "come out of her" was more urgent than ever at the time he was writing.[7]

Dennett also links the spiritual system of Babylon in this publication with the Church in Laodicea (Rev 3:14–20), those "lukewarm" Christians who believed they were rich and needed for nothing but really were poor, pitiful, blind and naked.[8] He uses this link between Babylon and Laodicea as another way of exhorting his readers to "come out of her."

In one of his numerous entries to the Brethren Periodical the *Christian Friend* Dennett compares Ephesians 2:22, which speaks of the Christian being a "dwelling place" for God's spirit, with Revelation 18:2 which castigates Babylon for being a "dwelling place" for demons and evil spirits. He writes, "Now Babylon is that which the professing church of God on earth has become . . . It is for the spiritual mind to discern how far Christendom has already become morally the home and dwelling-place of demons."[9] Here Dennett identifies Babylon not simply as the Roman Catholic system but as an entity encompassing something that is far wider and much more extensive than one mere denomination, namely, all those on earth who profess to be the true church of God but are morally and spiritually demonic. Christendom is, in other words, a church of worldly Christians, those "mixed up with all this frightful formality, self-complacency, and indifference . . . empty profession."[10]

In *Blessed Hope* (1879) Dennett continues this theme and uses the image to draw a distinction between the worldly churches and his own community. In the process he discusses apostasy and the antichrist. The final form of Laodicean apathy will be Babylon the Great, a place where

> the Church in its outward form, i.e. the profession of Christianity, will still remain . . . There will therefore be thousands (not to say millions) of mere nominal believers left behind . . . the churches and chapels, and other places where professing Christians meet, will carry on as before their religious services. The bells will ring, and the congregations, though thinned by the absence of those who were the children of God, will assemble; and hymns will be sung, prayers repeated or made, and sermons delivered.[11]

7. Dennett, *Visions of John in Patmos*, 232.

8. Dennett, "Revelation," 10–14.

9. Dennett, "Revelation," 24.

10. Ibid., 14.

11. Dennett, *Blessed Hope*, 62.

This is a major development, for Dennett here touches on one of the really substantial Brethren contributions to end-time thinking, and one that was to have a massive and continued influence, namely, the doctrine of the "Secret Rapture of the Church." This will be discussed in detail in chapter 9 below and we note it here only in passing. Suffice to say, Dennett paints a picture of a corrupt "left behind" Church from which the true believers have been translated to the heavens. What remains on earth is a church made up of mere professors of the faith, not true believers. In this context it is important to note the distinction Dennett makes between "real Christians" and "mere nominal believers." The Brethren compose the church of real Christians but nominal Christians are found throughout the many churches and chapels in the land. The use of the phrase "churches and chapels and other places where professing Christians meet" gives us an insight into where Dennett believes the daughters of Babylon may be found. The apocalyptic Whore is not limited to the great cathedrals of Roman Catholicism, or even the old, Established Churches of Anglicanism. Rather, through her progeny she may be found also in the "chapels" where the Non-Established Protestant denominations such as the Unitarians, Methodists, Baptists and the Non-conformists and Dissenters meet to worship. Dennett also adds "other places" to the list so as to be fully comprehensive in his charge against all denominations: to involve the Quaker Friend's and the Puritan Meeting Houses, Catholic shrines, and the meeting of Independent groups in private homes or schoolrooms as daughters of Babylon. Such groups, for Dennett, represent the "near outsider" and as such the threat is closer to home.

It would be easy to list further evidence of Dennett's evolving views, but such is not necessary. Already the broad outline of this thinking is plain. For him a distinction needs to be made between the true church (the Brethren) and the false one (Babylon). The former is the church built by God and the latter, Babylon, is the church built by man.[12] The former is the church where God is inside and the latter, Babylon, is the church inhabited by demons.[13] Terrible judgment awaits those who remain inside such Babylonian churches, yet there is hope for it is not too late, according to the futurist hermeneutic of Dennett, to "come out of her" and enjoy "complete separation."[14] Thus for Dennett "Babylon" may be used as a tool with which to both launch a vilifying attack on both the near (Protestant) and distant (Catholic) outsider and also used as a warning of impending danger to the

12. Dennett, *House of God*, 37.
13. Dennett, "Revelation," 26.
14. Dennett, *Blessed Hope*, 62.

uncommitted insider. The broad paradigm remains operative, but within it the details are changing.

KELLY

As we have seen in the previous chapter Exclusive division leader Kelly began his exegesis of Revelation chapters 17–18 on a religious level by identifying Papal Rome, in no uncertain terms, as the Great Whore.[15] Unlike the vast majority of Protestant Reformers before him, however, Kelly was to move beyond this designation and he quickly became much wider ranging in his exegesis, for although for Kelly Babylon was clearly Rome she was also "the parent of ecclesiastical corruptions outside herself yet akin to her."[16]

Kelly sees Babylon in the churches all around him and describes her influences in numerous ways but above all Babylon is deceptive. She deceives the church attendee by her pleasant outward appearance but underneath she is something foul and evil, for under "the fair guise of Christendom the woman was . . . most corrupt and hateful to God."[17] She has deceived religious men in cunning and wily ways, for "the delusion of Satan [is] not alas! outside, but in Christendom . . . the subtlest snare for man. It is Babylon . . . All Christendom . . . How blinding is worldly religion!"[18] This demonstrates Kelly's belief that Babylon is ubiquitous throughout all of Christendom, an institution he defines as "professing man, without life in Christ."[19] Yet Christendom cannot have always been Babylonian, as Kelly understands that Babylon is the "corruptness of Christendom,"[20] implying that at one time the church was not corrupt. Thus for Kelly Babylon is a church, but a church that has lost its true nature and calling, going back to that well-worn Old Testament link between religious apostasy and harlotry: "having the profession of being espoused to Christ, but really setting up to be mistress of all before the marriage to the deep dishonour of the future absent Bridegroom."[21] How then did Kelly believe that a once true and pure

15. See ch. 5 above.

16. Kelly, *Babylon and the Beast*, 4.

17. Kelly, *Exposition on Revelation*, 199.

18. Kelly, "Jesus the Son of God," 197. See also Kelly, "Judgment of Babylon," *BT*, 11.224. W. R. writes in to ask Kelly to help in "clearing up one or two of my difficulties," and Kelly responds by identifying Babylon as all of Christendom.

19. Kelly, "What Is God's Kingdom Like?," 356–57.

20. Ibid., 319.

21. Kelly, *Babylon and the Beast*, 3.

church had been corrupted by Babylon and become a hollow shell of faithless, professing Christendom? It was through religious idolatry:

> The unclean spirit of idolatry . . . [the] cause of the captivity in
> Babylon . . . will surely return . . . the nations of Christendom
> will be no better. . . . They have not continued in God's goodness
> and must also be cut off. They are largely idolatrous already, and
> this will grow to greater ungodliness.[22]

Such idolatry has left the church as a broken, ruined institution. As
well as her deceptive appearance she is useless in functioning as a true
church because she has lost her effectiveness, or to use the Matthean analogy, "saltiness," and can no longer act as salt and light to the nations as Jesus commanded in Matthew 5:13: "When Christianity vanishes and only
a savourless Christendom remains . . . so it will be when the final blows
come for Babylon."[23] Such an analogy implies that at one time she may have
been the true salt of the earth but now the salt has lost its savor. Instead the
church is in a similar state to that of Israel when captive in Babylon: "the
present broken state of the church" is "morally ruined . . . Nehemiah was
just as truly raised up of God for the return from Babylon . . . in this evil day
. . . no boast is more vain than that of possessing all the outward apparatus
of the church of God."[24]

Thus although Kelly clearly goes beyond just identifying the Catholic
Church alone as Babylon he remains vague regarding just who it is that
corrupt Christendom actually includes, other than that it includes "all."
This entirely comprehensive charge includes the Irvingites who in Kelly's
work *The Catholic Apostolic Body, or Irvingites* (1890–1891) are linked with
Christendom, which is then, in turn, linked with Babylon. He writes that
Drummond and Irving are guilty of "leading away the society into more
fatal depths . . . than was found in any other sect . . . [it] is confessedly
Babylon."[25]

This is an example of the book or Revelation being used in a highly
individual way. The entirely comprehensive charge of "all" even includes
other Brethren outside of Darby and Kelly's Exclusive division such as the
excommunicated congregation at Bethesda in Bristol who in 1848 were
accused of supporting Newton's Christological heresies.[26] Those who

---

22. Kelly, "Blasphemy of God's Power in Christ," *BT*, N1, 263–64.
23. Kelly, "Salt of the Earth," 86–87.
24. Kelly, *Lectures Introductory*, 113–14.
25. Kelly, "Catholic Apostolic Body," 57–73.
26. Darby, "Bethesda Circular," 253–58.

were originally insiders became, through a vituperative attack using the language of Babylon, near outsiders. Kelly was seeking to erect some very clear boundaries to define his own group, not just with regard to the wider Protestant and Catholic churches in general (the extreme outsider), but also with those who were actually quite close to Kelly's faction. This latter group, who would go on to become known as the Open Brethren, were exhorted to "come out" of Babylon by Kelly: "Scripture is not silent to their great sin. 'Come out,' therefore, brother, that you partake not of the sins, and so not receive God's strokes."[27] The members of the Bethesda assembly had allowed Babylon to creep into their meetings unawares in the form of confused and corrupt doctrines carried like a germ or virus from Newton's Ebrington Street assembly in Plymouth to their assembly. Bethesda chapel had been contaminated by heretical doctrine simply through supporting members of Ebrington Street and thus they had allowed themselves to be taken into Babylonian captivity.[28]

Kelly, then, represents a further development of the Babylon interpretative paradigm within the Brethren. The image is being used now even to sharpen the focus of ecclesiological self-identification further and to distance the "Exclusives" from those who would later become the "Open" faction. Intriguingly however Kelly never builds on the "mother-daughter" of Babylon idiom to describe the relationship between the corrupt denominations of Christendom and Papal Rome but, rather, Rome is the source of the corruption of a once true church, not of the genesis of an originally Babylonian daughter, as this would implicate his own "Exclusive" sect which itself gave birth to the "Open" sect.

TROTTER

The next Brethren author considered here is the renowned Brethren author on prophetic subjects, William Trotter. Some brief biographical details on Trotter have been given in chapter 4 above, but his biblical interpretation has never before been critically examined to this point. Trotter draws a sharp distinction and differentiation between the two entities he sees around him that confess to be that institution known as "the church" and, like Dennett and Kelly before him, makes a comparison between "the true church" and "the false professing body."[29] This false church, or false professing body, is

27. Kelly, *Doctrine of Christ*, 16.

28. The link between Babylon and Doctrinal Contamination will be taken up in much more detail in ch. 6 below.

29. Trotter, "Recapitulation," 428. See also, Trotter, "Christ and the Church," 81.

described by Trotter as "Nominally Christian . . . [an] outward adoption of Christianity . . . presented to us in the Apocalyptic vision—Babylon the Great. . . . this vast system of worldly Christians, of a Christian profession."[30]

Thus the superficially external and extensive worldly nature of the fake church in Trotter's understanding can be seen. He continues to depict this hypocritical institution in such terms as: "Ecclesiastical corruption . . . the Gentile professing body . . . Christendom . . . nothing remains for it but to be cut off."[31] Babylon is also portrayed as "the fallen church . . . professing Christians . . . the nominal professing body."[32] In using such terms Trotter is reiterating his views that the false church is made up of Christians who are merely professors of faith and not truly regenerate. His use of the verbs "fallen" and "corruption" to describe the false church suggests however that it once occupied a place higher and a status purer than it does now.

Trotter is very clear that Scripture predicts a "false church." She is Babylon the Great: "The mystic Babylonish woman . . . profession of Christianity."[33] She is "Babylon . . . the false church."[34] Again, then, we can see the use of Revelation's Babylon image being used among key Brethren writers and being used primarily in a way that reinforces the group's own sense of purity and faithfulness to God through vilifying the outsider, in this case both near and far, as Babylon.

For Trotter, the false Babylonian church has replaced the true church on the earth: "The one Church, existing as Christ's witness on earth, [has] been set aside, and some other body taken its place . . . [it will] be spued out of Christ's mouth."[35] Here Trotter is using the language of Revelation chapter 3 and the rebuke brought against the lukewarm church of Laodicea, a church which God will ultimately spit out of his mouth, to condemn the church he sees around him.

Harking back rather to the views of Roger Williams (ca. 1603–1683),[36] Trotter identifies the Established Church in England, with its civil relationship, as being the church in Pergamos (Rev 2:12–17), a church which has

---

"The doom of Christendom . . . the Church of God . . . Christendom has assumed this place, and pretends to be nothing less than this Church of God." Trotter, "Coming Crisis," 60. Here professing Christendom is contrasted with the true church.

30. Trotter, "Recapitulation," 428.

31. Trotter, "Ecclesiastical Corruption and Apostasy," 243.

32. Trotter, "Doom of Christendom," 63.

33. Trotter, "Times of the Gentiles," 210–11.

34. Trotter, "Last Days of the Gentile Supremacy," 278.

35. Trotter, "Apocalyptic Interpretation," 349.

36. Froom, *Prophetic Faith*, 3.51. Froom identifies Williams as the first author to identify the Church of England as Revelation's church of Pergamos.

been enticed into immoral practices and teachings. The church of Thyatira (Rev 2:18–27), on the other hand, is the "Popery of the Dark Ages."[37] Such a sequential reading of the Seven Churches was an unusual development in Brethren hermeneutics and as such represents a movement outside of the futurist Brethren interpretative community on these issues for Trotter.[38]

Trotter specifically condemns the Protestant Church of his own day but rather than criticizing the Protestants for being lukewarm, like the charge leveled against the Laodiceans in Revelation 3, he identifies them as the church in Sardis described in Revelation 3:1–6, who, although a few true believers remain in that church and although they have a reputation for being alive are in fact really dead.[39] Trotter levels the same charge against Protestantism as the Apostle Paul leveled against the Church of Galatia, that of allowing "false brothers infiltrating their ranks" (Gal 2:3–5). The infiltration is that of allowing Roman ordinances, or Catholic law and rules, into the Protestant church: "Romanism is avowedly a system of ordinances . . . but what of the multitude on their way to Romanism, who lay full as much stress on ordinances as Romanists themselves?"[40] Here he is undoubtedly referring to the Oxford Movement, or Tractarian Movement, led by John Henry Newman and E. B. Pusey, among others. They sought to reabsorb all the various English denominations back into the Roman Church in a kind of "anti-reformation" process, undoing the work of the Reformers who had already, in the words of the Babylon motif, "come out" of Rome.

Trotter is very clear that the exegesis of Babylon should not be confined or limited simply to the Reformation interpretation of Papal Rome. He states that Babylon is more than just Catholicism, it includes other Christian religions also: "The doom of Babylon the Great . . . I do not confine it to the Church of Rome."[41]

37. Trotter, "Israel in the Approaching Crisis," 255.

38. See Surridge, "Seventh-day Adventism," 24–29. Surridge notes that most historicists understood the first four churches to exist sequentially throughout the past and the last three: Sardis, Philadelphia and Laodicea, to coexist at the same time in the present. Outside Adventist exegesis a truly sequential reading of the Seven Churches was not very common before 1856 and the work of James White.

39. Trotter, "Israel in the Approaching Crisis," 253, 255–56.

40. Ibid., 248.

41. Trotter, "The Spared Remnant," 278. N.B., also in this publication, "It has been the habit to interpret all these things of Popery . . . Babylon doubtless symbolises Popery; not Popery alone, but chiefly . . . Popery with every other form of ecclesiastical corruption." Also, Trotter, "Christ and the Church," 118: "The great professing body, including Romanism, and all else that ostensibly bears the name of Christ"; and, Trotter, "Ecclesiastical Corruption," 255: "Leaving Rome aside, and looking at the national churches of Christendom, and the great professing bodies which have branched off

Obviously aware of the Protestant stream of exegesis that has gone before him, Trotter enters into a dialogue with his reader concerning the identity of the false Babylonian church:

> "Ah, but it is of Rome that you are speaking; and what has Rome or Romanism, to do with Christ and the Church?" . . . no doubt Romanism is the principle part of that which mystic Babylon represents. But it is not the whole . . . does not Romanism embrace the greater part of what professes to be the Church?[42]

Thus while it is clear that Rome Papal is the starting place for his interpretation of the Babylon motif, Trotter does not remain there but quickly moves on to use the image of the Great Whore to describe the wider, nominal church, using Babylon to vilify not just the extreme outsider but using Babylon to vilify the nearest outsider, who perhaps, being closer to home poses a greater threat.

His wider understanding of who Babylon is, enables him to identify churches as Babylonian in countries where geographical and territorially Catholicism had not spread or at least had only an insignificant influence, thus he states: "I speak not now of Romanism, but of what bears the name and sustains the responsibilities of the Church in countries where Romanism is not predominant."[43] Trotter goes on to question exactly what it is that "holds together the very framework of society in these so-called Christian countries?"[44] Rather than being a true light and converting the world "those countries where Christ is nominally owned"[45] have instead been converted by the world, forming a union with the world, and it is for this reason that professing Christianity will be judged for she has become "nominal, national Christianity . . . a vast and monstrous world system as is said in the 18th of Revelation."[46] National Christianity here, as for Dennett, is perhaps referring to the civil, established and state sanctioned denominations.

The real identity of these false, nominal, national churches can be found in his prophetic paper *The Doom of Christendom* (1854) in which he lists Romanism, the Reformed Christianity of England, Europe and America, the Established Dissenting, Protestant and Greek churches as the recipients of the indictment against Babylon. Through their union with the

---

from them . . . the Protestant part of Christendom . . . what is it but the world under a Christian name and profession."

42. Trotter, "Christ and the Church," 117.

43. Ibid., 118.

44. Ibid.

45. Trotter, "Approaching Judgments," 35.

46. Trotter, "Second Coming of Christ Pre-millennial," 45.

world they shall be judged during Babylon's overthrow.[47] Yet Trotter goes even further than simply to present a list of the false churches he believes to be Babylonian. He challenges all who listen to his sermon or read his paper to judge whether they are in any way guilty of association with Babylon for "it becomes every one of us to consider how far he may be in anywise associated with it."[48]

At this point one may begin to see a trend, and indeed a new paradigm, arising within the specifically Brethren movement when compared with wider exegesis. For this community were not only concerned with defining themselves over and against Rome, the preoccupation of the wider Protestant movement, but with defining their own place on the map Christendom. The Whore of Babylon motif is used to spell out very precisely where the Brethren are: both "spatially" (i.e., where the movement is relative to other Christian groups, both near and far in terms of the threat of boundary transgression) and temporally (i.e., where the movement comes in the history of the world). This latter point will come more clearly to the fore in chapters 8 and 9 below.

BELLETT

For Bellett Christendom is an entity that has "corrupted itself" and thus will be judged according to the judgments foretold in the Apocalypse that befall Babylon.[49] Christendom attempts to "regulate the world" and is "full of the falsest thoughts," a place of "strange alliance" between "ease and indulgence and self-pleasing."[50] Such a church is worldly, fleshly, sensual and decadent. Bellett further describes Christendom as a place of "strangely inconsistent elements . . . [of] anomalous materials" a mixture of "clean and unclean vessels."[51] By this he means that Christendom is a place of confusion of thought and doctrine. This harks back to the older use of "Babylon" to mean confusion as seen above, and is an important development which is explored in detail in chapter 7 below where it is shown that the Babylon image is used also to argue that the other churches are in "Doctrinal Confusion." This again brings the Brethren into sharp relief against their perceived ecclesiological background.

47. Trotter, "Doom of Christendom," 76.

48. Trotter, "Predicted Corruption of Christianity," 204–5.

49. Bellett, "Introduction to Isaiah," 229–32, 243–45.

50. Bellett, *Woollen and Linen*, 31.

51. Bellett, *Witnesses for God*, 18–19.

Christendom is, according to Bellett, on its way to a place of apostasy, that is, the professing church is in a position of falling away from the truth.[52] Bellett is clear, the church of the last days will deny the Lord and become corrupt to such an extent that it should not even really be called a church, for "the Christendom that we see around us is . . . far from the church."[53] However, Bellett describes this false church in dichotomous terms as a "victorious corruption."[54] Perhaps referring to how this ecclesiastical impostor has formed a civil and ecclesiastical unity[55] in which the church controls and subjugates the world which supports it.

To be overly religious or to be enticed with external traditions and correct worship in the church is a sure sign that the believer has gone back into Babylonian captivity. Thus Bellett writes: "Not that we are to go back to Babylon . . . we may be beguiled into moral relaxation through satisfaction in our ecclesiastical accuracies."[56] He then goes on to quote one of the woes to the Scribes and Pharisees found in Matthew 23:23 which criticizes the hypocrisy of being religious in action only and neglecting to act out of justice, love and faithfulness.

In his exegesis of the Babylon motif Bellett differs somewhat from the other authors in this chapter and also from the Reformers before him in that he never openly identifies Babylon as something papal or Catholic. This is rather surprising given the entrenched tradition and suggests to some extent that Bellett was more concerned with the threat from the near outsider rather than the threat from the extreme outsider, that is, the danger on his own doorstep rather than the distant danger from Rome. Bellett does, however, identify Babylon as a religious entity and he specifically identifies Babylon as Christendom: "this was Babylon, and in spirit this is Christendom."[57] Thus corrupt, false, fleshly, inconsistent and civil religion is for Bellett the Christianity of Babylon the Great. This view is just as clear in *The Potter's Broken Vessel* (1880) where Bellett unequivocally understands Babylon and Christendom as straightforward synonyms meaning exactly the same thing.[58]

---

52. Bellett, *Notes from Meditations on Luke*, 106.

53. Bellett, *Witnesses for God*, 49.

54. Bellett, "Rightly Dividing the Word of Truth," 87.

55. Bellett, "Potter's Broken Vessel," 32.

56. Bellett, *Witnesses for God*, 37.

57. Bellett, "Babylon," 26.

58. Bellett, "Potter's Broken Vessel," 32. See also Bellett, "Rightly Dividing," 83–92. Here Bellett links Babylon with the corruption of the "Great House." Also Bellett, "Zechariah," 104. Here Bellett links the vision of the woman with the ephah in Zechariah 5, with Babylon and states, "This 'wickedness' is hidden . . . under a profession . . .

However Bellett does not become any more specific than this in his designation of who is actually in Babylon and of which churches make up Christendom. What he is clear on, unlike Dennett and Trotter, is that the Established Church, formed through its union between the religious and the civil, is not necessarily Babylonian. He states that

> the Establishment is not a Church ruin; it is an important thing in the earth . . . [it] has linked His name with the government and men of the world, but God's dear people are there . . . it may not be a Church ruin . . . Christendom is not to be mistaken for Church ruins . . . [a few] call on the Lord out of a pure heart from the Church ruins . . . Ruins are weak things, but still they tell of the original building.[59]

Thus Bellett's interpretation here is somewhat at odds with the growing Brethren exegesis which understands an established link between the church and the state, such as that held by the Church of England, as being a principle of Babylon.

Bellett does not highlight any one particular denomination or tradition as being Babylonian but rather perceives Babylon as being indicative of the whole of professing Christianity in which true and vital Christians reside like wheat among the tares of nominal Christianity. Alluding to the parable of Matthew chapter 13 they must, according to Bellett, be allowed to grow together until harvest and judgment.[60]

Simply "coming out" of Papal Rome like the Protestant Reformers of the sixteenth century did is not enough to escape Babylon. The Reformation alone was not enough, for as Bellett states: "Reformation will not do. So it is with Christendom . . . mere Protestantism will not do."[61] Although he admits that the Reformation was "a kind of return from Babylon"[62] the act of reformation itself did not restore the churches purity.[63]

Finally, he reiterates his view that Babylon is in all of Christendom. The church is compared to Israel during her Babylonian captivity where some retained their purity but others were corrupted by Babylon's pernicious influence. The true church at the end of the age is, in a dispensational and recapitulatory way, an image of Old Testament Israel: "captive in the

of the name of Christendom but it is really Babylon at the end." Also Bellett, *Notes from Meditations on Luke*, 57. He again Christendom is linked to Babylon.

59. Bellett, "Extracts from Letters," 166.
60. Bellett, *Woollen and Linen*, 7.
61. Bellett, *Notes from Meditations on Luke*, 57.
62. Bellett, *Witness for God*, 32.
63. Ibid., 47.

dungeons of Babylon." Bellett uses the judgments of Revelation chapters 17–18 as a warning to those true believers inside Babylon of the imminent "waning, fading, evening shades of Christendom, which are soon to close in the midnight of Apocalyptic judgments."[64]

WOLSTON

Wolston refrains from limiting his religious identification of Babylon simply and singularly on the Roman Catholic Church but rather identifies Babylon as a "false church." He writes of this fake ecclesial entity's destruction as "the fall of Babylon . . . the judgment of the false Church."[65]

In the style of the emerging Brethren hermeneutical pattern Wolston sets his identification of Babylon on a much broader level than the Reformers before him, for Rome was not the only threat to him; the danger was much closer. Unlike Kelly, Trotter, and Bellett discussed above, but in line with Darby, Dennett, and Miller, Wolston makes use of the Babylonian "mother-daughter" idiom in working out his views. The key difference between these two exegetical lines is that of whether the Protestant denominations were "born corrupt" and thus were always Babylonian by virtue of their mother being corrupt, or, were the Protestant denominations "born pure" but at some point experienced an apostasy after corruption by Babylon thus becoming Babylonian. Wolston is to be found in the former camp. Thus we read of the Babylonian family: "The time has come when the whore with all her children are cast into the fire. That is her judgment. Babylon falls, in the 18th chapter."[66] Such a warning is leveled to the outsider, both near (Protestant) and far (Catholic).

Yet Wolston also uses the Babylon motif to warn the insider for apostasy, or falling into Babylonian captivity, is still a possible risk *intra muros*. The true church becomes false by its association with the world. When the church becomes mixed up in the affairs of the world then it becomes Babylon, and it is with regards to such a relationship that Wolston writes,

> It is therefore a very serious thing if God's people be mixed up with the world, even though it be religious . . . "Come out of her, my people . . ." What is Babylon? It is the world-church. And you and I must not forget that while there is the Church of God, the real thing, there is also the world-church. And therefore we

64. Bellett, "Mornings of Scripture," 8.

65. Wolston, "Stone Cut Out," in *SC*, 6.126. See also Wolston, "Candlestick and the Bride," 213. He writes of "the false church system of the world, Babylon."

66. Wolston, "Stone Cut Out," in *SC*, 6.131.

should see what it is. It is a serious thing if the saints of God get mixed up with the world or the world-church, which is Babylon.[67]

The call of Revelation 18:4 is thus not only a call to "come out" of the world but also to "come out" of the world church, a view which will be explored in more detail in chapter 8 below. Thus for Wolston Babylon is a tool used in vituperative attack, both *extra muros* as the charge of being a "false church" by birth is directed to the near (Protestant)[68] and extreme (Catholic)[69] outsider (for which Wolston uses the "mother-daughter" idiom), and *intra muros* as the danger of being corrupted by Babylon by association may lead to the insider falling away.[70]

While Dennett associates the corrupt Babylonian world church of his own day with the lukewarm church of Laodicea (Rev 3), Wolston, along with Baines, identifies the church they see around them as the church of Thyatira (Rev 2) who is seduced by Jezebel's corrupt doctrines:

> In Thyatira the Church ruled the world . . . Rome as the ecclesi-
> astical mistress of the nations of Europe, could excommunicate
> monarchs, and go the length of compelling a king to go and kiss
> the Pope's toe. Thyatira runs on to the Lord's return . . . and the
> papacy will continue till then without doubt.[71]

The Roman Catholic Church has historically been, according to Wolston, the Thyatiran church who ruled and exercised authority over the world yet the seducer Jezebel has infiltrated other churches in the present time of Woslton's writings with her pernicious and deadly doctrines and as such has caused other churches to fall away into Babylonian captivity in particular through church-state relationships.[72]

Wolston, like Dennett, uses the image of the church in Laodicea but whereas Dennett identifies this passage as referring to his own day Wolston understands the Laodicea motif as describing the latter-day corrupt church. The empty, lifeless Laodicean church is destined to become, in the future, Babylon the Great:

> When the Lord takes away the candlestick, with every mark of
> detestation as to the state it has fallen into, as in Laodicea, Satan

67. Wolston, "King David's New Cart," 226.
68. Wolston, "Established and Endowed," 96.
69. Ibid., 97.
70. Ibid., 95–99.
71. Ibid., 97.
72. Ibid., 98–99.

will take up what is left of the profession, then become his fitting tool for the development of that frightful church-world system afterwards portrayed in Babylon.[73]

The true church must "come out" of the false house of God for the evil of Jezebel's seductive doctrines entered the house God clandestinely and the risk of falling into Babylon is high. The Church is now like Thyatira; full of seduction, it is heading towards becoming like Laodicea: full of "luke-warm" persons who are not accepted by God. For those who remain in such a church the judgments of Revelation chapters 17–18 are ripening. This is a powerful composite image and would have given those who adopted it a powerful sense of the importance both of their own community and the work they had to do in calling people out of the Jezebel-corrupted, luke-warm Babylon that was now nothing short of a "hold of every foul spirit, and a cage of every unclean and hateful bird" (Rev 18:2). For Wolston the Brethren were like the captive Israel in the time of Nehemiah; the faithful must leave Babylonian captivity behind.[74]

It would be easy to extend this list of Brethren interpreters who saw in the Babylon image a picture of not just Rome but of the wider Christian community too. Such views are embedded in the literature which has been investigated in this book, much of it for the first time from this perspective. However, the presentation of further extensive detail on this point seems hardly necessary. In what follows, therefore, only the key points where the emerging exegetical paradigm seems to undergo further modification will be discussed in any detail. As we shall see, among Brethren writers this image of the Whore of Babylon and her daughters was a very useful and indeed powerful one. As the movement struggled to its feet and sought a clear sense of its own identity it was to the biblical text that they turned to seek out their own identity before God and the text, in the hands of these imaginative readers, did not disappoint.

WIGRAM

Wigram identifies Babylon as a religious institution or system but never explicitly narrows down his identification to singularly Catholicism, rather, like others in the tradition, he identifies Babylon in much broader terms as

---

73. Wolston, "Candlestick and the Bride," 197.
74. Wolston, *Handfuls of Purpose*, 272–73.

the "professing Church."[75] For Wigram such professing churches were not "born" Babylonian, but became such through an apostasy or falling away.[76]

Wigram makes a further contribution to Brethren exegesis of Revelation chapters 17–18 when he contrasts the image of the Bride of Christ found in 2 Corinthians 11:2 and Revelation 19 with the image of Babylon the mother of Harlots. The Great Whore is "filled by Satan for the world, with the lust of the flesh, the lust of the eye, and the pride of life," whereas the bride is the dwelling place of God, the home of God's children, a place of unity in fellowship, doctrine, and action. Here, emphasizing the vast difference between the two, he concludes: "What a difference between all this and a modern 'Independent church!'"[77] By "Independent church" Wigram seems to have either the post 1874 independent Open Brethren group in view or the 1876 independent Kelly Division, rather than the Independents, that is, as in the Congregationalist denomination.[78] This again shows how in the hands of a determined interpreter the image can be used to bring great clarity to the question of precisely which group is God's true community. Wigram, it seems, is more concerned with using Babylon to vilify the near outsider, those who pose an immediate threat to the boundaries of the nascent Brethren movement, than the extreme outsider such as Rome, yet he also uses the text to vilify the insider, or at least those who were once inside, and perhaps were even at one time held in high esteem (such as Kelly) but now have been "put out" or excommunicated.

BAINES

As we have seen in the previous chapter Baines identifies the Harlot of Revelation chapters 17–18 as a *future* Roman Catholic system. He does not,

75. Wigram, "Corruption of Christianity," in *Memorials of the Ministry of G. V. Wigram*, 1.127–32. N.B., He does however say, "The Holy Catholic Church . . . [was] dishonoured and Ichabod (where is the Glory) became stamped on the company professing to be the church." Thus identifying Catholicism as part of his overall umbrella designation of Babylon as the wider "professing church," in Wigram, "Church: Its Present State," 103.

76. Wigram, "Corruption of Christianity," 1.127–32.

77. Wigram, *To the Christians in New Zealand*, 10.

78. The "independence" of the Open Brethren in terms of autonomy to decide on matters of doctrine and fellowship is attested to in Burnham (2005), 208. Of the Kelly Division, Wigram states: "Of this I am sure, that the so-called religion of 1876 is part of Christendom, and is not Christianity," in Wigram, "Coming Kingdom," 61. Either group would fit the charge but the important thing to note is that Wigram is now using the Babylon motif not to merely "vilify" the outsider but to castigate *intra muros* within the Brethren group itself.

however, limit the designation to Papal Rome alone but rather uses the "mother-daughter" idiom to broaden the charge. He notes that "she is also called 'the mother of harlots and abominations of the earth' for not merely is she an idolatrous system herself, but she has given birth to other idolatrous systems scattered over the world."[79] Her daughters, though not named by Baines at this point, are ubiquitous in their presence. He also develops the identification of the church around him as the church of Thyatira: a church seduced by the harlot Jezebel.[80] His exegesis is in keeping with what others in the movement were now saying and the use within the group to which the image was in general being put. There is little in Baines' work that adds much to the paradigm, though it is apparent from that work that he was able to synthesize a good deal of what had gone before and was going on all around him. Not only is the Babylon image used, but so too are the themes of "Laodicea," "Thyatira," and the "mother-daughter" idiom as the group become more and more comprehensive in their designation of exactly who "Babylon" is. Not only is the distant outsider, Papal Rome, Babylon, but now like the tightening rings of concentric circles, the near insider, Protestantism and all of its denominations is also being identified as "Babylon." Furthermore the use of the text as a form of vituperative rhetoric to attack the outsider has become internalized and it is starting to be used *intra muros* to attack the Babylon within the Brethren.

OTHER AUTHORS

The authors mentioned above were perhaps among the most significant standing authors in the Brethren movement but some lesser known, or at least less prolific, figures from within the tradition also had something to say on the issue.

The figure of Newton needs brief mention here too. Newton did not have much to add to the paradigm, though his status within the movement may well have helped to recommend it to others. According to this interpreter, Babylon consisted of all corrupt Christendom and not the papal system only.[81] For him such churches are Babylonian not because they were "born" that way from a Babylonian mother but because they had been corrupted and tainted; mainly by ritualism.[82] The Churches of Rome and Eng-

---

79. Baines, "Glorious Coming and Kingdom of Christ," 225.

80. Ibid., 197–98.

81. Newton, *Prophecy of Habakkuk*, 5–7.

82. Newton, *Olive Tree and Its Branches*, 6–7. Also, Newton, *God and "the Heathen*," 2–3, 9–10.

land as well as the Non-conformists are all identified as Babylon.[83] These views, as we have seen, he shared with many other Brethren writers. It was of course towards both Newton and Kelly after the 1874 and 1876 schisms that the Darbyite Exclusives such as Wigram used the language of Revelation chapters 17–18 to launch a vituperative attack on those once well loved and highly respected insiders.

Thomas Tweedie, a former clergyman who after seceding from the Church of England joined the Brethren movement and became a missionary to British Guiana, argued that the identification of Babylon is much broader than some have thought. Tweedie was in line with his more prolific fellow believers when he wrote of Babylon that she is: "The professing church, loving the world and seeking a portion in it, is in all this opposed to the bride."[84] Similarly F. W. Grant, the English Brethren author, who was instrumental in guiding the 1885 schism of the Exclusive Grant division in North America from the Exclusives led by Darby in England, through linking the "strange woman" of Proverbs 5 with the Great Whore of Revelation chapters 17–18 concluded that

> the enemy is well versed in this terrible warfare . . . Nothing is more common than to see him in the clothing of religion . . . In the battle with him, we should always keep in mind what Proverbs 5: 6 says of the strange woman; "lest you should ponder the path of life, her ways are changeable that you should not know them."[85]

Thus for Grant we see that it is all religion in general that is Babylonian; religion is the clothing of Babylon, the superficial facade that hides the truly satanic character that lies underneath. A similar interpretation is taken by Thomas Newberry in his commentary on Revelation.[86]

Little biographical information is known of brethren author William Lincoln, although we do know that he was an ordained Anglican minister who, on November 23, 1862, seceded from the Church of England to become part of the Brethren movement.[87] Writing between 1861 and 1916 he produced some twenty-six publications and of these six were primarily

83. Newton, *Probable Course of Events*, 5.

84. Tweedie, "Mystery, Babylon the Great," 94–95.

85. Grant, *Divine Movement*, 46.

86. For Newberry, Babylon represents the whole of "apostate Christianity," outwardly bearing the name Christ as a cloak or covering of respectability which hides something much more sinister and devilish underneath. Newberry, *Notes on the Book of Revelation*, 97–98.

87. Lincoln, *Address of the Rev. W. Lincoln*.

on the subject of the book of Revelation and the end times. The majority of his publications appear to be in the form of lectures and sermons, thus it is highly probable that his views on such matters were widely disseminated as they were not only read but also heard preached from the pulpit. At some unknown period of the late nineteenth century, Lincoln published a series of pamphlets on the book of Revelation titled under the series title *Lincoln's Leaflets.*

In pamphlet ten, Lincoln speaks of an entity he calls simply "Christendom," a term he uses like many of those above, to describe the union of the professing church with the world. He is critical of the way that the clergy of nominal Christianity have shown no signs of Christian regeneration but rather have not only tolerated worldliness but actively looked to the world for help and support rather than looking to Christ:

> As then Jericho fell, so now Babylon falls. As the literal Babylon perished by the drying up of its great river; so the Peoples of Christendom finally and deliberately reject every vestige of Christianity, and its unregenerate clerics and professors receive no more countenance or help from the world on which it had leaned for support.[88]

Lincoln goes on to use the "mother-daughter" idiom in ways not dissimilar to those noted in other authors above. Indeed, he specifically identifies the daughters of the Great Whore as the "world's churches," and, continuing in the developing tradition of understanding Babylon on a systemic rather than a personal level, identifies the daughters of Babylon as luxurious religious systems, which he in turn links with the church of Laodicea:

> In the former chapter we behold the harlot of Babylon and her daughters, i.e. the world's churches, in all their luxury . . . and their religious systems extirpated violently by the newly elected emperor and his ten kings . . . In 18 God's hand is seen in these judgements on the ecclesiastical apostacies of Christendom. In 3 Christ had warned he was about to vomit the professing Church, in her last or Laodicean phase, out of His mouth.[89]

Thus Lincoln continues in the newly emerging tradition as for him Babylon and "lukewarm" Laodicea are the same thing.

In a letter to a certain Mr. Howells dated 1829, Lady Theodosia Powerscourt identified Babylon as all of those professing Christians who remain

88. Lincoln, "Book of the Revelation," 10.3.

89. Ibid.

silent on important social and political matters. This is a slight variation on the general theme in favor of the importance that, from the author's perspective, God places on social witness and is somewhat at odds with the underlying premillennial pessimism of the Brethren, particularly those who held more Exclusive views. However, such matters were an important part of the Albury Park prophetic conferences, of which Lady Powerscourt had attended on a number of occasions.[90] Lady Powerscourt believed that to be "in Babylon" was for the church to be silent on such political matters as emancipation. To act in such a way is to "take our lot with Babylon."[91] When she discusses emancipation in this letter she is probably referring to the Roman Catholic Relief Act of 1829, the overwhelming response to this Act was one of despair at the socio-political situation.[92] Powerscourt also uses the analogy put forward by Grant and Newberry of wearing "religious" clothing as a way of describing those who confess Christ with their lips but deny him by their actions. Here she identifies Babylon as all of the professing Christians who indulge themselves in immoral religion through their lack of social action: such people wear Christianity as a fake veneer. We read:

> Christianity is so much more profession than confession. We strive to live our doctrines, instead of confounding the world by the contradiction of our walk and our belief . . . We wear Christ too like a loose garment, to be put on and taken off as convenience offers—denying him, by not confessing him.[93]

Very little biographical information can be gleaned about the life of the Brethren author Hugh Henry Snell (1815–1891) who authored some eighteen publications, of which three were on the subject of prophecy and the end times.[94] Like all of the Brethren authors that have been examined in this chapter Snell broadens the identification of Babylon on a religious level to include all of corrupt Christianity, drawing a sharp distinction between the false church and the true church and stating, "We do violence to truth to limit Babylon to Romanism."[95] He thus uses Babylon to castigate, not just the distant outsider, but the near outsider too; the enemy on his own doorstep. However his description of the Babylonian church as

90. Burnham, Story of Conflict, 115.

91. Powerscourt, Letters and Papers, 23.62.

92. Oliver, Prophets and Millennialists, 140–42.

93. Powerscourt, Letters and Papers, 23.62.

94. Pickering, Chief among Brethren, 119.

95. Snell, Notes on the Revelation, 161.

the "false and corrupt one"[96] suggests that Snell believed the outsider had "become" Babylon rather than being "born" Babylon, a view reiterated by the absence of the "mother-daughter" idiom in his exegesis. The apostasy comes through any connection between the church and the world.[97] Such a union leads the church into Babylon.[98] Snell however does not go as far as Dennett and others to say that any formal arrangement between the church and the world, such as in the civil-religious relationship of the Established Church of England, is specifically Babylonian, yet he does clearly identify both Catholics, who were "supported by the world" in the Roman Catholic Relief Act of 1829, and Anglicans, who were "supported by the world" when the monarch was pronounced as their head in 1534, as being Babylonian. He writes that "Romanism is certainly a large example of Babylon . . . be assured that Babylon the Great abounds also in Protestantism, or wherever the world's support is resorted to in connection with the name and work of the Lord."[99]

The exegesis of the Babylon motif by Brethren author C. H. Mackintosh is important as it has been noted above that it was through Mackintosh that Brethren, particularly Darbyite, hermeneutics and doctrine was spread throughout North America. In essence Mackintosh took on board the Brethren views on Revelation, views which he took with him to America, enabling American Brethren to set them within that new context.

Mackintosh follows closely the emerging outline of exegesis traced above. He too broadens the designation of Babylon to include more than just the Roman Catholic Church. Babylon is found throughout the "professing church,"[100] both in "popery, and in every section of Protestant profession."[101] He even applies the text to the Irvingites of his own day,[102] a group who attended the same prophetic conferences as many notable Brethren and had much in common with regards to their premillennial outlook. Thus

96. Ibid., 157.

97. Ibid., 161.

98. The concept of worldliness will be examined later on in ch. 8.

99. Snell, *Notes on the Revelation*, 165.

100. Mackintosh, "Letters to a Friend," 201. See also Mackintosh, *Assembly of God*, 27–28; Mackintosh, "Church: Ephesians 1 and 2," in *Occasional Papers*, 48; Mackintosh, *Remnant: Past & Present*, 14. Here he notes "the professing Church is a hopeless wreck."

101. Mackintosh, "Fifth Letters to a Friend," 320.

102. Mackintosh, "Fifteenth Letter to a Friend," 14. He writes: "Do I want to see the church restored to its Pentecostal glory? By no means. This was the delusion of poor Edward Irving. I never expect to see the church restored." See also Mackintosh, *Notes on the Book of Numbers*, 187.

the language of Babylon is being used closer and closer to home with the progression of time, to denigrate ever nearer threats from outsiders.

Mackintosh also continued the emerging Brethren tradition of interpreting Babylon in light of the Letters to the Churches pericopae found in Revelation chapters 2–3. He does not do this in a historicist way, which would suggest that each of the churches in Revelation exist in different periods of Christianity's history, but rather in a simultaneous way suggesting:

> [In] Thyatira, we find Romanism . . . Sardis, Protestantism . . . Laodicea is loathsome to the heart of Christ . . . He will spew out of His mouth, and Satan will take it up and make it a cage of every unclean and hateful bird—Babylon! Wherever you find pretension, assumption, self-assertion or self-complacency, there you have, in spirit and principle, Laodicea.[103]

This development is significant insofar as Mackintosh clearly identifies Roman Catholicism as Babylon, thus a link is made with Thyatira and Papal Rome. Also Mackintosh here clearly identifies Protestantism as Babylon, thus a link is made with the church in Sardis. Both Babylonian churches exist simultaneously rather than sequentially. In some way Laodicea is seen by Mackintosh as the combined total of the churches of Thyatira and Sardis. Here Mackintosh seems to be weaving together the combined exegesis of Dennett, Lincoln, Wolston, Trotter and Baines, on Revelation chapters 2–3, all of which are in some way Babylonian, but for Mackintosh they are combined together in Laodicea, the final corrupt religious system of which Revelation chapters 17–18 describes.

SOME CONCLUDING REMARKS ON "BABYLON" AS ALL OF CORRUPT CHRISTENDOM

It is clear that here in this chapter, just as in the previous chapter, the Brethren have been using the Babylon motif as a form of vituperative rhetoric, to vilify the religious outsider in order to define the self. The major difference in this present chapter is in the spatial location of that vilification. Whereas in the previous chapter the text was used polemically against Papal Rome: the extreme outsider, here in this chapter we have seen how the Brethren used the text to malign those closer to home, that is, Protestantism and all of her denominations. Even other nondenominational sects, the nearest

---

103. Mackintosh, "God's Fullness for an Empty Vessel," in *Miscellaneous Writings*, 5.10.

outsiders, are identified as Babylon. In both cases the text is used *extra muros*, that is, against the outsider.

The work related here perhaps gives a further insight to the inner workings of a new religious group in the period during which they emerge from a parent body. Such movements are naturally concerned with the question of their own ecclesiological status and it is often the case that they will perceive themselves as uniquely significant in the history of God's dealings with humankind. Given this fundamental understanding the competition for such status must be undermined. We see that clearly with the Brethren but it has been noted before. For example, one reason that Collins gives for the historical vilification of the Jews by Christians in Revelation is that "insofar as Christian messianism appeared to be a new and separate phenomenon, it had no status. Thus the two groups competed for status."[104] This is surely what was happening with the newly formed Brethren movement. They too, as a new phenomenon, had no status and had to compete for it with the vast number of Protestant denominations around them. Such a struggle is seen reflected in the Brethren interpretation of the biblical text.

There have been a number of new developments highlighted above in the use of the text, the first being from the pen of the Exclusive Brethren writer Wigram, who, following the lead of Kelly and Darby, turned the direction of attack from the outside to the inside using Babylon *intra muros* to castigate other Brethren. As Collins notes, the original "use" of Revelation was not only to vilify the extreme and near outsider but also "Christian rivals" inside.[105] More specifically she suggests the specific text used by the Christians to whom John wrote Revelation to vilify their own Christian rivals was the Letters to the Churches in Revelation 2–3, and in particular the image of Jezebel in the church in Thyatira.[106] It is perhaps not surprising then that the other new development in Brethren exegesis seen in this chapter is that of the interpretation of Babylon in conjunction with the Letters to the Churches pericopae in Revelation chapters 2–3. Just as the first Christians used the image of Jezebel the prostitute to vilify their own Christian rivals so too the Brethren used this image, in conjunction with the Babylon motif, to vilify their own Christian rivals.

After the split between Open and Exclusives (1848) and the split between the Darbyite Exclusives and the Kelly faction (1879), the Brethren were no longer only concerned with the extreme and near outsider but also

104. Collins, "Vilification and Self-Definition," 314.
105. Ibid., 316.
106. Ibid.

the "otherness within."[107] As such the vituperative rhetoric of "Babylon" began to be applied not just to Papal Rome and the Protestant denominations outside but to other Brethren within. Green has noted that for any "textual community," a category into which the Brethren fit, "the most threatening kind of otherness [is] the otherness within."[108] This is indeed true for the Brethren whose own history has been one marked with schism and sectarianism and it is of no real surprise that the Babylon motif begins to be used *intra muros* in order to vilify the otherness within.

Collins notes that a primary factor in the composition of Revelation was "the experience of trauma."[109] It would not be unreasonable to describe the Plymouth dispute of 1846, the Bethesda schism of 1848 or the numerous other schisms of the 1880s and 1890s as traumatic events for the Brethren movement. The example of trauma that Collins gives is the destruction of the temple and Jerusalem at the hand of Rome in 71 CE. She suggests that it was this experience of social and religious trauma that led the author of Revelation to speak of Rome as Babylon, the Great Whore.[110] The experience of trauma within the Brethren movement also led to using the vitriolic language of Babylon against those who had been perceived to destroy the unity of the early Brethren movement. Thus in many ways the similar use of the text by the earliest Christians and the nineteenth-century Brethren grows out of a shared *Sitz im Leben*. Both groups experienced trauma, thus, both groups sought to reinforce their own identity by using the texts to denigrate the other. As Simmel has noted in his work on conflict: "the unifying power of the principle of conflict nowhere emerges more strongly than when it manages to carve a temporal or contentual [*sic*] area out of competitive and hostile relationships."[111]

The language of Babylon provided a deadly arsenal for attack in such a competitive and hostile religious environment. It was used primarily for the extreme outsider: Papal Rome, then for the near outsider: Protestantism and her offshoots. Finally it was used for the insider: the enemy within, the Open and Kelly Brethren factions. In each case, just as was the case for the Christians who first received the text, Babylon was the perfect tool to assail the other and thus "carve out" a corner in nineteenth-century British premillennial millenarianism.

---

107. Green, "Otherness Within," 49.

108. Ibid., 69.

109. Collins, *Crisis and Catharsis*, 99.

110. Ibid.

111. Simmel, *Conflict*, 102.

7

"Babylon" Is Doctrinal Confusion

In the previous two chapters it has been demonstrated that the Brethren identify Babylon as either Papal Rome or all of what they believe to be the corrupt churches around them, thus defining the difference between the "insider" and "outsider" on a religious level. The Whore of Babylon motif was used by the group to reinforce "self identification" by denigrating the "religious other." In this chapter an account is given of how the Whore of Babylon motif is used by the Brethren commentators to distinguish on an epistemological level between the "insider" and "outsider," that is, between those that have the truth (themselves) and those who do not (outsiders).

It has also been noted above that a number of Brethren authors link the exegesis of the Babylon motif with the exegesis of the Letters to the Churches (Rev 2–3). Wolston and Baines, for example, identified the Babylonian church as the same as the church of Thyatira (Rev 2:18–29), a church which allowed in a woman called Jezebel to teach and beguile the believers with corrupt Satanic mysteries.[1] Thus already it is becoming apparent that some link was made by the Brethren between Babylon and some type of confusion or deception concerning matters of truth and correct teaching.

This is perhaps unsurprising given the linguistic competence and biblical literacy of many of the Brethren writers who were quick to spot a potential link between the story of the tower of Babel and the descent into "confusion." Such commentators included even such major figures as S. P. Tregelles (1813–1875) who joined the Brethren movement in 1835, married into Newton's family and was employed by Wigram to carry out biblical

---

1. See Wolston and Baines in ch. 6 above.

textual criticism, an employment that resulted in the publication of *Heads of Hebrew Grammar* (1852) and a translation of *Gesenius' Hebrew and Chaldee Lexicon* (1881).[2] Tregelles notes that Babel means "confusion" particularly "confusion of speech, stammering."[3] This becomes extended in Brethren exegesis to mean "confusion" more generally, including doctrinal error and is linked not only to Genesis chapter 11, but to the Whore of Babylon from Revelation as well.

The ancient story of the tower of Babel also acts as a picture of human rejection of the word of God and rebellion against the divine will. The Brethren writers picked up on this theme using Babylon to symbolize not only doctrinal confusion, but also rejection of, and rebellion against, their own understanding of the word of God in Scripture. Of course they were not the first expositors to link the Babylon of the Apocalypse with the tower of Babel story in Genesis chapter 11[4] but, as we note in this chapter, they do appear to have been among those who made the most of this potential link; and they did so to great effect. Perhaps the most important Brethren author in this context is Darby himself who not only understood Babylon to be linked to Babel, and hence symbolic of confusion, but also developed a coherent and systematic doctrine based around this idea. This is developed further below.

DARBY, "BABYLON" AND THE ROOTS OF THEOLOGICAL DISCORD

It is not important here to develop at length the detail of doctrinal dispute that entered into the Brethren movement. We note only in passing that such disputes were initially focused upon events that took place in the late 1840s during what became known as the "Erbington Street" controversy in Plymouth and the "Bethesda" controversy in Bristol.[5] An examination of those controversies, which in the end led to the split between "open" and "exclusive" Brethren parties, indicates that they had as much to do with issues of authority as they did with scriptural interpretation but, as is common, it was ostensibly over the interpretation of Scripture that the battle was fought. In short, Christological, ecclesiological and eschatological differences arose,

---

2. Other notable publications by Tregelles in the area of biblical textual criticism include, *Hebrew Reading Lessons*; *A Collation of the Critical Texts of Griesbach and Others*; and *Codex Zacynthius. Greek Palimpsest Fragments of St. Luke*.

3. Tregelles, *Gesenius' Hebrew and Chaldee Lexicon*, 101.

4. See ch. 3 above.

5. A complex issue explored in detail in Burnham, *Story of Conflict*.

particularly between the leading figures of Darby and Newton. The majority
of publications on the Brethren, and in particular from those authors who
have made use of the material at the Christian Brethren Archive, tend to
focus in detail on the minutiae of such disagreements.[6]

What is more important than this doctrinal detail, however, is the way
in which the participants in the dispute sought to "read into" the Bible their
understanding of what was happening and to "use" the Bible in their account
of it. For example, Darby, believing Newton's error to have had a confusing
and polluting effect on the whole of the Ebrington Street assembly, used the
call of Revelation 18:4 "come out" as a tool for excommunication. Darby's
sectarian use of Revelation 18:4 is clear:

> Come out from among them . . . There is evil unconfessed and
> unjudged; evil (I judge) of the very worst kind, speaking of evil
> in a Christian assembly; and I suppose there must be scriptures
> for leaving it, or we should never have been gathered at all.[7]

The perceived Christological heresy taught at Ebrington Street, Plymouth caused Darby to declare that the Bethesda assembly in Bristol should
also be excommunicated. Why, then, did Darby think that this assembly
too needed casting out for heretical belief, since Newton had not taught his
doctrinal "errors" there? The answer is perhaps to be found in Darby's evolving understanding of doctrinal corruption and heretical teachings. Darby
began to develop a system of belief that understood confused truth as something contagious, something infectious, something that could be passed on
from one person to another—and from one assembly to another—almost
through a kind of miasma, or germ, or virus of corruption. This frightening possibility of almost a doctrinal plague that Darby saw infecting some
of those even within the broad Brethren movement, itself has apocalyptic
overtones and it is hence unsurprising that it is the Apocalypse that provided Darby with some of his language to describe it.[8]

6. See in particular Burnham, *Story of Conflict*; Coad, *History of the Brethren
Movement*; Turner, *John Nelson Darby*; Miller, *Brethren*; Noel, *History of the Brethren*;
and Dickson, *Brethren in Scotland*.

7. Darby, "Narrative of the Fact," 106.

8. Brethren historian Coad has noted the underlying fear of heresy held by Darby.
Darby believed that heresy was a real, tangible thing, not just an abstract notion which
expresses a divergent opinion. Coad, *Prophetic Developments*, 122. Burnham has more
recently drawn attention to how such heresy was, in Darby's thought, in some way
contagious or transmittable from person to person and congregation to congregation, Burnham, *Story of Conflict*, 208. Embley notes that "the Exclusive idea of 'contamination' developed until it became something like the early Old Testament idea of
holiness—almost a physical contagion. 'Evil' could be transferred *ad infinitum* from

Darby was deeply committed to the exegesis of Scripture and in particular the correct understanding its prophetic sections. It was, primarily, Darby's exegesis of the Whore of Babylon motif in Revelation chapters 17–18 that provided for Darby a divinely sanctioned basis for this doctrine of the nature of heresy. This can be seen easily enough. For example, immediately prior to his description and exegesis of the Fall of Babylon (Rev 14:8), in his *Synopsis of the Books of the Bible* (1877), Darby comments on the remnant described in Revelation 14:3–6, the 144,000, who "have not defiled themselves with women" and who "in their mouth no lie was found; they are blameless." Darby informs us that they were "characterised by purity from surrounding contamination" and that "corruption and falsehood they had been kept free from, openly confessing the truth."[9] He then goes on to describe Babylon, the city of corruption's fall. Although for Darby, these pure ones were undoubtedly Jewish and not of the church, we can determine a link here between how Darby understood purity and contamination in terms of truthfulness and the contagious spread of impurity.

In a letter written to J. G. Deck, the date of the composition of which is uncertain but was received by Deck on August 29, 1851, Darby writes that Scripture gives divine warrant to the excommunication of whole assemblies on account of evil and not just individuals, for "Babylon" is a place "from which I am called to come," and the appropriate response to such evil is "separation," to "put them out—unless recovered by and to the truth."[10] Darby is clearly linking not only individuals but also whole congregations that hold corrupted understandings of the truth as Babylonian.

Similarly, in a letter written to R. T. Grant[11] composed in Glasgow in 1865, Darby describes Babylon as Church corruption and then informs Grant that there is "a recrudescence on the Bethesda question," that is, Darby uses a medical term for a reoccurrence of symptoms, and urges Grant to break with the evil in order to "keep it out."[12] To allow such a reinfection of the evil of corrupt doctrine to re-contaminate the believers there would be to "put a positive sanction upon the evil which man has brought in." Extreme separation was the only way out of Babylon.

The place that such confused Brethren were going, Babylon, was a place where the truth had been corrupted. It was "the city of confusion, or

assembly to assembly throughout the world," Embley, *Origins and Early Development*, 116, 190.

9. Darby, "Revelation," 574.

10. Darby, *Letters*, 1.98.190–95.

11. This is not the same person as F. W. Grant who led the Grant division in North America. Little biographical information is known about R. T. Grant.

12. Darby, *Letters*, 1.255.414.

Babylon, which are synonymous terms . . . the city of confusion, or Babel."[13] It was ruled and governed by "the king of Babylon . . . the virtual headship of confusion."[14] Thus for Darby there is a very strong link between the Babylon of the Apocalypse and Babel, the place known as "confusion": a place inhabited by believers who have been contaminated by corrupt and evil doctrine and teaching.[15] Babylon is responsible for "chaining men's minds,"[16] for she is the source of seductive heresy[17] and of "unfaithfulness to a known truth": truth prostituted, corrupted and tarnished.[18]

For Darby, the spirit of Babylon was responsible for the corruption and confusion of Christian teaching in general. As we have seen in chapter 5 above, Catholicism is the place that Darby primarily locates Babylon. Yet it is Catholic doctrine in particular that is, for Darby, especially Babylonian with Catholic teaching on absolution of sins, the priesthood and Mariology being highlighted as significantly Babylonian.[19] Such doctrines represent for Darby the very contents of Babylon's golden cup of abomination and filthiness.[20] However "Babylon" does not stop there. To the list of Babylonian corruptions he includes also Judaism, heathenism, Puseyism, and Latitudinariansim.[21]

For Darby, one of the greatest ways that Babylon seduces believers away from the truth is with regards to confusing the Brethren over the true status and position of the church. Undoubtedly the doctrine of the ruin of the church is central to Darby's ecclesiology and to a certain extent an incorrect understanding of the church is perceived by Darby as being a symptom of Babylonian confusion. Thus with reference to an incorrect understanding of the church held by a "Romish Priest," Darby described that person as "being delivered into the hand of the king of Babylon."[22] Elsewhere Darby goes on to castigate, using language clearly drawn from the Apocalypse, all who do not share his own understanding of what constitutes the true church

13. Darby, "Living Water," 29–30.

14. Darby, "Jeremiah," 91, 93.

15. Darby, "Third Dialogue on the Essays and Reviews," 295. See also Darby, "Thoughts on Romans 11," 500, 512.

16. Darby, "Fragmentary Thoughts," 351.

17. Darby, "Reading at Notting Hill on 1 Corinthians 1," 123.

18. Darby, "Dialogues," 69–71.

19. Darby, "Fragmentary Thoughts," 339, 340, 346–47.

20. Darby, "What Is the World," 182–83.

21. Darby, "Fragmentary Thoughts," 347–48.

22. Darby, "Romanism," 51, 64. A similar view is expressed in Darby, "Christianity Not Christendom," 271.

and what is true doctrine.[23] Targets included not only the Roman Church itself but the Oxford Movement and many more besides.[24] What is more, as we have seen above, as fear of the "doctrinal plague" took root in his mind Darby turned his pen, *intra muros*, even against those from within the Brethren movement. His undiplomatic language mirrored that of the biblical text as he sought to name the enemy that was once without, but had now, in the person of Newton, entered within.

What we see in Darby here is the way in which texts can be used both to provide the language of expression and also to imply divine sanction to views that are always evolving. As the Brethren movement matured a little and became secure enough to be able to engage in a power struggle from within, the very tools that were used to draw a dividing line between "us" and "them" (where "them" means "other Christians") were redeployed. "Babylon" is now not just "Rome" but "doctrinal confusion," even where that confusion is found *intra muros* among those once thought to be fellow Brethren.

KELLY

Kelly continues Darby's exegesis of the Babylon motif linking Babylon with doctrinal confusion and the corruption of truth in over fifty of his publications. He clearly identifies the Babylon of the Apocalypse using the language of Genesis chapter 11: "God . . . allowed Babel to come forth once more. It was that same system of confusion; but now in a new form."[25] For Kelly, then, in a recapitulatory sense, the same principle of bewilderment that first caused misunderstanding on the plain of Shinar is at work in confusing the church in his own day. He further reiterates this point by saying: "The origin of the application of Babylon seems to be this; the essence of the name consisting in confusion, the meaning is a system of confusion."[26]

23. Darby links Babylon with confusion of doctrine in the following documents: Darby, *Commentary on Greek New Testament*, 589. Darby, "Fragmentary Thoughts," 339. Darby, *Synopsis of the Bible*, 581. Darby, "The Mystery," 108.

24. Darby identifies both individuals and denominations as Babylon in the following documents: Darby, "Examination of the Book," 132. Here Rev. Jukes, an Anglican clergyman, is in Babylon. Darby, "Analysis of Dr. Newman's, 'Apologia,'" 185. Here Cardinal Newman and the Oxford Movement are in Babylon. Darby, "Letter to a Clergyman," 24–28. Here the Newman Street congregation are linked explicitly with Babylon. Darby, "Remarks on the Pamphlet," 430, 434–35, 454. Here an individual, Mr. Olivier, is described as Babylonian in his exegesis.

25. Kelly, *Lectures on the Second Coming*, 2.

26. Kelly, "Amos," in *Lectures Introductory . . . Minor Prophets*, 128.

Further links are made between Apocalyptic Babylon and the tower of Babel in, for example, Kelly's lecture on Zechariah, where the point is made that Babylonian confusion is a source of great hidden evil for the Brethren.[27] It is found also in his lectures on the book of Revelation where he describes Babylon as the "special corruptress of the truth."[28] But for Kelly, Babylon is not only a symbol of "Gentile confusion,"[29] that is the confusion of the *ethna* or nations, Babylon is also in herself confusion personified; "confusion being here the characteristic element." She is both the source of "every kind of confusion of truth and error, of good and evil, intoxicating, corrupting and seducing," and the one responsible for blurring the lines between what is true and what is false, perplexing people over matters of doctrine, through her ability to make drunk. She is the place of confusion, the "city of man's confusion."[30]

For Kelly, Babylon is the fountain of corruption where "the streams of professedly Christian doctrine that spring up form Babylonish principles." They constitute the main corruption of Christianity.[31] Yet Kelly insists that such a corruption of the true teachings and doctrine of the church is not in itself a falsehood or lie. It still contains some truth, just contaminated truth. The creed, for example, is essentially an orthodox representation of Christian belief, yet it has been slowly and incipiently polluted by hypocritical and heretical influences: "truth is held in the creed of Christendom but the leaven of the Pharisees has worked through it so it is held without faith or righteousness."[32] In Kelly's commentary on Revelation *Lectures on the Book of Revelation* (1897) his views on the distorting and twisting influence Babylon has on truth is explored fully. Babylon is responsible for "every blot or error which creeps in to the word of God."[33]

While Kelly, as a fundamentally evangelical Protestant, would deny that there could be any error in the actual written word of God there is of course plenty of room for error in the exposition, interpretation and application of those words by an individual who has come under Babylon's

---

27. Kelly, "Zechariah," in *Lectures Introductory . . . Minor Prophets*, 460–61.

28. Kelly, *Lectures on the Book of Revelation*, 348.

29. Kelly, "Answers to Questions," *BT* 11, 239.

30. Kelly, *God's Inspiration*, 595. See also the following places where Kelly inextricably links Babylon with confusion. Kelly, *Eleven Lectures on the Book of Job*, 63; Kelly, "Elements of Prophecy," 63; Kelly, "Joshua," in *Lectures Introductory . . . Earlier Historical Books*, 91–92; Kelly, "Luke," in *Lectures Introductory . . . Gospels*, 256; Kelly, *Exposition . . . Thessalonians*, 8–9.

31. Kelly, "Micah," in *Lectures Introductory . . . Minor Prophets*, 257–58.

32. Kelly, "What Is God's Kingdom Like?," 356–57.

33. Kelly, *Lectures on the Book of Revelation*, 323.

pernicious influence. Her *modus operandi* is through making those who read Scripture so "drunk" that they cannot sensibly and sagaciously make sense of who God really is. Babylon is an "active source of corruption, intoxicating men and drawing them away from the living God."[34] Babylon does not refer to darkness and blindness to Scripture, in that the Scriptures are simply unknown, but rather Babylon refers to what is known and true yet fraudulent, twisted, and manipulated. She represents "the use and abuse of revealed light . . . look at Babylon: she is evidently the great corrupt and corrupting power in religion . . . producing confusion . . . seductive to men."[35] Babylon is the corrupt and licentious woman who, with no doubt, is the source of religious corruptions.[36]

Kelly lists a number of specific doctrines that are held by the churches around him as being corrupt and confused. Legalism, ritualism, Gnostic confusion, monasticism and asceticism are described by Kelly as the "fatal mischief" of Babylon.[37] The Catholic doctrine of sin is particularly Babylonian according to Kelly,[38] as is the authority of tradition.[39] Catholic sacramental theology is also connected to Babylon, with Holy Orders, Baptism, Confirmation,[40] Eucharist,[41] marriage as a sacrament,[42] extreme unction[43] and penance[44] all being described as Babylonian confusions of the truth. The role of canonization,[45] and the adoration of saints, Mary, and the consecrated elements are described as Babylonian too.[46]

34. Ibid., 326.

35. Ibid., 335.

36. Ibid. For further examples of links between Babylon and corrupted truth, see also Kelly, "Coming," in *Three Prophetic Gems*, 87; Kelly, *Church of God*, 243; Kelly, *Babylon and the Beast*, 5.

37. Kelly, *Exposition of the Second Epistle to Timothy*, 251.

38. Kelly, "Jesus the Son Of God," 197–98. Also Kelly, "Amos," in *Lectures Introductory . . . Minor Prophets*, 161.

39. Kelly, "Philadelphia and Laodicea," 286.

40. Kelly, *Is the Anglican Establishment*, 2–3. See also Kelly, *Eleven Lectures on the Book of Job*, 132–33.

41. Kelly, *Purpose of God for His Sons*, 16.

42. Kelly, *Exposition . . . Titus*, 32.

43. Kelly, "Encyclical Letter of Pope Leo XIII"; Kelly, *Exposition of the Epistle of James*, 185–86; Kelly, *Lectures . . . Galatians*, 95–96, 125; Kelly, "Second Advent Before," 137.

44. Kelly, "Encyclical Letter."

45. Kelly, *Sanctification*, 17–18.

46. Kelly, *Judgment, Not Reunion*, 3.

Like Darby, Kelly believes that an incorrect and confused understanding of the church is a sign of Babylon's influence. In particular, a common
mistake is of confusing the scriptural promises, admonishments, warnings
and future hope of the church with Scriptures that should only be applied
to Israel; the covenant people of God.[47] However, simply having a correct
understanding of what the church is, is not enough on its own. If one is
a member of an Established church then the truth of one's ecclesiological
doctrine has been corrupted: "Membership of a church is the vast error of
Christendom. Rome, I presume, was mother of it . . . the church . . . fell
back on the State to resist the Papacy . . . Babylon [is] the corruption of
the church."[48] The view is reiterated when Kelly states: "Membership of the
Church of England, [is] . . . in a word, BABYLON."[49]

It is not surprising that the Established Church comes under particular attack here given Kelly's own historical context. As has already been seen
above, the Brethren viewed all of Protestant Christendom to be, in essence,
the daughters of the Great Harlot. Anglicanism, arguably the eldest of Babylon's daughters and the least distant from the Roman church would have
shared particularly in her mother's characteristics. Thus it is clear that just as
the term Babylon, when used in the book of Revelation, had already taken
on new significance for those who originally read the text, so now the open
ended term came to mean new things for those who read it in new situations
and whose biblical interpretation shadowed their sectarian tendencies.

For Kelly the source of such confused and corrupt doctrine is to be
found in false teachers. He describes such counterfeit instructors as bringing shame on the truth and being responsible for encouraging a great exodus from the truth. Such teachers have a ubiquitous influence, and although
the specific details of their confusion and corruption may differ, they are at
least united in their liberal and critical approach to Scripture. He condemns
them thus:

> What can bring a deeper stigma on "the way of the truth" than
> . . . these accredited teachers? . . . Babylon and the false teach-
> ers, with . . . well-turned words have all along drawn the mass
> into departure from the truth . . . [the] false teachers which is
> now poisoning the fountains of Christendom . . . They may dif-
> fer each from the rest doctrinally in other respects; but they all
> agree to let in scepticism as to scripture . . . Now where is there
> a single denomination free . . . [of] that deadly error . . . in our

47. Kelly, *Righteousness of God*, 43–52.

48. Kelly, "Churches and the Church."

49. Kelly, *Is the Anglican Establishment*, 6–8.

day we see how those who are false in doctrine are bold enough
to set conscience at defiance . . . they abandon the truth which
they had solemnly pledged themselves to preach and teach.[50]

Kelly then goes on to identify some of these co-called false teachers,
both on a denominational and personal level. Kelly identifies Babylon, the
symbol of confusion of truth, as the parent of the religious corruptions of
Catholicism and Protestantism who both alike have departed from the word
of God and consecrated error.[51] Yet, he does not remain quite so general
about his identification of the place where the false teachers may be found,
going on to identify the popes in particular as a source of doctrinal confusion: "The Popes . . . build up their tower of Babel . . . there is no excuse for
the confusion of theologians."[52] Here, in one of the few cases where Brethren
authors are "anti-pope" (individual) rather than "anti-papal" (institutional)
in their exegesis, he explicitly states that individual popes are confused over
doctrine through his use of the Tower of Babel motif, the place that we have
already determined to refer to the source of confusion. Within Catholicism
it is not simply the popes who cause such confusion over matters of truth.
All "Catholic expositors . . . [have a] false interpretation [of Scripture because they have been] misled by some ancient fathers . . . we do not know
to what confusion and error we may be led."[53] Evidently the whole process
of Catholic doctrine formation is confused from the Fathers through to the
theologians and expositors through to the popes. The Protestants do not get
off lightly from the charge of being false teachers. Comparing the Reformers
to the children of Israel leaving their Babylonian captivity Kelly states that
Lutherans, Calvinists and Puritans never recovered the truth and are still
in darkness.[54] They may have come out of Babylon but her corrupting and
darkening effect on truth is still active in their churches.

It is not just the mainstream denominations that are accused by Kelly
of being places like the tower of Babel, that is, places where one becomes
confused over matters of the truth. The Catholic Apostolic Church, a
Dissenting and Independent Christian movement contemporary to the
Brethren movement, whose founder Edward Irving and benefactor Henry
Drummond would have been personally known to Kelly and other Brethren
through their prominence at the Powerscourt and Albury conferences, are
given special attention here. Here we see a struggle to define very precisely

50. Kelly, *Second Epistle of Peter*, 126–27.
51. Kelly, *Babylon and the Beast*, 5, 12.
52. Kelly, "Encyclical Letter."
53. Kelly, *Jeremiah*, 51.
54. Kelly, "Joseph," 86.

the borders of the "true" community of God's people. Kelly suggests that the Irvingites hold in high regard the perplexing doctrines of Babylon: "Babylon, the great confusion and corruption of truth . . . seems at this time to have risen into no small honour in Irvingite eyes."[55] Yet the same may be said to be true not just of "Irvingism; but in all sacerdotalism, Puseyism, Ritualism," for whenever the church is run by a priesthood it will always "lead to the final catastrophe of Babylon."[56] Again the Oxford Movement of the 1830s and 1840s comes under attack again from the Brethren, but this time specifically the Reverend E. B. Pusey who took over from Newman as leader of the Oxford Movement in 1841. Their High Church "Romanistic" tendencies to ritualism and their sacerdotal emphasis on the holy orders Kelly found to be Babylonian. The criticism could be very precise indeed. The Bishop of Carlisle, for example, is condemned by Kelly for teaching people about Babylon and the antichrist yet failing to preach salvation and the gospel,[57] whereas Dr. Driver, Regius Professor of Hebrew at Oxford, is criticized for "hankering after Babylon," since in Kelly's view Driver's historical-critical approach represents "the hateful, impious, and blasphemous spirit of error" found in Babylon.[58] Another individual picked out by Kelly for espousing confused and corrupted teaching is the Rector of St. Saviour's, the Reverend R. P. Carey, who disagrees with Kelly over whether or not offenders within the church should be excommunicated. Carey believes that "any decent man of the world" should be allowed fellowship and thus be considered a saint. For Kelly, Carey's views show a confusion over the correct understanding of the church (he sees it as a politico-religious institution), and also a confusion over what it means for God to call his people to come out. Carey believes the "call out" to refer to Jerusalem, but Kelly sees this as an example of scriptural error, a misinterpretation. The call is to "come out" of Babylon, which for Kelly represents any system of confusion.[59]

To be in fellowship with Babylon, either by virtue of association with individual false teachers or denominations that hold confused doctrine, means to be in danger of being deceived and ruined: "dense delusion . . . ruinous infatuation . . . Babylon . . . the Gentile city of confusion . . . it becomes them to inquire whether they may not have fellowship with her

55. Kelly, "Catholic Apostolic Body," *BT*, 17.315.
56. Kelly, "Receive Ye the Holy Ghost," 133–34.
57. Kelly, *Feasts in Deuteronomy*, 26–27.
58. Kelly, *Interpreter* 1.1 (1905) 238–40.
59. Kelly, *Church of God*, 5, 71.

sins."[60] The use of "fellowship" here is strongly hinting at the interaction between brethren in an assembly. Kelly writes that "no man or woman guilty of such shameful impropriety would be allowed a place in fellowship." He refers to the excommunication of the Bethesda assembly in similar terms, in particular drawing attention to "a former Fellow of Exeter College, to whom we refused fellowship."[61] This could refer to either Newton (fellow 1826–1832), or Harris (fellow 1815–1829). Both were part of the excommunicated assembly in Bethesda.[62] Kelly goes on to say that the reason that the Exclusives such as he, Wigram and Darby acted the way they did towards the Brethren at Bethesda, or the reason for making so called "assembly judgments" which excommunicated both individual persons and whole assemblies for doctrinal error, was that "errors if unredressed might be fatal."[63] Thus we see that Kelly believes that by having fellowship with either a person on an individual level, or an assembly on a corporate level, that has been seduced from the truth by Babylon, that the sinful delusions and confusion and corruption over truth, regardless of moral uprightness and character, can lethally threaten other believers.

For Kelly the danger of Babylon is "fatal to the soul,"[64] more so than any other spiritual danger,[65] and must be guarded against. Babylon is trying to seduce and corrupt the souls of the Brethren and care must be taken, presumably care over the correct meaning of Scripture, to safeguard oneself: "take good care that our own souls are preserved from the contaminations of Babylon . . . guard against the seductions of the enemy!"[66] She is plotting to cause believers to descend into error, for this is the "chief conspiracy of Babylon—the false lady."[67] Her teachings are so virulent that physical contact alone through fellowship is not the only way her dangerous teachings can contaminate the believer, Kelly writes: "Beware of reunion with the city of confusion . . . beware even of looking back,"[68] thus almost implying an airborne vector of transmission.

60. Kelly, *Notes on the Second Epistle*, 50–51.

61. Kelly, *Plymouth Brethren*, 44, 49.

62. N.B., Richard Hill was also a member of the Bethesda assembly at Plymouth who had studied at Exeter College (1799–1880) but he, unlike Newton and Harris, was never made a fellow.

63. Kelly, *Second Epistle of Peter*, 74.

64. Kelly, *Mystery of Godliness*, 3.

65. Kelly, *Lectures on the Book of Revelation*, 357.

66. Ibid., 389.

67. Kelly, *Lord's Supper*, 10–11.

68. Kelly, *Judgment, Not Reunion*, 13.

Simply ceasing contact with such a confused believer is not enough, for "those who assume that just because they have separated themselves from Babylon they are no longer exposed to her dangers are deceiving themselves."[69] The virulent, "malarial," disease-like character of Babylonian confusion is developed at length as a warning to Brethren against associating with those who adhere to false teachings.[70] The source of the Babylonian disease is "the woman of Revelation," the virus of her teaching is the "spread of nominal, faithless doctrine and creed," and the symptoms of this Babylonian disease "affects men's mind and feelings."[71] The cure from contagion and deadly confusion of the truth is to follow the words of the angel of Revelation 18:4: "Come out." Such a medicine is offered to a certain Reverend F. Whitfield, who Kelly informs us, was once with the Brethren, but after the 1850 Dublin split sided with the Bethesda party before eventually recanting his secession and rejoining the Anglican church. Kelly writes to Whitfield: "'Come out of her my people . . .' renounce Babylon . . . leave every other error and evil . . . unquestionably the wicked are to be put out."[72] The use of the text here is highly individualistic.

We may conclude that Babylon, for Kelly, is a symbol of confused and corrupted truth and doctrine, including confusion over sacraments, Christology and ecclesiology, presented by false teachers from false denominations, she is deadly and seductive, virulent and contagious and the only prescription for safety is complete isolation from the germ or fatal doctrine, to "come out."

Kelly's understanding of Revelation's Babylon motif as pointing to the confused doctrine of his competitors has been treated here in some detail here. This detailed account was necessary however as it illustrates something of the complexity, depth and scope of the use made of the Babylon motif by this particular Brethren author, who was not alone. As we have seen, Kelly is not content to use the biblical palette to paint in overly broad brush strokes a picture of contemporary Babylon, but he is concerned to trace in precise and painstaking detail an outline of the specific doctrines held by particular individuals which he believes to be Babylonian. Brethren exegesis once again rides the crest of the wave of historical circumstances.

---

69. Kelly, *Priesthood*, 101–2.

70. Kelly, *Church of God*, 28. See also Kelly, "Christian Hope," 40.

71. Kelly, *Exposition of the Gospel of Luke*, 231.

72. Kelly, *Brethren and Their Traducers*, 31.

WIGRAM

Wigram, as someone who devoted much time to the study of Hebrew Scripture, was well aware of the semantic link between Babylon and Babel in Genesis 11, the entry point for confusion into the world. In the second of three lectures he delivered on *The Coming Kingdom* (1876) he asks a rhetorical question: "What is Babylon?" He answers,

> The city and tower built in the plain of Shinar, where the Lord confounded their language . . . Babel, or confusion . . . Nebuchadnezzar's strange confusion of mind and actions . . . in the Revelation . . . a corrupt, lascivious woman . . . the most fruitful and least suspected root of evil corruption, was in confusing civil power in the world . . . and the power in the church . . . to blend, or try to blend the two distinct and opposite things in one, was to make a new system, and a system of confusion.[73]

Here he links Babylon with a number of types of confusion, namely confusion of language, confusion of mind and action, and confusion of doctrine. Here he is not defining Babylon simply as wrong language, incorrect thought and action, or erroneous doctrine, but rather as subtle confusion, misunderstanding and uncertainty over things that contain a kernel of truth, albeit truth blended in with lies:

> Romanism, as a church system, is based upon truth; pure error is rarely found in her, but truth mis-stated and perverted . . . each of her doctrines may be aptly compared to some adulterated compound consisting of so ingenious a mixture of truth and falsehood, so entangled and intimately blended, that the falsehood is [in chemical phase] *held in solution.*[74]

The fact that Wigram did not appear in chapter 5 of this book is indicative of the fact that this Brethren interpreter did not single out Catholicism as specifically Babylonian. Wigram did however include Catholicism in the pandenominational phrase "professing church" which he used as a catchall label. Wigram's concern, however, to identify Babylonian doctrinal error did mean that the Catholic church came into his sights when interpreting Revelation chapters 17–18, since he highlighted the specifically Catholic doctrines of unity, infallibility and absolution as specific examples of truth mixed with falsehood. Corrupted doctrine and confused teaching is combated in the assembly by Brethren being in agreement over issues of truth,

73. Wigram, *Coming Kingdom*, 58–59.
74. Wigram, "God's System of a Church," 199.

but as Babylon is a mystery who tries to exert a mystifying influence over issues of truth and true unity in doctrine, she poses a hidden danger.[75] We perhaps see here a concern for truth which borders on near paranoia and that gives rise to an interpretation of the text with nightmarish qualities. The biblically saturated world in which Wigram and his fellow Brethren are now inhabiting is a dangerous place.

Like Baines and Wolston in the previous chapter, Wigram, who from the very earliest period of schism within the Brethren community identified himself with the Exclusive sect led by Darby, found a contemporary application for the Letter to the Church in Thyatira (Rev 2). In particular he saw in the Babylon-related image of the woman Jezebel, who seduces members of the church with false teachings and the mysteries of Satan, a spiritual explanation for the presence of confused doctrine within the assemblies such as Bethesda: "There is a farther thing in the Church at Thyatira, where Jezebel is teaching. If an assembly take the position of covering over evil it is like this."[76] Wigram also uses the image of Balaam's "enticing" teachings, which he combines with Jezebel's "misleading" teachings, to add further weight to his warning against confused doctrine in an assembly. He uses the sectarian language of Numbers 22:10, "Do not go with them," as a warning to his Brethren to stay away from Bethesda.[77]

Wigram's support for Darby's project of excommunicating whole assemblies for doctrinal error can be seen in *The Present Question 1848–1849*, a compilation of three letters written by Wigram in response to the Bethesda schism. In these letters Wigram systematically lays down his own views on the danger of heresy, its contagious nature and the need to excommunicate not only individuals but also whole assemblies who have been contaminated by the confused doctrines. Wigram recommends "holy separation from evil around" as the appropriate response to Bethesda, for such Brethren carried with them the unseen germ of confusion, thus "no one could be received from thence save upon the understanding they were clear from evil." The offensive and evil doctrine held at Bethesda was contagious: "able to spread . . . and put sincere souls off their guard." The only solution available to prevent infection from this spreading, contagious and corrupting teaching was to withdraw from contact with the evil altogether. Those at Bethesda, Newton and even his supporters have been "tainted with the doctrine" and thus the only possible way to halt the transmission and widespread infection of the diseased doctrine was complete "separation from Mr. Newton

75. Wigram, *To the Christians in New Zealand*, 11–12.
76. Wigram, "Notes on Scripture," 158.
77. Ibid., 168.

and his views."[78] In the second letter, in reference to the "evil of Bethesda" Wigram writes: "In Babylon, as such, the animating energy was clearly of Satan, with all untruthfulness, lying, and cunning craftiness. It was molded clearly on corrupted truth."[79] If a person remains in fellowship at Bethesda then they are "shareholders" in this evil. Wigram makes a reference to the May 1848 meeting about the Bethesda dispute held in Bath where some hundred leading Brethren met to discuss what should be done in the wake of the Plymouth disorder.[80] Darby, Kelly, Trotter, Wigram and other soon-to-be-Exclusives insisted that the only way forward they could see was to excommunicate Newton, members of the Ebrington and Compton Street chapels in Plymouth in which Newton preached, members of the Bethesda assembly in Bristol which had received members from Plymouth, and also anyone who had any contact with them:

> It was an unwise and unholy act of Bethesda to cut itself off . . . to identify itself with and endorse that work of Satan by receiving and retaining the emissaries of it . . . [Bethesda] not only has let in the jesuitical system of Compton-street, and given currency to the doctrine of Mr. Newton, but it has done so in acts which exhibit the very same evil system . . . it has made the whole body of its members, as such, commit themselves to the evil.[81]

Not all Brethren agreed with this sectarian response. One such Brethren was Andrew Jukes, founder of the first Brethren assembly in Hull (1842), who on attending the Bath meeting about Bethesda questioned the decision to excommunicate George Müller: one of the leaders of the Bristol assembly who was noted not only for his moral uprightness but also for his radical social action work with orphans in the Bristol region. Wigram argued that Müller, in accepting contaminated Brethren from Plymouth into his Bristol assembly, had tacitly sanctioned the heresy, for "he stands connected with an immoral spiritual system, [it] would be impossible [to receive him] until he has confessed his error and removed the evil."[82] For Wigram the "sin of receiving and sanctioning" those who had become "tainted with the blasphemous errors" was just as bad as holding onto the errors oneself.[83] He writes that "being individually free from the error in doctrine mattered not" for there are many Brethren "who repudiate with

78. Wigram, *Present Question*, 1.4.

79. Ibid., 2.8–9.

80. Coad, *History of the Brethren Movement*, 157.

81. Wigram, *Present Question*, 2.7.

82. Ibid., 11.

83. Ibid.

horror the doctrine, and perhaps do not hold it, and who yet are under the power of this spell."[84] Thus even if an individual rejected the erroneous doctrine, as Müller did, this made no difference as the evil could still spread. Müller, by receiving Brethren from Plymouth into his assembly in Bristol, had sanctioned the heresy and become tainted by it. Whereas for Darby the power of the doctrine to taint was like an infectious contaminating poison, and for Kelly the power of the doctrine to pollute was like a poisonous or contagious disease, Wigram perceived its effects as its power to bewitch, like being under a spell or enchantment. Other notable Brethren, who, although Wigram conceded did not hold onto Newton's Babylonian heresy, were still condemned through the language of Babylonian contagion included Robert Chapman,[85] Henry Craik,[86] Feltham, Meredith and Aitchison.[87]

OTHER AUTHORS

Grant, who formed the Exclusive Grant division of Brethren in America on a principle of excommunication similar to that of Darby and Kelly in Britain, links the allowing in of the woman Jezebel into the Thyatiran church with confusion of fellowship, concluding that it is thus necessary to judge the character of those allowed fellowship according to the truthfulness of their faith. He states,

> Suppose all Christians accepted your invitation and you were really able to assemble all the members of Christ at the Lord's table with their jarring views, their various states of soul, their entanglements with the world and with their evil associations . . . your "gathering" would be a defiance of the holy discipline. It would be another Babel (confusion). Do you think that outward unity is so dear to Christ that He would desire it apart from true confession, cleansing and fellowship in the truth?[88]

Here he puts forward certain qualifications for being accepted into fellowship around that central act within all Brethren assemblies, namely the Lord's Table, including truthfulness of what one confesses, purity and accuracy of association. For Grant, to accept one into fellowship who could

84. Ibid.

85. Wigram, *Appeal to Saints*, 7, 10, 11, and 15.

86. Wigram, *Answer of G. V. Wigram*, 22. Here Wigram asks when Craik will be delivered from the evil of Bethesda and Newton.

87. Wigram, "Letter of the Ten," 33.

88. Grant, *Divine Movement*, 34.

not meet such requirements, even though still a Christian, would lead to confusion, just like the coming together of all the nations in defiance of God on the plain of Shinar (Gen 11) and in the seduced church of Thyatira (Rev 2).

Newberry, in his exegesis of Revelation 17:4, draws attention to the fact that the Great Whore is "dressed in purple and scarlet and is glittering with gold." Such attire, he argues, is a reference to confused, corrupt and false doctrine, for

> purple, the combination of scarlet and blue, is emblematic of authority which unites the heavenly and the spiritual with that which is earthly and carnal. False doctrine is, for the most part, a corruption of Divine truth—error overlaid with thin layers of truth, like base metal gilded.[89]

He, like Darby and Kelly earlier on in this chapter, does not accuse Babylon of outright lies and blatant falsehood but rather sees her as much more seductive and incipient in her influence, taking truth and distorting it, corrupting and confusing the truth, mystifying and intoxicating the truth with subtle lies.

This pernicious influence can be seen in the writings of Tweedie, who in an entry to the *Northern Witness* on the subject of Babylon as a Mystery, writes: "I think the strong delusion to believe a lie comes here on those who, in the days of the great whore, believed not the truth but had pleasure in unrighteousness."[90] Thus although he does not write that Babylon's lies have a veneer of truth, she does, for Tweedie, influence and seduce believers into delusion and misunderstanding, perhaps as a result of her intoxicating wine causing drunkenness with regards to matters of truth.

Lady Powerscourt also understands Babylon as the source of falsehood and lies but she is closer to Darby and Kelly than Newberry in her understanding of the nature of such confusion in that these errors are not simply lies or untruths, but corruptions and distortions of truth. She writes in a letter: "misunderstanding scripture . . . wonderfully blind . . . to take up our lot with Babylon . . . every principle of error seems to have its representative . . . contradictory opinions, each proved from scripture . . . a perceptible mixture of error and prejudice."[91] This suggests that Babylon's lies may even have their origin in Scripture and may be argued from the word of God but, through misunderstanding, blindness and prejudice, are erroneous and

---

89. Newberry, *Notes on the Book of Revelation*, 98.
90. Tweedie, "Mystery, Babylon the Great," 94–95.
91. Powerscourt, *Letters*, 23.62.

contradictory. She clearly links this confusion of truth in with the tower of Babel pericopae in Genesis chapter 11 as she writes that "Babel destroyed itself by its confusion"[92] thus supporting the recapitulatory views indicative of wider Brethren exegesis.

The concept of a Babylonian veneer of truth which gilds lies and thus produces confusion can be seen in Snell's commentary on the Revelation. When discussing Babylon the Great he writes: "The devil's powers of mimicry; his artful ways of having something outwardly resembling what is of God," but they result in "deceiving the world."[93] Babylon represents the church on the outside, the veneer of Christianity, but on the inside is the "false and corrupt one."[94] She does this by making believers drunk and thus too inebriated to discern what is really true from what is, not merely openly false, but what is secretly masquerading as true on the outside. He writes of the golden cup of abominations found in the harlots hand (Rev 17:4), which will "deceive and intoxicate."[95] Drinking from her cup makes one feel emotionally and sensually like one's religious needs for forgiveness have been fulfilled but in reality the cup has no real power or salvific effectuality. Here Snell alludes to the ritualistic partaking of the Eucharist and the confused belief that such a sacrament itself can actually make one holy. The sacramental chalice is, for Snell, a "bewitching cup."

Snell continues in the tradition of interpreting Apocalyptic Babylon in light of the tower of Babel story in Genesis chapter 11,[96] yet he does not confine the story to its historical context but applies it to his own day: "we must conclude that Babel, or confusion, must be wherever the Lord is not wholly followed."[97] Such confusion primarily comes through the mixing of "church and world," it is indeed a "deadly poison."[98]

Brethren authors Baines and Wolston add little to the growing hermeneutic. Babylon is the corruption of religion[99] and the source of confusion.[100] Baines does contribute a new idea to the emerging Brethren interpretative outline in that he adds that Babylon is a symbol of the great apostasy or falling away from truth. Baines writes, "Men will be given up to

---

92. Powerscourt, *Letters*, 78.234–35.

93. Snell, *Notes on the Revelation*, 156.

94. Ibid., 157.

95. Ibid., 160.

96. Ibid.

97. Ibid., 166.

98. Ibid., 174.

99. Baines, "Glorious Coming," 226. Wolston, *Handfuls of Purpose*, 122–23.

100. Baines, "Glorious Coming," 221. Wolston, "Notable Birthday," 42–43.

strong delusion that they should believe a lie . . . and more especially that deadly delusion symbolised by the plague of bitter waters."[101] He does not however call for an assembly to be excommunicated or put out of fellowship if an individual adheres to heretical teachings, rather he simply understands that assembly to be a false church, a place where confusion makes itself at home and where people sincerely believe that they hold onto the truth but that their truth is a delusion—a fake imitation. Babylon is "a false thing . . . the counterfeit . . . the false church is the harlot . . . the false church is Babylon, the habitation of confusion."[102]

Trotter, a strong supporter of Darby and the Exclusives, used Babylon as a tool to berate and excommunicate the epistemological other. Like for many of his Brethren above, Babylon was, for Trotter, both the symbol and source of doctrinal confusion.[103] His views are important for he provides an eye-witness account of the Plymouth and Bethesda controversy, and in particular officially records Darby's views on this matter. He notes that

> Mr. D. [i.e., Darby] . . . was obliged, in order to keep a clear conscience himself, to withdraw from the assembly . . . there was evil allowed in the assembly . . . separation became unavoidable . . . the corruption of moral integrity, and the system of intrigue and deception which attended the evil . . . Thus far the evil had been confined to the undermining all the truths . . . most corrupting in their effects on others . . . false doctrines . . . Strange things were known to have been taught.[104]

He also adds to the developing Brethren exegesis of Babylon as "confusion" by interpreting Revelation chapters 17–18 in light of the parable of the wheat and the tares (Matt 13:24–30), of which he notes that the tares have a "specious but spurious resemblance to wheat" and that the tares represent the "children of the wicked one . . . counterfeit and spurious . . . hypocrites . . . false professors."[105] He also interprets Revelation chapters 17–18 in light of the parable of the leaven (Matt 13:33). The leaven is, according to Trotter, heretical teaching "secretly and clandestinely introduced." The source of such heresy is the "mystic woman of Revelation 17" she has secretly introduced confused teaching into the Church which has "openly developed at last in the foul system of Babylon."[106]

101. Baines, "Preliminary Judgments," 117.
102. Baines, "Glorious Coming," 291.
103. Trotter, "Last Days of Gentile Supremacy," 275.
104. Trotter, *Origins of (So-Called) Open Brethrenism*, 11–15.
105. Trotter, "Predicted Corruption of Christianity," 191–92.
106. Ibid., 195.

Bellett continues in the emerging hermeneutical stream of Brethren exegesis that identifies Babylon as confusion, using such language as "strangely inconsistent" doctrine,[107] idolatrous doctrine[108] and lies[109] to describe Babylon's effects on truth. Although he concedes, "there may be much evangelic truth confessed in systems which will be judged at Babylon,"[110] there is much incorrect teaching there and Brethren must purge themselves from such "incorrect teaching": the "canker" and "error" of Babylon.[111] Bellett adds to the growing interpretative trend by linking Revelation chapters 17–18 with Joshua chapter 7, the story of Achen's sin. Although this theme, it will be seen in chapter 8, is picked up by other Brethren authors to vilify the world, here Bellett uses the story of the hidden Babylonian garment to warn of the danger of hidden Babylonian heresy. The Babylonian garment brings a curse and leprosy on the people. Bellett writes, "The cursed thing has been again and again and ever taken. His responsible creature, has linked himself with pollution."[112]

SOME CONCLUDING REMARKS ON "BABYLON" AS DOCTRINAL CONFUSION

This chapter has demonstrated quite clearly that one of the ways that the Brethren use the Whore of Babylon motif is to vilify *intra muros* those who believed confused, corrupt and heretical doctrine. In doing so the group is strengthened from within as it is such "rhetoric of accusation and retribution" which on a sociological level "ties the individual tightly into community bonds and scores on his mind the invisible fence and paths by which the community co-ordinates its life in common."[113] The change in interpretation from the previous two chapters in which the Brethren used "Babylon" to eke out their own space among all the other Christian denominations of their time to identifying the "Babylon within" as the source of heresy, reflects the change in *Sitz im Leben* of the group. The Brethren use of Babylon in the way shown above is in many ways remarkably similar to the way medieval European society used the charges of witchcraft and leprosy to

---

107. Bellett, *Witnesses for God*, 18.

108. Babylon, "Babylon," 1.25.

109. Bellett, "Letter–Jeremiah," 29. See also, Bellett, "Potter's Broken Vessel," 32.

110. Bellett, "Extracts from Unpublished Letters," 37.

111. Bellett, "Rightly Dividing the Word of Truth," 89.

112. Bellett, *Notes on Joshua*, 44–45.

113. Douglas, *Risk and Blame*, 27–28.

force out certain members of society who posed a risk to the internal order and to reinforce the social hierarchy inside.[114]

Additionally, the Brethren understanding of Babylon as a hidden miasmatic danger is remarkably similar to contemporary attitudes to technological and environmental danger in the United States, for as Douglas and Wildavsky have noted, the essential elements of risk and danger are that "danger is involuntary (we should not willingly accept them), irreversible (there is no turning back), and hidden (we shall not know we are encountering them)."[115] Each essential component of danger is met, according to the Brethren, in heresy. Heretics like Newton and his circle should not be willingly accepted into fellowship, to do so may result in the heresy being transmitted miasmatically to other Brethren. Heresy, like technological and environmental danger, is also irreversible. The Brethren from the Plymouth and Bristol controversies of the late 1840s set out on a path of division and dissent, for as Knox has noted of the centuries preceding the Brethren movement: "Schism begets schism" and the first split of a sect necessarily entails the next.[116] Heresy, like technological and environmental danger, is hidden. The Brethren described heresy as a Babylonian garment "hidden" under a tent (Josh 7) and a wicked Babylonian woman "hiding" evil in an ephah—a measuring utensil (Zech 5).

Once more the charismatic and authoritarian personality of Darby drives the community interpretation. His dealings with Ebrington Street and Bethesda show a coercive form of social control and perhaps even a political exercise of power as he used the language of Babylon to excommunicate Newton and those who looked to Newton and not Darby as their leader.[117] Darby's doctrine of contamination, which was influenced by his reading of Revelation 18:4, and his vehement application of the language of Babylon to those who differed to him doctrinally can be seen in socio-religious terms as an intolerance of ambiguity or "confusion." Darby and other Exclusive Brethrens' feelings about Babylonian confusion is quite clear, for the group "the ambiguous or unstructured situation is avoided as it usually precipitates unpleasant emotional reactions ranging from uneasiness to anxiety" manifest not just at cognitive level but also at an "interpersonal or social level."[118] As such, an examination of the exegesis of Darby and his

114. Ibid., 84–99.

115. Douglas and Wildavsky, *Risk and Culture*, 16.

116. Knox, *Enthusiasm*, 1.

117. Darby uses "Babylon" to coerce the Brethren. For a study of the way that powerful figures coerce others and control their freedom see Rosenbuam, *Coercion and Autonomy*.

118. Block and Block, "Investigation of the Relationship," 303.

Exclusive circle reveals something of a hierarchy of "authoritarian person-alities," where "Ego-control" represents the individual's characteristic means of handling or mediating both his "internal need tensions" and the demands imposed upon him by the "external world." As we have seen here in this chapter, such is evidently correct. The Exclusive Brethren use Babylon to give divine sanction to their own authoritarian desires to control who is inside and who is out.

The authors in this chapter have been, predominantly, from the Exclusive factions of the Brethren movement whose sectarian ecclesiological tendencies have been reflected in their use of the text. There is of course an obvious point to make here and one that shall not go unnoticed. The fact that the tradition to which this group of Brethren writers belonged became known as "Exclusive" is an indication of their strict ecclesiological stance. In the hands of such authors, Revelation chapters 17–18 took on particular significance as they read into the text their own experiences, fears and interests. The task was not a difficult one since in many ways the experience of the Brethren, at least as they perceived it, was not unlike the experience of the community for whom Revelation was originally written, both existed within a threatening world (perceived or actual) characterized by impurity, religious fornication and danger. Thus the relationship between what had been written and what had been read was a fairly close one and for the Brethren this divine confirmation of their status and the call to maintain purity was a powerful imperative.

8

"Babylon" Is Worldliness

So far in this book it has been argued that the Christian Brethren of the nineteenth century used the Whore of Babylon motif as a form of vituperative rhetoric against those who do not belong within the group. This has been clear in the primarily religious interpretations of the Whore of Babylon motif examined in chapters 5 and 6 in which Babylon was used polemically against both Roman Catholicism and against all of the so called "corrupt" denominations of Christendom. In the previous chapter attention was drawn to the use of the Babylon motif to define on an intellectual and epistemological basis who, for the Brethren writers, was "in" the group and who was "out." It was shown in that chapter that a significant part of this was centered upon an attempt to draw a line between those who, from the perspective of the writer, believed what was "true" and those who believed what was "false." The concept of Babylon here proved to be a useful way of understanding the outsider who, according to the Brethren, held onto confused and heretical doctrines. This present chapter, by contrast, is concerned with what might be termed "secular" or "worldly" interpretations of the Whore of Babylon motif among Brethren interpreters. As will be shown, the vituperative use of the text to vilify the enemy need not only be leveled against the religious or epistemological "other," for the image of Babylon would prove to be a convenient tool to be used polemically to warn the Brethren of the dangers of the very world in which they lived.

This method of tapping into the psychology and dynamics of an emerging sectarian community reflects Newport's suggestion that *eis*egetical schemes provide a useful way into the thinking of religious groups.

Newport draws attention to Tyrrell's famous remark that "those seeking to reconstruct a life of Jesus are all too often in the position of looking into a deep well only to see there a faint reflection of themselves."[1] However, Newport goes on to note that "those distorted images at the bottom of Tyrrell's well surely have some value, if not to the biblical scholar of the historical-critical school, at least to the historian of ideas, and perhaps to the literary theorist as well."[2] Newport's work is helpful in that it makes this argument generally with reference to a variety of different groups. Inevitably, however, his work does not go into great detail concerning any one of them. In this book the method is used with reference to one relatively small group and one particularly narrow text. The results, therefore, are less broad but significantly deeper.

Any new sectarian Christian denomination faces the problem of both defining and representing the "self," that is, who they are, and of defining and representing the "other," that is, who and what it is from which they have seceded. The question to be addressed here is: "What does it mean for one to be a part of the Brethren movement?" The exegesis of the Whore of Babylon motif is a significant way in which the Brethren community tried to solidify their own identity and answer that very question as a dangerous, bloodthirsty enemy provides on a sociological level "unification on the basis of conflict." Babylon, a "danger which is always threatened but never materialized" can thus be seen as "especially apt to strengthen the feeling of unity" in sociological terms.[3]

Anthropologist Mary Douglas, in *Purity and Danger* (1966), while discussing theories about the concept of pollution with particular reference to bodily refuse notes that social structures, for example Christian denominations, are vulnerable around their margins or boundaries. All such margins, or places where contact with the "outsider" occurs, could be viewed as dangerous and it is crucial to her analysis not simply to "treat bodily margins in isolation from all other margins" as "there is no reason to assume any primacy for the individual's attitude to his own bodily and emotional experience, any more than for his cultural and social experience."[4] For a Brethren interpreter his experience of the wider world occurs on the margins of his own social existence and is thus a potentially dangerous one.

Douglas' now classic work may be helpful here too. According to her theory such margins and boundaries are vulnerable because they are the

1. Newport, *Apocalypse and Millennium*, 21.
2. Ibid.
3. Simmel, *Conflict*, 103–5.
4. Douglas, *Purity and Danger*, 121.

place of interface between the insider and the outsider. The boundary is a permeable or porous area, a place susceptible to allowing danger in through contact with the "outside" and, as such, can lead to feelings of anxiety from within about the integrity and security of the group as it participates, willingly or unwillingly, in an exchange of ideas and values at this interstitial border. In this chapter it is argued that in the hands of the Christian Brethren interpreters, the book of Revelation helped to ease the sense of "danger" that came through contact with the outside world; a danger that might lead to impurity. Just as "pollution rules" within a culture ensure "the order in external physical events,"[5] so too for the Brethren, the prophetic text of the Apocalypse which revealed the future to the group, gave order and meaning to the external physical world. It also identified clearly the source of danger: Babylon.

Douglas herself leans in this direction in showing that the notion of boundary transgression, or "pollution" as she defines it, has its origin in the social construction of entities with highly defined boundaries. The exegesis of the Apocalypse for the Brethren authors, just like the exegesis of Leviticus for Jewish authors, provides, so it is argued here, "a positive pattern in which ideas and values are tidily ordered" and "above all . . . has authority."[6] Thus if such boundaries are transgressed, for example, by not conforming to the standard Brethren exegesis of the Apocalypse or not adhering to the authority of prominent Brethren such as Darby, a person becomes symbolically dirty or polluted and "is matter out of place."[7] They become "outsiders" because of divergent beliefs. Douglas states that "a rule of avoiding anomalous things affirms and strengthens the definitions to which they do not conform"[8] and, although she does not talk about the Brethren specifically as is the case in this chapter, her theories when applied to this group suggest that the Brethren would have a rule of some kind about avoiding the world and the things of the world. Such a rule strengthens the Brethren view that they are not of the world but merely strangers passing through. The call for separation is of course explicit in the angelic voice of Revelation 18:4: "come out of her my people," the text which follows is full of images of ritual pollution for Babylon is "unclean," "detestable," and has "plagues."

Douglas is helpful in another way in this chapter. Her "matter out of place" theory can be applied further to the Brethren movement insofar as the Brethren, through their imminent eschatological expectations,

5. Douglas, "Pollution," 339.
6. Douglas, *Purity and Danger*, 38–39.
7. Ibid., 35.
8. Ibid., 39.

considered themselves to be "matter out of place." The boundary with which they interface is not just a religious boundary but also a secular one for the Brethren define themselves not just against other denominations but also against the world. This world, they believe, is not the home of the true saints, but heaven is their home.[9] The Brethren are just passing through this world and must do so undefiled. Thus they may be considered, in Douglas' terms: "matter out of place."

Douglas has also applied her cultural theory of pollution and contamination to the secular tenets of contemporary Western society. According to Douglas, and her colleague Wildavsky, the concept of boundary transgression as pollution is "an instrument of control" that gives "the central establishment . . . the monopoly of explaining the natural order."[10] Thus, "from the point of view of the central political establishment, the socially inferior are morally and physically contaminating, to be segregated and forcibly confined, punished if they try to break out."[11] For the Brethren this punishment does not just come from within the group (as was seen in the previous chapter and the use of Babylon in Darby's project of excommunication), but it comes also from without. The punishment for transgressing the boundary between the Brethren and the world is to be counted as being "in" Babylon on the day of her judgment; to "share her sins," to "receive her plagues" and thus be judged by God.

The Brethren movement is an entity which has its own religiously and culturally particular rituals. The primary example of this is the celebration of the Lord's Supper. Beliefs are important too and here it would appear to be an inaugurated futurist eschatology and a sectarian ecclesiology which are foremost. Unlike many other religious groups, social practices were relatively unimportant for the Brethren writers. With the exception of the notable work of Müller and Barnardo, who established orphanages for children, much Brethren activity showed the outworking of a premillennial pessimism. This makes sense: if, after all, the world is soon to end, what point is there in trying to fix it up? The world is not getting better but gradually worse and heading for judgment.

In this sense the Brethren's struggle against this world can be seen as a struggle to maintain cultural identity among a rapidly changing religious, political and economic milieu. The Catholic Emancipation Act of 1829 and the efforts of Newman and Pusey to re-Catholicize the Church of England

9. For example, Wolston, in *Handfuls of Purpose*, 340–41, asks: "What is a stranger? A stranger is a person who is away from home. Where is our Home? It is the place where Jesus is. That is home. He is not here. He is up there."

10. Douglas and Wildavsky, *Risk and Culture*, 47.

11. Ibid., 47.

was understood by the Brethren to be a return to Babylon (this has been clearly demonstrated above). Yet forming their own religious movement was only a religious response to a religious problem. The world in which the earliest Brethren authors lived was a world that appeared to fulfill the darkest predictions of a dispensational schema. The French Revolution was the source of widespread uncertainty within English political and social circles, which, when combined with the war between America and England during the first decade of the 1800s and that fact that most of Europe was engaged in the Napoleonic wars, caused many to turn to Scripture and in particular the apocalyptical portent of "wars and rumors of wars" to explain their own *Sitz im Leben*.[12] Similarly, a ubiquitous European cholera infection reinforced such a belief further, again being seen as a sign of the world's impending doom and of God's great displeasure. For the Brethren, then, the world was an unsafe place and the book of Revelation was a guide to those who found themselves trapped in it.

Thus the use and influence of the Whore of Babylon motif can be seen in how the Brethren invented their own identity. The Whore of Babylon motif enables the Brethren authors to pursue the question of how one comes to know the "other." The "religious other" is, in this case, Papal Rome and her many daughters; that is, the sum total of all corrupt Christendom. The "secular other" is the world in which the Brethren live. The ability to comprehend the complex dynamics of any community, whether religious, secular, geographical, ethnic, small, large, is always a significant activity, and, as anthropologist Geertz has noted, one can never really get to the bottom of things as the final interpretation of any text will not elicit the same exact meaning for everyone.[13] The group of Brethren authors here examined did not have a simple, one-layer answer to who Babylon was, but rather they understood the identity of Babylon on a number of levels. The exegesis occurred over a number of complex layers. While the identification of Babylon highlighted in chapter 7 above presented a warning to the Brethren about incorrect and confused exegesis, it is somewhat ironic that the community as a whole appears not to have held onto a single "right" interpretation of what Babylon was, but rather held a number of simultaneously "right" interpretations.

---

12. Matt 24:6; Mark 13:7.

13. Geertz, *Interpretation of Cultures*, 313.

DARBY

This tendency to adopt a number of different interpretations of the Babylon motif, all of which were simultaneously thought be right, can be seen in no less central a figure than Darby. As has been noted above, Darby identified Babylon as the Roman Catholic Church, yet also as the whole of corrupt Christendom, and simultaneously as corrupt and confused doctrine. However in this chapter it becomes clear that Darby also interpreted the Whore of Babylon motif as referring to the world and worldliness, thus drawing the boundaries not just within the Christian tradition but also without.

Darby writes quite clearly that "the great principle seen in Babylon was worldliness"[14] and that "Babylon [is] a thing of this world."[15] But somehow Babylon is more than just something in or of the world. She is representative too of the power and authority of the world and for this reason Darby writes: "The government of the world . . . [is] Babel and violent power,"[16] and also: "Babylon is . . . [the] power of the world."[17] Here Darby is using government not just in a political sense, insofar as he perceives Babylon to be behind the political, legislative and administrative agency of the world, but in more general terms as that which has authority and power over things. Babylon represents the secular "other," the physical world and its authority, power, and control. The language of religious boundaries, the distinction between self and other, is apparent when Darby writes of the "outward worldly glory of Babylon."[18] Babylon represents an "other" external world or sphere of existence to the internal world in which the Brethren exist.

For Darby Babylon symbolizes a lust for the beauty or attractiveness of the world. She represents the dangerously attractive external world outside of the Brethren's internal world: "See how people are attracted by the external . . . [by] the woman . . . the spirit of the world."[19] She is a thing which allures man: "Babylon . . . the beauty which attracts man but disgusts God . . . it is the world."[20]

Darby draws attention to Babylon's designation as a prostitute or whore. She is the one who entices and allures men, causes them to lust after

14. Darby, "Notes on the Apocalypse," 97.

15. Darby, "Exposition of the Epistle to the Romans," 191; See also, Darby, "Isaiah," 10: "the Fall of Babylon . . . the darkness of this world"; and Darby, "Fragmentary Thoughts," 352: "Babylon, the world-church."

16. Darby, "Genesis, Typically Considered," 123.

17. Darby, "Notes on Isaiah," 46.

18. Darby, "Practical Reflections on the Psalms," 325.

19. Darby, "Fragmentary Thoughts," 346–47.

20. Ibid., 344.

her and then seduces them: "the woman was gorgeously and imperially arrayed, had every human glory and ornament on her, and a rich cup of prostituting . . . [the] source of all seduction to Men."[21] Her sexuality is seen as a threat to Brethren purity. Douglas notes that in certain cultures lethal punishments are inflicted on those who have engaged in adultery "in the interests of maintaining the social structure"[22] and this is certainly the case for Babylon who, because of her prostitution and adultery, is judged and destroyed. Thus continuing with Darby's fourth layer of exegesis, this world, which Babylon symbolically represents, seeks to seduce the saints and thus will be judged and destroyed to maintain the social structure of the true church of the Brethren. Babylon is: "the strange woman" who represents all "the snares and attractions of corruption . . . seeking to satisfy one's lusts by violence and corruption . . . self-will . . . full gratification . . ." This "strange woman" has "the ruin of man written on her forehead."[23]

In Joshua chapter 7 we read of how Achan the Israelite acted "unfaithfully" or adulterously, not as a result of engaging in a sexual act outside of marriage, but because he hid a Babylonian garment under his tent. He was taken outside of the camp and burned. Darby comments on this: "What of . . . the Babylonish garment? That was merely the people gratifying their lust with the things of the world,"[24] thereby linking the act of holding onto something made in Babylon with lusting after or sexual desire for the world. In Revelation 17:16 and 18:8 the Whore of Babylon is burned with fire and in Genesis 38:24 and Leviticus 21:9 burning is the punishment for prostitution. Douglas notes that in some cultures fear of sex pollution is "mediated by contact with fire."[25] Clearly on an anthropological level this kind of view is behind the Israelite punishment for prostitution, the apocalyptical punishment of Babylon and, *vis-à-vis* Brethren exegesis, the judgment waiting the world and those who engage in intercourse with the world.

21. Darby, *Synopsis of the Books of the Bible*, 5.581–82.

22. Douglas, *Purity and Danger*, 131.

23. Darby, "Practical Reflections on the Proverbs," 342–78, 355–56; see also "a strange woman . . . This was mere corrupt lust . . . The heart, allured by evil . . . following the path of lust to death . . . The special warning (v. 8) is withdrawal, not coming near the door of her house . . . [do] not go in the path of lust, nor [let] lust have occasion to seize hold of the will . . . The evil too, as it was reckless, was shameless." Ibid., 373–37; and, Darby, "Practical Reflections on the Psalms," 221. "The church of God is . . . formed of people who are of no account in this world . . . the grandeurs of the . . . Babylons, which God judges, eclipse it in our sight? . . . Is the appearance and vain show of this world of weight with us?"

24. Darby, "Readings on Joshua," 434.

25. Douglas, *Purity and Danger*, 154.

Douglas also notes a commonly held belief which she defines as the "Delilah Complex," a "belief that women weaken or betray,"[26] found among many groups and cultures throughout the world. The name of course refers to the story of Samson and Delilah in Judges chapter 16. Delilah, perceived in popular exegesis as a prostitute, seduces Samson to give up his position as a Nazerite, one who is set apart for God. For Darby, the true church is, like Samson, set apart for God. The apocalyptic prostitute, Babylon, like Delilah, seeks to seduce the believer away from God and into the world. One way that she does this is by mixing the church and world together. Babylon blurs the distinction between the two worlds. The porous boundary between the sphere of the church and the sphere of the world, the place where they meet, the interface, margin or boundary between the Brethren community inside and the outsiders in the world is a dangerous, vulnerable place. Darby writes: "The church and the world cannot go on together . . . 'Ye are not of this world'"[27] and that "everything not heavenly is mixed up with her."[28]

For Darby, this illicit union and adulterous relationship between the church and the world can be seen in no clearer terms than in the formation of the Church of England and its church-state affiliation. In no unclear terms Darby states "the union of church and state I held to be Babylonish"[29] and that "the position and worldliness of the church . . . disqualified it for being an agent of the gospel in the country."[30] So, whereas Dennett, Trotter, Wolston, and Newton identify the church-state relationship as a religious corruption of Babylon further defining the community's religious boundaries, Darby uses the church-state relationship in a secular way to define the community's secular boundary. For Darby, the Church of England is no longer a church but has been completely subsumed by the world. Further evidence of this view can be gleaned from his exegesis of Zechariah chapter 5. He writes of "the ephah and the woman . . . the union of the Church in the world . . . the woman in the world . . . the professing Gentile Church now simply buried in the world."[31]

Douglas highlights a number of specific things that, from an anthropological perspective, belong outside of the boundaries of many societies and cultures which when brought inside ritually defile and make one dirty and

---

26. Ibid., 154.

27. Darby, "Fragmentary Thoughts," 351–52.

28. Ibid., 348.

29. Darby, "Analysis of Dr. Newman's 'Apologia,'" 156.

30. Darby, "Thoughts on the Present Position," 79.

31. Darby, "Zechariah," 217–18. See Darby, "Christian Liberty," 116–17; Darby, "Claims of the Church," 314; Darby, "Reply to the Remarks," 244.

impure.[32] The Brethren have their own list of specific worldly things that exist at the interface between their own community and the world which similarly pose a threat and danger to those inside. Darby's list includes pride,[33] learning and numbers,[34] worldly prosperity and advantage,[35] selfish enjoyment and lust,[36] drunkenness[37] and lasciviousness.[38] Involvement with these things, which exist on the margins of the Brethren world, is categorized as dangerous and the image of the Whore of Babylon is put to use by Darby to warn his brethren of such danger and potential defilement.[39] There are other ways in which Darby uses the Babylon image. For example, he can use it in a geographical sense to describe the location in which he lives.[40] He also uses Babylon to refer to the act of commercial business, particularly within the geographical confines of England.[41]

It is plain then that in the work of arguably the most significant person from the movement here under discussion, we can see the book of Revelation in general, and the Whore of Babylon Motif in particular, being put to great use. The text serves Darby well as he looks to it to provide him with the guidance needed on matters relating to those points in the world where danger and potential impurity are to be found.

32. Douglas, *Danger and Purity*, 121.

33. Darby, "Thoughts on Isaiah," 309.

34. Darby, "Fragmentary Thoughts," 255.

35. Darby, "Revelation," 584.

36. Darby, "The Proverbs," 293.

37. Darby, "Christianity Not Christendom," 253.

38. Darby, *Closing Days of Christendom*, 3, 5. See further Darby, "Testimony of God," 513–14; Darby, "Church and Its Friendly Subdivisions," 250; Darby, "Altar of Abraham," 103–4; Darby, "Hints on the Book of Genesis," 135; Darby, *Letters of J.N.D.*, April 1867, 1.495–96. In each of these publications Darby uses Babylon to warn against a list of specific forms of worldly attitude or behavior.

39. For further examples of how Darby uses Babylon to warn his brethren of the dangers of the world, see Darby, "Scriptural Criticisms," 20. "Babylon has no need to be sorrowfully and separately waiting . . . the true-hearted believer . . . will, as separated from the world, wait for Him in whom his hope is, in the spirit of holy separation." Darby, "God For Us," 250; Darby, *Letters of J.N.D.*, February 5, 1874, 2.254; Darby, "General Remarks," 361–62.

40. Darby, "Thoughts on Isaiah," 309; Darby, *Letters of J.N.D.*, August 11, 1873, 2.236.

41. Darby, "Fragmentary Thoughts," 328, 338.

DENNETT

Dennett, like Darby, links Babylon with the world. It has been demonstrated in chapter 6 that Dennett identified Babylon with the church in Laodicea which he interpreted as a warning to the daughters of Babylon. Further, in *Expository Jottings* (1883), Dennett describes Laodicea as the "worldliness of the assembly,"[42] thus linking Babylon with the world. For him Babylon represents worldly glory and the worldly church[43] and he draws a distinction between the community of the Brethren, which are the true heavenly church, and the Babylonian "other," that is, those who make up the world church.[44] Both those inside and outside must remain together until the time of judgment as the parable of the tares and the leaven foretell.[45]

For Dennett, Babylon is ultimately something intrinsically selfish. He describes Babylon variously as self-exaltation, self-gratification, self-confidence, self-glorification and self-sufficiency. Babylon is seeking one's own happiness, acquisitions and stability in this world.[46] Babylon lives a life of pleasure, gratifying her worldly desires,[47] whereas the true church of God is heavenly in character and does not belong to the earth.[48] Such selfish attitudes do little to reinforce a unified social order within the Brethren community, whereas loyalty towards other Brethren and the Brethren hierarchy fosters *communitas*, symmetry and inner coherence, helping maintain order and reinforce the boundaries.

In a variation on the general Brethren theme, Dennett uses the "Babylon-is-the-world" idiom to traduce those who engage in philosophical study. The very origin of philosophy, Dennett states, is Babylonian and even in modern times retains this character. Students seeking "learning and wisdom" can be lead into spiritual declension and even backsliding through the worldly influence of Babylon philosophy.[49] As we have seen in chapter 7, heretical or confused thought is dangerously contagious and the Brethren need to protect their boundaries from epistemological defilement. Here, once again, the image of the Whore of Babylon is used to mark out the areas where it is unsafe for the faithful to go.

42. Dennett, *House of God*, 17.
43. Dennett, *Visions of John in Patmos*, 226.
44. Ibid., 221.
45. Dennett, *Blessed Hope*, 61.
46. Dennett, *Visions of John in Patmos*, 234.
47. Dennett, "Widow Indeed," 125.
48. Dennett, *Visions of John in Patmos*, 221.
49. Dennett, *Daniel the Prophet*, 12, 16.

After exploring the threats that Babylon poses to Brethren purity Dennett finds, in the biblical character of Daniel and his friends Hananiah, Mishael, and Azariah, examples of how purity and distinction can be maintained even when Babylon (which in the Daniel story is of course literal Babylon)[50] is pressing hard on the boundaries of the Brethren community. Daniel was, according to Dennett, a "true Nazarite" who walked "undefiled amid the Babylonish seductions and corruptions." The Nazirite is one who, according to Numbers chapter 6, has made a voluntary and special vow of separation to Yahweh. He or she will follow strict laws of separation including abstaining from alcohol, not cutting one's hair, and avoiding corpses. Dennett states of the Naziriteship of Daniel that "an application may be made to ourselves" and that his Brethren readers must walk "a path of holy separation."[51] After linking the book of Daniel with the Apocalypse, Dennett then exhorts his readers to "maintain the place of separation outside of all the alarms and confusions of the world." Thus for Dennett true separateness and true holiness can only be found outside the world, that is, inside the Brethren conceptual sphere. Samson was also a Nazirite yet, as we have noted earlier, he lost his set apartness and distinction, an event which Douglas uses to develop her "Delilah Complex" theory. Such a theory sheds light on how those who have separated themselves from the external world perceive the outside world as a threat of impurity, particularly in the form of the sexualized female, to which category Babylon is antitypical.

Ultimately Dennett's view of the world is fuelled by his premillennial pessimism linked to a dispensational worldview. Babylon represents the societal, governmental and commercial power of the world. Such worldly things the Brethren must avoid as their destruction is foretold in Revelation chapters 17–18. Babylon, this world, will be judged, rendering the nations powerless and unstable and shattering the very framework of society. As such, no improvement in the state of the world should be expected or even worked towards, indeed it would be a waste of time for a Christian to engage in any kind of political action in the vain hope of trying to improve the world. To this end, Dennett writes,

> Will any political changes or legislative enactments alter the moral character either of human governments or of their subjects? . . . trace the course of human governments from the days of the kingdom of Babylon up to the present time . . . some individual monarchs have been pious men; but . . . whatever their

50. Or at least understood by a noncritical reader as literal Babylon.
51. Ibid., 14–15.

piety, they could not change the course or the character of their governments.[52]

Clearly then Babylon, this world and all that it represents is, for Dennett, a place to which the Brethren do not belong.

MACKINTOSH

Mackintosh was very aware of the dangers posed at the vulnerable margin between the internal world of life within the Brethren movement and the world "outside." He warns his reader of the inherent risks at such interstitial places, for example, in his work *Jehoshaphat: A Word on World-Bordering* (n.d.) he blames the proximity of the kings of Israel to the Babylonian nation around them for Israel's Babylonian captivity.[53] Like Dennett he also uses the concept of the Nazirite, which he defines as people who "separate themselves from Babylonish pollutions . . . apart from the world's defilement,"[54] to warn his Brethren of the dangers of such "World-Bordering," to borrow Mackintosh's phrase. After exhorting his reader to "have nothing to do with rank in this life," and to separate from "everything which directly savours of the flesh and of the world" he turns his attention to childcare, something he designates: "the management of our children,"[55] for they too can be found in Babylon:

> The music master, and the dancing master, are surely not the agents which the Spirit of God would select to help our children along, nor do they, by any means, comport with that high-toned Naziriteship to which we are called . . . shall I be so base as to train my children for the devil and the world? . . . If my children savour of Babylon, I savour of it myself.[56]

Like Dennett and Darby, Mackintosh treats the concept of the civilization of society with disdain. He says that there was much to be found in Babylon that

> was attractive to the nature's eye. The arts and sciences were cultivated amongst them. Civilization had reached a far loftier point amongst those ancient nations than we moderns are

52. Ibid., 59–60.
53. Mackintosh, *Jehoshaphat*, 9–10, 13, 15, 32.
54. Mackintosh, *Discipleship in an Evil Day*, 9.
55. Mackintosh, *Thou and Thy House*, 31.
56. Ibid., 32.

disposed to admit. Refinement and luxury were probably carried to as great an extent there as amongst those who put forth very lofty pretensions.[57]

Such civilized, sophisticated and refined things in life are, according to Mackintosh, merely the gilded bait on a Babylonian hook. The true Christian should learn from Hezekiah's mistake and be "raised above the influence of the world's polite attraction."[58]

Just as a Durkheimian analysis of a society suggests that "dangerous powers imputed to gods are, in actual fact, powers vested in the social structure for defending itself,"[59] so here dangerous powers imputed to the world are used by the Brethren to defend the insider from the secular other, that is, the world. It is important to note that when such a "closed community" as the Brethren speak of the world they "invoke the idea of the evil outside as a theological image, justifying their separation from the established order."[60] Above, Mackintosh uses examples from Scripture of the physical threat that geographical Babylon posed to literal Israel as a warning of the threat that symbolic Babylon, this world, poses to the true church. The world is evil and to designate it as such reinforces the boundary between insider and outsider for such a "sense of border is inherent in the consciousness of the people [like the Brethren] who perceive their lives as . . . essentially critical of some defined other part of human society where power resided."[61]

BELLETT

Bellett continues to use the emerging Brethren exegesis of Babylon to warn of the dangers of contamination from the world but becomes highly specific as he describes one particular activity as being especially Babylonian. He writes: "Now, this moment you are called to the admiration . . . of the world's greatness . . . It calls itself a 'great exhibition of the world's achievements' . . . no part of scripture can help us to understand it better than this . . . the 17th chapter."[62] To this, the editor of the pamphlet adds: "Bellett was speaking in February 1851 at the 'Great Exhibition.'" Bellett clearly uses Revelation chapters 17–18 to explain why such a "Great Exhibition" is tak-

57. Mackintosh, *Notes on the Book of Numbers*, 28–29.
58. Mackintosh, *Work In Its Right Place*, 44.
59. Douglas, "Pollution," 339.
60. Douglas and Wildavsky, *Risk and Culture*, 102.
61. Ibid., 103.
62. Bellett, *Belshazzar's Feast*, 16.

ing place in the Crystal Palace, Hyde Park, London. The Victorians, proud of their industrial, military and economic achievements which had made Great Britain arguably the greatest world power of its time, arrived in their millions to see some thirteen thousand exhibitions dedicated to British accomplishment. The events struck such a chord with Bellett that he dedicated an entire publication to identifying the Exhibition as Babylon. In *Belshazzar's Feast in Its Application to the Great Exhibition* (n.d.) we read: "The mind turns with these thoughts to the present moment . . . to the subject of 'The Great Exhibition' . . . The Exhibition is therefore in full collision with the mind of God. Christ exposes the world; the Exhibition displays it."[63] The reason why such an exhibition disagrees so strongly with what Bellett perceives to be God's thoughts is based on his pessimistic outlook that is so often indicative of a premillennial worldview; namely that trying to make the world better is a waste of time.[64] Such an event is therefore against God's divine will and could perhaps be seen as rebellion against God, if not even as antichristian. The very same project was undertaken in Genesis chapter 11 according to Bellett. The Great Exhibition is a modern day rebuilding of the tower of Babel.[65]

The danger of going to the Great Exhibition is that it is the very epitome of all that is worldly, earthly and carnal and as such represents a grave danger of pollution to those who cross its margins and enter the Crystal Palace. It is the "great shop of the world's ware," a place where "man's works are displayed there. Man's art is enthroned there, and man expects to be admired and wondered at there . . . It is a mirror in which the world is reflected in a thousand attractive forms . . . It is full of the spirit of the last days."[66] Ultimately the Great Exhibition is a symbol of the Great Whore of Revelation. Bellett writes of "the world's advancement, the jubilee of Babylon . . . the woman of Revelation 17 glorifies herself, and lives deliciously in the earth." Thus, Bellett writes that the true Christian should remain separate from the exhibition. Just as Daniel remained separate from the feast of Belshazzar, so the Christian must be separate from the worldly temptations displayed in the Crystal Palace, for God requires "separation of His own out of the world." Furthermore, this is not just a spiritual separation but also a physical "separation from the earth."[67] He concludes by exhorting his readers to ask themselves: "If we have a pulse of affection or allegiance to Jesus, can we

63. Ibid., 9–10.
64. Ibid.
65. Ibid., 12, 16.
66. Ibid., 14–15.
67. Ibid., 16.

glory in this present moment with all its costliness and pleasures?"[68] Thus implying that attendance equates to betrayal of Christ himself.

It will be clear by now that the identification of Babylon in Brethren exegesis is becoming more and more specific and systematized as the Brethren's ecclesio-social structure becomes more systematized and the boundaries of the movement more well defined. Douglas has noted that "pollution rules indicate areas of greater systemization of ideas"[69] thus the more complex the pollution rules, the more systematized a group's ideas will be. This is indeed true of the Brethren exegesis unfolding in this book.

OTHER AUTHORS

It has been shown above that a number of Brethren authors linked the symbol of "Babylon" to "worldliness." In doing this they achieved further clarification of where they stood before God. As was seen in the previous chapters, for the Brethren "Babylon" was "false religion" not just in general, but even in the context of "false" members of the Brethren movement itself. They used the symbol of Babylon to draw a line, perhaps more accurately a circle, in the sand. But they used the same symbol to distance themselves from the world and hence to bring themselves out in even sharper relief against the presumed wicked and worldly backcloth. It was not just the four writers above who did this. Rather the view seems to have been pretty well embedded with the movement as a whole. In an attempt to show how, so it seems, such views were stitched into the very fabric of the Brethren movement and how the symbol of Babylon was used widely both to facilitate and communicate this view, a very brief summary of some of those other writers will now be presented.

In the four publications in which Wigram can be seen to link Babylon with the world his main emphasis is on worldliness within the church.[70] The church becomes Babylonian when it looks to the world for its power.[71] To try and "blend" the world and the church together leads only to confusion. Such confusion, on an anthropological level, is indicative of pollution

---

68. Ibid., 24. The only other Brethren author to comment on the Great Exhibition is William Trotter. See, Trotter, "Millennial Reign of Christ," 84. "Think, my brethren, of what the pride of man's heart is doing at this very moment, in concentrating the wealth and energies of all nations in making one grand display to all the world of what man's skill and energy can effect!" He does not, however, link the Exhibition with Babylon.

69. Douglas, "Pollution," 339.

70. See Wigram, "Notes on Scripture," 159. "Babylon signifies confusion, mingling with the world."

71. Wigram, "Church: Its Present State and Prospects," 25–26.

in many cultures, and if, for example, one takes the ancient Israelites as an example, such confusion can lead to ritual defilement as was the case in Leviticus and the abomination laws. Here the Hebrew word *tebel* (e.g., Leviticus chapters 18 and 20), translated as "contamination" or even "incest" may be understood as synonymous with perversion, mixing, confusion, pollution, or loosing distinctiveness.[72] Awareness of such Hebrew linguistics was not beyond Wigram.

Miller identifies Babylon as something secular on three occasions yet in each instance he stresses, like Wigram, that Babylon is the mixing of the church with the world.[73] The place where the church and the world meet is a dangerous place, a boundary where ideas are exchanged. The importance of maintaining a distinction between "insiders" (the Brethren) and "outsiders" (the world) is stressed, as the place where the two worlds meet is unsafe thus boundaries must be reinforced.

Grant insists that those who merely call themselves Christian but do not maintain a separation from the world should not be allowed to take part in that most defining of all Brethren rituals: the Lord's Supper, because of "their entanglements with the world . . . it would be another Babel."[74] Lincoln insists that "not only must there be separation from evil . . . but separation entire in this specified manner from the religious world."[75] Newberry likens association with the world to prostitution. Worldliness is: "the prostitution of Christianity to secular ends . . . spiritual fornication. The union of the carnal and the spiritual, the human with the Divine, the earthly and the heavenly . . . [it is] the wine of Babylon's fornication."[76] These authors maintain the importance of distinction, of not allowing the things of the world to mix with the things of the church. There must be no homogenizing, to do so would make one guilty of the Levitical sin of *tebel* of uncleanness through mixing or confusing things which leads to ritual impurity.

Lady Powerscourt links Babylon with worldliness in five of her *Letters and Papers* (1872). She warns of the danger of Brethren taking "our lot with Babylon . . . to feast the world; to nestle themselves as the world."[77] For her, the call of Revelation 18:4, "come out of her," is a warning spoken to

72. Bailey, "Tebel," 664.

73. Miller, *Meditations on the Beatitudes*, 16–17. See also, Miller, *CH*, 1.355. "The church . . . shakes hands with the world, and sinks into its position . . . Babylon spiritually." Miller, *CH*, 2.195–96. "The very essence of Babylon [is] the unhallowed mixture of Christ and the world."

74. Grant, *Divine Movement*, 34.

75. Lincoln, "On the Value of the Third Epistle of John," 8.2.

76. Newberry, *Notes on the Book of Revelation*, 97.

77. Powerscourt, *Letters and Papers*, 23.62.

the church in the world who surround themselves with ungodliness.[78] Like Darby and Mackintosh, Powerscourt draws reference to the Babylonian garment of Joshua chapter 7, we should: "treasure no Babylonish garment however goodly"[79] as to do so leads to ritual defilement and contamination. Powerscourt urges her reader to remain faithful, virginal, and separate in order to retain distinctiveness from Babylon.[80] To associate with Babylon is to be the opposite of these virtues, to be unfaithful, promiscuous and in alliance with the world.

BRETHREN PERIODICALS

Periodicals often give a rather better sense of what is happening "on the ground" of a religious tradition. This is so since they often contain the views of authors who may never actually write a substantial book and through such things as brief comments and letters to the editor they can be a more accurate barometer of the spiritual pressures within a denomination. For this reason significant time has been spent during this research looking at Brethren periodicals, a source that has not heretofore been much examined by scholars. A brief summary of that material is found below.

Time and time again the theme of maintaining distinctiveness from the Babylonian world around arises in the popular Brethren magazines and periodicals of the nineteenth century. For instance in the *Christian Witness* the London Missionary Society is criticized for following "worldly objects of pursuit," holding "worldly association" and of going "to the world for aid."[81] Again this boils down to a question of authority and of who is in charge, Christ or man, for "in appointing a committee or being appointed to it [they are] . . . indirectly interfering with the headship of Jesus."[82] The author of this article uses Babylon to warn any Brethren who would consider being involved in such evangelistic and socially beneficial groups of the importance of remaining "separate" from such "unholy and disobedient" groups for risk of world-contamination.[83]

Another article in the *Christian Witness* asks: "Is the Exercise of Worldly Authority Consistent with Discipleship?" The answer comes: "Has the scripture written nothing respecting Babylon?" In particular "stations of

78. Ibid., 57.157.
79. Ibid., 60.191; See also "Paper on Genesis 22," 257–58.
80. Ibid., 78.234–35.
81. Harris, "Religious Societies," 92–93.
82. Ibid., 93–94.
83. Ibid., 96.

power or influence in the world" are given as specific examples of boundary transgression into Babylon.[84] Salvation itself is seen here as "extrication" from Babylon and "from the principles and systems of this evil age." Another Brethren author, possibly C. Brunton, warns of "the terrible danger of being of the world at all . . . Babylon is for the world, and the world for Babylon."[85]

The equally popular *Northern Witness* periodical connects Babylon with the world on a variety of occasions. The editor of the magazine, Caldwell, writes an article called *Separation from the World* (1878) during which he warns the church against forming an "alliance of any kind with the world." The secular sectarian language can be seen further when he exhorts his readers to "maintain the path of separation" otherwise Satan may "entangle the child of God, and drag him into hurtful association with the world."[86] The forbidden bond between church and world that many have entered into culminates in Babylon the Great.[87]

Other contributors to the *Northern Witness* continue on the same lines. Bland warns those who tolerate the evil of this world that the impending judgment of Babylon awaits them,[88] whereas an author known as W.P.L. notes that just as Lot in Genesis chapters 11–13 made a good start in his walk with God he soon fell away as he "prospered in worldly matters." Such "worldly advantage . . . cost him very dear."[89] There is a lesson here for the Brethren, so the author states: meeting with Brethren is more important than home, market place or work.[90] In each case a link is made between the world and Babylon. Tweedie, in a contribution to the *Northern Witness*, focuses on the carnal, worldly and sensual attractions of Babylon: "earthly pleasures, riches, and excitement . . . Babylon claims in the flesh. Babylon rejoices in earthly prosperity . . . [Babylon is] loving the world and seeking a portion in it."[91] Bellett, who has above been identified as seeing Babylon in the Great Exhibition, contributes to the *Northern Witness* by urging his reader to "retire from the world to admire Jesus . . . the secret of their victory [over the world is] retiring from the world's idolatry."[92] He is referring here

---

84. Newton, "Is the Exercise of Worldly Authority," 258.
85. Brunton, "Land of Shinar," 286.
86. Caldwell, "Separation from the World," 81–83.
87. Ibid.
88. Bland, "Babylon," 53.
89. W.P.L. "Love of the World," *NW*, 9.76–8.
90. Ibid., 78.
91. Tweedie, "Mystery, Babylon the Great," 94.
92. Bellett, "Revelation," 86.

to the saints who in Revelation chapter 21 have survived the Babylonian threat of the previous three chapters. They kept away from the vulnerable margin so as not to risk the dangers of boundary transgression and pollution. Hence they are the ones whose will be like a virgin bride, beautifully dressed in white robes, both externally and internally uncontaminated.

A GEOGRAPHICAL BABYLON REDIVIVUS

The broad flow of Brethren interpretation of the Babylon motif when applied to the world that has been sketched in above has been highly literalistic. This is seen particularly in the work of Bellett, who looks for and finds, a contemporary, literal equivalent to the biblical "Babylon." But there were other views, even in the context of the broad parameters of the Brethren view that "Babylon" was (among other things) a symbol of worldliness. This can be seen in the Babylon *redivivus* theme, to which attention is now turned. As we shall see, this view too was highly literalistic suggesting (as in some contemporary Rapture fiction, for example the *Left Behind* novels) that literal Babylon must first be rebuilt in order to be destroyed again by God.

Such fundamental literalism can be seen in a number of Brethren authors who identify the Babylon of the Apocalypse as a literal, geographical entity, that is, as ancient Babylon *redivivus*. Bergin, for example, predicts that Babylon will be a literal city with the Antichrist for its secular king.[93] He believes that Babylon must be literally rebuilt because prophecies concerning its destruction have not yet been fulfilled. He notes that "*sudden destruction*" was to come on Babylon, but no such thing has yet happened.[94] On the contrary, Babylon like many Eastern cities of the ancient world "gradually decayed until it became almost uninhabited. But now there is a town of considerable size, called Hillah, on the ruins of ancient Babylon . . . there are bricks bearing . . . Nebuchadnezzar's name."[95] Bergin is aware that such an idea is somewhat divergent both to the Protestant norm and the emerging Brethren hermeneutic of identifying Babylon as Rome but argues that because of Babylon's commercial and maritime nature, London is closer to the city described in Revelation chapter 18.[96] Turning to the newspapers, Bergin sees that the construction work for the building of Babylon has already begun with "engineers . . . sent down the valley of the Euphrates . . .

93. Bergin, *Babylon to Be Rebuilt and Destroyed*, 161.
94. Ibid., 162.
95. Ibid.
96. Ibid., 163.

making a railway." The completion of the urban project of the regeneration of Babylon, and therefore the fulfillment of Revelation chapter 18, is imminent, for "it will not take long to rebuild the land of Shinar . . . eastern opulence uniting with western wealth, would make it a city such has never been seen, and we have no reason to think it would take many years."[97] Yet the imminent completion of this evil city brings with it the imminent threat of danger. Bergin asks: "When there is an advertisement for clerks to go out to the railway down the Euphrates valley, will any stop? A few will have ears to hear the words, 'Come out of her my people' . . . but most will rush there."[98]

An equally literalistic interpretation of Revelation chapter 18 is purveyed by Bland and Habershon in their papers delivered at the Women's Branch of the Prophecy Investigation Society ca. 1915. Bland quotes the *Morning Star* of the 1st of February 1913, which states: "The bricks used in the construction of the Hindia Dam were everyone of them stamped with the words 'Nebuchadnezzar King of Babylon.'"[99] Such a discovery leads these authors to examine "Babylon" in a number of Old Testament prophecies from which they conclude that the sudden and perpetual destruction of Babylon is as yet unfulfilled in a literalistic sense.[100] They conclude, like Bergin, that the literal rebuilding of the city of Babylon will happen very soon and may have begun already.[101] Further evidence of this event Bland and Habershorn find in the *Sphere* on the 7th February 1914, which through its description of irrigation work in that area further convinces these authors that the Chaldean city of Babylon is to be literally rebuilt on the ruins of modern day Hillah.[102]

Variations on this general theme are found in the work of William De Burgh and an author known only as "F.G."[103] Similarly, the author of the article "Is the Exercise of Worldly Authority Consistent with Discipleship?" (1837), possibly B. W. Newton, holds a futurist and literalistic view arguing that, contrary to the views of some he mentions, Babylon is a literal worldly

97. Ibid., 163–64.

98. Ibid., 164.

99. Bland, *Babylon, Past and Future*, 5.

100. Ibid., 6.

101. Ibid., 10–11.

102. Bland, "Babylon," 51–53. Here Bland takes more of a moderate hermeneutical stance whereby he distinguishes between Babylon in Rev 17 and Babylon in Rev 18. The former is Rome, the center of religious apostasy, the latter is a literal Babylon—a city to be rebuilt on the river Euphrates.

103. De Burgh, *Exposition of the Book of the Revelation*, 295. "F.G.," "Babylon," 282–85.

power and a real geographical location and city which is yet to come.[104] If the author of the 1837 publication is Newton, and we have only the penciled annotation of the original owner of the *Christian Witness* by which to go, then such a view would be entirely in keeping with Newton's massive 642-page book *Babylon: Its Future, History and Doom, with Remarks on the Future of Egypt and other Eastern Countries* (1890), which is a sustained and detailed argument for the literal revival of the physical kingdom of Babylon in order for the events of Revelation chapters 17–18 to be literally fulfilled in the future.[105] This would also be entirely consistent with Newton's views on a literal kingdom of Babylon *redivivus* in the *Patmos Series* of pamphlets in which he interprets Revelation chapter 18 along the literal, geographical lines above noted.[106]

Not all of the relevant literature has to this point been presented on this theme. This is inevitable. The materials in the Manchester Christian Brethren archive are copious and the apparent interest in "Babylon" among Brethren writers significant. There were others, for example Brunton, the author of "The Land Of Shinar" (1837), notes that "while the attention of the Church has been much drawn to the name and nature of Babylon, little stress has been laid on the location of it."[107] He continues in the emerging hermeneutical trend of predicting "a literal Babylon, to be erected in the land of Euphrates."[108] Bellett too, noted above for his identification of Babylon as the "Great Exhibition" understands Babylon to be a commercial power, arguing along lines similar to the above noted authors.[109] Likewise Baines, in his *Preliminary Judgments* (1905), interprets Babylon as being religious, political and commercial in nature.[110] However he rejects the views of Bellett, Bland, Habershon, De Burgh, Rossier, Brunton, "F. G." and Newton, that this will be expressed as a physical rebuilt city of Babylon on the site of Hillah, in favor of suggesting that the commercial and political aspect of the great whore is symbolic of mankind's independence of God in the world. That being said Baines adds something new to the exegesis in that he understands the judgment and doom pronounced upon the city and empire of Babylon in Revelation 18 inaugurated in the recent events in Europe, with

104. Newton, "Is the Exercise of Worldly Authority," 258–60.

105. Newton, *Babylon*.

106. Newton, *Time of the End*, 7.

107. Brunton, "Land of Shinar," 282.

108. Ibid., 282–85.

109. Bellett, "Potter's Broken Vessel," 32.

110. Baines, "Preliminary Judgments," 114; "Glorious Coming," 221.

"the great French Revolution" and "Napoleon" both being mentioned in his exegesis of Babylon.[111]

However not all Brethren authors accepted the secular interpretation of Babylon. Snell, for example, in *Notes on the Revelation: With Practical Reflections* (1866) argues that the Babylon of Revelation 18 "could not be understood to be a material city."[112] Although the above noted authors argue that Babylon must be both a woman and a city Snell concludes that she is literally neither, rather she is a symbol. Wolston was of the same opinion as Snell interpreting the city of Babylon in Revelation 18 in a "figurative way"[113] concluding: "Do not suppose that Babylon is a built city, or the New Jerusalem either. Both are figures."[114]

Perhaps the Brethren author most vehemently opposed to the literalistic interpretation of Babylon is William Kelly. Writing on a favorite passage for those Brethren authors who argued for a literal revival of a Babylonian superpower, that is Zechariah 5, Kelly states that "from Shinar religious corruption came, and thither it must go . . . sent back to Babylon . . . It is all no doubt a symbolical prophecy . . . I should take the vision as a symbolical picture."[115] Thus although it has been noted many times in this present book that Kelly reads Scripture from a highly literalistic hermeneutical stance he does not do so to such an extent as Baines, Bellett, Brunton, Bland, Bergin, de Burgh, Rossier and Newton above who await a literal revival of the Babylonian kingdom in modern day Iraq. For Kelly, to identify the Apocalyptic Babylon as the same as the Old Testament Babylon would be to fundamentally misunderstand and misinterpret Scripture. He gives further evidence against the above shown literalistic understanding of a physical rebuilding of the city of Babylon by arguing from a close reading of Scripture but nothing further is gained here from examining such extracts in detail other than to note in passing that those Brethren who do foresee Babylon *redivivus* are, in Kelly's opinion, "pseudo-literalists." Such exegesis is futile and appeals only to "the curiosity of learned men."[116] Perhaps Kelly is specifically referring here to Newton and those above who believe Babylon will be literally revived, on this cannot we cannot be certain, however it is for certain that

---

111. Ibid., 228, 230.

112. Snell, *Notes on the Revelation*, 171.

113. Wolston, "Candlestick and the Bride," 216.

114. Wolston, "New Jerusalem," in *SC*, 9.198.

115. Kelly, "Zechariah," in *Minor Prophets*, 457–58.

116. Kelly, *Prospects of the World*, 47–49. In the following publications Kelly explicitly denies that the Apocalyptic Babylon could be literally rebuilt as the Old Testament city was built on a plain and the apocalyptic Babylon sits on seven hills: Kelly, *Lectures on the Book of Revelation*, 364; Kelly, *God's Inspiration on the Scriptures*, 2.48; 6.10.

Kelly categorically dismisses their views saying: "'Mystery' teaches us that here it is in no way a question of a heathen city with any amount of political influence . . . Neither pagan Rome nor modern commerce, nor a future city rising on the Euphrates, can possibly answer to such a designation."[117]

SOME CONCLUDING REMARKS ON "BABYLON" AS WORLDLINESS

It is plain both from this chapter and the two before it that the interpretation of the Babylon motif was far from static in the Brethren movement. A satisfactory reason of why this is the case can perhaps be found in the work of the phenomenologist Wolfgang Iser. Iser's reader-oriented approach has been examined in chapter 2 above where it has been applied to the general reading of Revelation. The conclusion arrived at there was that Revelation contains many narrative "gaps" or areas of vagueness. And the Babylon motif is such place of indeterminacy. All Brethren interpretation is simply an attempt to understand those "gaps."

Iser states of a text that "one automatically seeks to relate it to contexts that are familiar,"[118] and this is certainly true in the area of biblical exegesis and in particular the interpretation of the Apocalypse, whether that be the interpretation of those Brethren who had seceded from the Catholic church identifying Babylon as Papal Rome, or those who had seceded from other denominations identifying Babylon as all of corrupt Christendom, or those who, like Bellett, looked at the Great Exhibition and identified Babylon thus. Each person seeks to relate Babylon to a familiar context. The world is the example *par excellence* of that which is familiar, and the context in which each and every person, Brethren or not, find themselves writing. The vilification of the world as Babylon is merely a method employed by the Brethren to maintain social and religious integrity amid a rapidly changing world, a world which in its government, politics and commerce was at odds with the groups otherworldliness.

In chapter 2 of this book, three types of "gaps" in the book of Revelation were identified. The first is the gap that is created by the author failing to name, or positively identify any of the specific motifs and symbols found there. For example the author described Babylon as a city (Rev 17:90), but doesn't name the city, rather stating that understanding its identity calls for wisdom. Failing to provide any real detail for this city thus invites and entices interpreters to attempt to fill in the gaps, thus becoming part of the

117. Kelly, *Babylon and the Beast*, 5.
118. Iser, *Act of Reading*, 22.

text and composing the meaning through suggesting what the name of that place must be.

The second type of gap found in the Apocalypse is that the author fails to give specific times when things will happen, thus in participating in the composition of the text the Brethren interpreter of the nineteenth century will fill in the gaps and suggest that the prophecies are being fulfilled in his own time. We have seen in this chapter that the Great Exhibition, the French Revolution, the building of a railroad through Iraq and the construction of irrigation systems from the Euphrates have all been put forward as being the fulfillment of the Babylon passages. The issue has been further complicated by those Brethren authors who sought to apply Old Testament prophecy about Babylon's sudden and permanent downfall to the Babylon of the Apocalypse. These writers argued that as the literal geographical city of Hillah was never suddenly and permanently destroyed, then the city must be first rebuilt in order for those prophecies to be fulfilled.

The final type of gap left in the text of the Revelation is a failing to give specific places where things will happen. Again this has led to a debate between Brethren authors over the place where Babylon will arise. Some have suggested the plain of Shinar, others Rome, others have argued over the topographical details of Revelation 17:9 compared to the topography of Genesis 11.

Yet after all this has been said there are striking similarities in the ways that the Brethren authors interpret Babylon as the world. Here the work of Stanley Fish is useful. The Brethren are an "interpretive community." Individual Brethren interpreters cannot interpret texts by self-consciously trying to figure out idiosyncratic responses but rather interpretation is a collective and sociological phenomenon bound within the context of the Brethren community. The "right" explanation of Revelation chapters 17–18 in the Brethren movement is the one which the community accepts as "corporately right," that is, the "Community Interpretation." The common link is the call to "come out," whether Babylon be a symbol of the world, or acting in a worldly manner, or the Great Exhibition or a physical city, to be found in such places would be a form of boundary or border transgression and thus lead to ritualized pollution.

Similarly this chapter has shown how paying attention to the *eis*egesis of a religious community may be helpful in viewing the world from their perspective so one can understand something of the pressures the community faced, both from without and from within. Hence, the outline work of Newport can be seen to provide another possible impetus for the further development of the area of *Wirkungsgeschichte* within biblical studies and for a further justification of the primary importance of the reception history of the text in understanding millennial groups.

9

"Babylon" and the Secret Rapture
of the Church

The previous chapters of this book have all been concerned with the identity of Babylon. In chapter 5 it was noted that the Brethren, like the Reformers before them, identified Babylon as the Roman Catholic Church. However, whereas the Reformers saw Babylon as Papal Rome alone, the Brethren understood Rome to be the source of other Babylonian churches through the use of the "mother-daughter" idiom. In chapter 6 the Brethren understanding of the identity of these daughters of Babylon, so called, was explored. Within Brethren exegesis Revelation's Babylon motif was taken as a representation of all corrupt Christendom and none escaped this designation. In both chapters 5 and 6 it was shown that the Brethren adopted the line of interpretation that they did in order to identity the "religious other." Chapter 7 highlighted the way that Brethren authors understood Babylon as a confused, corrupt and heretical understanding of Scripture and doctrine. As such Babylon was identified as the "epistemological other." Finally in chapter 8, Babylon was identified as the world, either through embracing worldly values and engaging in worldly pastimes, or more literally as the ancient kingdom of Babylon *redivivus*. Here Babylon represented the "secular other." It is plain then that the Brethren used the Babylon motif to define themselves through vilifying the "other." The question remains, however, not only of the specific identity of Babylon, but also of the response that should be made towards her. It is argued in this chapter that it is concerning that response that the Brethren line of interpretation breaks substantially new ground. It is argued also that it is on this point that the text can be seen to exert an influence on the reader, rather than the reader reading into the text. Here then, we have an example of *Wirkungsgeschichte* and not simply *Auslegungsgeschichte*.

The variety and range of interpretations held among the group have been explained to some extent through an application of Iser's phenomenological reader-oriented approach to the text and its meanings. There is, however, in contrast to the variety of identities that Babylon has, only one common community response—that is, "come out of her my people" (Rev 18:4).

The Brethren sought to "come out" of Babylon on a number of levels, as though through a series of concentric circles of exegesis, each hermeneutical circle being increasingly sectarian and increasingly exclusive. First, they came out of Babylon insofar as they identified themselves with the Protestant Reformers who had "come out" of Papal Rome in the sixteenth century, then, they came out of the various Protestant denominations to form their own movement. The Brethren also "came out" by defining their own particular doctrinal and ritual beliefs, enabling further reinforcement of the distinction between "insider" and "outsider." Finally they sought to "come out" of the world altogether and have nothing to do with, not only worldly practices and pursuits, but also nothing to do with the physical earth itself. Each time, they "came out," they solidified and consolidated their own identity over and against that which they identified as Babylon.

Babylon was, it will be clear by now, something highly unpleasant. She is clearly an anti-Christian power described throughout Revelation chapters 17–18 as, among other things, a prostitute, an abomination, filthy, hated, desolate, naked, a sorcerer, a drunkard, bloodthirsty, fallen, foul and unclean. She will be eaten, burned, judged, receive plagues of death, famine and fire. Yet in the account of her downfall and destruction it is clear that the church can do nothing to destroy her. On numerous occasions in Revelation the saints are seen as either resisting or destroying their enemies who are all overcome by the saints, either through tribulation resistance, or at the post-tribulation battle of Armageddon (Rev 16:16).[1] Babylon, however, is not destroyed by the church, rather it is the kings of the earth and the beast with its ten horns that turn on the whore and bring God's judgment upon her (Rev 17:16). Faced with such a prospect, the image of Babylon is terrifying indeed. She cannot be overcome by conflict or resistance, the only safety must be to escape from her. For the Brethren, then, the question became one of how to escape, not just spiritually, but physically, from this end-time foe. The answer was simple: they must leave the world.

1. See, e.g., Rev 2:2–6; 7:14; 9:4; 11:11; and 19:14.

BIOLOGICAL RESPONSES TO FEAR

It is a well-established principle in biological and physiological studies that "when a person is thrust in to a dangerous or unpredictable situation, hormones are involved in both the short-term and long-term responses. The short-term reaction [is] called the 'fight or flight response.'"[2]

Freeman uses the example of being confronted by a dangerous animal. He describes the scenario of "being chased by a grizzly bear." During such an encounter "action potentials from your sympathetic nerves would stimulate your adrenal medulla and lead to the release of epinephrine"[3] (also known as adrenaline). Thus fear, it seems, elicits a remarkable and powerful biological change in the human body. Trump and Fagle explain how the emotional feeling of anger can have a profound physiological effect on the body. They describe the story (which is quite possibly just a medical myth or anecdote, but the physiology is reasonable nonetheless), of a doctor "who saved a diabetics life by making him angry." In a medical situation where no drugs or food were available the doctor saved the patient's life by telling the diabetic "to stop complaining, that he was just pretending to be ill." The effect was to make the patient angry. This "anger caused the brain to send signals to the [adrenal] medulla . . . which responded by releasing adrenaline into the blood stream," the adrenaline caused the liver to produce insulin, which converted glycogen into glucose in the blood stream,[4] thus the anger saved his life by increasing the sugar levels in his blood.

Physical stress can cause hormones to be released into the blood having a physiological effect on the body. One cited example is that of the extended stress of the journey of a salmon moving upstream towards the ocean.[5] The strenuous and dangerous journey to the sea is fuelled by stress hormones increasing muscular activity. Thus fear, anger, and stress all effect the human body. Kimball has noted that "we have all heard of heroic deeds accomplished in times of danger or other emergency. The secretion of adrenaline and noradrenaline by the adrenal medulla is an important mechanism for making this possible."[6]

It is possible, particularly for a group who perceive the world to be a threatening and dangerous place and who interpret Scripture literally, that confrontation with a written text describing a bloodthirsty prostitute would

2. Freeman, *Biological Science*, 1082–83.

3. Ibid.

4. Trump and Fagle, *Design for Life*, 261.

5. Freeman, *Biological Science*, 1083.

6. Kimball, *Biology*, 206, 448–49.

provoke the same reaction of fear as confrontation with the grizzly bear above, or that the Great Whore's responsibility for the torment, grief, and killing of the saints would induce the same feelings of anger that doctor arose in the diabetic patient, or indeed that the physical stress or resisting her intoxicating drink and sexual advances would elicit the same physical stress response as that of the salmon above. In each case the "fight-or-flight response" is triggered by a threatening stimuli, and Babylon is indeed one such threatening stimulus.

There are a number of physiological "side effects" to this response, including "significant increase in pulse rate, blood pressure, and oxygen consumption by the brain." This gives the physical feeling of a "rush," and on a more emotional level "strong subjective feelings of anxiety and excitement," and "a state of heightened alertness and increased energy."[7] The more visible responses to a frightening stimulus include "the pupils of the eye dilate and there is a tendency for body hair to stand erect."[8] In relatively hairless humans this is often seen as "gooseflesh." The side effects include "the 'cold sweat' and nausea often induced by a fearful situation."[9]

Such short-term responses to acutely stressful situations are relatively short lived. Once an adrenaline "'rush' has worn off most people feel exhausted and want to rest," but if the stress continues for the long term, through extended periods of "starvation or fasting, prolonged emotional distress, or chronic illness" then the adrenal cortex produces the hormone cortisol which is "found in airline pilots and crew members during long flights, athletes who were training for intense contests, the parents of children undergoing treatment for cancer, and college students who were preparing for final exams."[10] In Brethren readers who read the Bible with deadly seriousness the hormones adrenaline and cortisol, it will be argued here, were released through a reading of Revelation chapters 17–18. Hence biology played some role in the development of the Brethren "secret rapture" theory and was an ingredient in the overall interpretive response to the frightening images found in the text.

PSYCHOLOGICAL RESPONSES TO FEAR

If such physiological reactions are created through responses to physical danger it is not unreasonable to presume that the same physiological

7. Freeman, *Biological Science*, 1082–83.

8. Kimball, *Biology*, 448–49.

9. Freeman, *Biological Science*, 1023.

10. Ibid., 1083.

responses may be created through response to psychological or emotional danger, that is, a perceived or hypothetical threat. In chapter 2 a brief examination of the work of Norman Holland's *Five Readers Reading* (1973) was carried out to shed light on how and why readers interpret texts in the way they do from a psychological perspective.

In particular the second principle of literary experience that Holland identifies in his book is relevant here, that "Defences Must Be Matched."[11] When readers, like the Brethren, interpret terrifying images like the Whore of Babylon texts there must be something in the work that reacts and responds to dangers and perceived threats in the same way that the reader reacts and responds to perceived threats. Individual readers have different defense mechanisms and different forms of verbal, physical and intellectual response in fight or flight situations. Thus in order for the reader to connect fully with the text, the literary characters must to some degree respond to danger in the same way the reader responds to danger. For the Christian Brethren this involved a desire to "come out" of Babylon, a flight or extraction response to the danger.

Holland, asked five readers to interpret William Faulkner's *A Rose for Emily* (1931) and from their different interpretations he identified five archetypal groups. Of these groups three are of particular relevance here.

The reader named "Saul" took particular pleasure from controlling women, describing the mother figure as frightening and terrible.[12] A reader from this "Saul" archetypal group, who had an underlying obsession with being controlled by frightening and terrifying women, would become completely absorbed by Revelation chapters 17–18, where we read of a perverse "mother" figure called the "Mother of Harlots." The grotesque nature of this "mother" would connect with "Saul's" fears and feed his fantasy: his simultaneous loathing and admiration about violent, terrifying "mothers." In particular Revelation 17:6, "I saw the woman drunken with the blood of the saints . . . I wondered with great admiration," would be a text that such a reader would find particularly absorbing. Readers of this archetypal group show "an obsession with control . . . who is big and powerful . . . searching for anything big or vague that might pose a danger . . . [they are] threatened by large sadistic women."[13] It is easy to see how the Great Whore of Revelation could exert a terrifying fascination on a reader like "Saul."

The next archetypal group that is relevant for this study are those which Holland identifies with a reader called "Shep." This group appeared

11. Holland, *Five Readers Reading*, 115–17.

12. Ibid., 79.

13. Ibid., 80.

to read the text in light of their underlying fantasies about violence, killing and blood, and the dangers of personal injury, of being watched by "big-brother," and of paranoia. Holland notes that many of Shep's interpretations "were hostile . . . of ripping and tearing apart"[14] and that "he had to remind himself that he was not under attack . . . like a small animal, he perceived reality in terms of threat."[15] Such a reader, in projecting his own paranoid fantasies about being under attack by a superhuman character, will find the imagery of Revelation chapters 17–18 absorbing to the point where they may identify themselves with those people who have been killed by Babylon and had their blood drunk. Holland observes that "Shep" felt threatened by "mother" type characters whom he believes to control him and cause him pain, anger and resentment for some type of sexual gratification.[16] A reader like "Shep" would easily identify with the kings of the earth who resent and abhor the "mother of harlots" even though they commit fornication with her (Rev 17:16; cf. Rev 18:3b). Readers from this group also simultaneously hate yet sexualize any perceived threat.[17] Such a reader would be easily absorbed by the image of the Whore of Babylon, allowing the fantasy of the text to be transformed into the fantasy of the reader.

The archetypal group represented by a student known as "Sebastian," would deal with threatening images by flight or denial, or alternatively he would sexualize a threatening image, particularly when interpreting aggressive material.[18] He often felt out of control and would often identify the controller as a "sexually desirable woman."[19] He wanted to avoid situations that could result in "massive, overpowering violence,"[20] and he needed to escape any kind of trap.[21] It is not an unfeasibly large assumption to make that a reader from this archetypal group would, upon reading of an aggressive and sexual prostitute called Babylon, be absorbed by the call of Revelation 18:4, "come out," as such an exiting would be an escape and an avoidance of the dangerous trap.

14. Ibid., 82.
15. Ibid.
16. Ibid., 85.
17. Ibid., 87.
18. Ibid., 91.
19. Ibid., 93.
20. Ibid., 97.
21. Ibid., 100.

THE DEVELOPMENT OF BRETHREN RAPTURE THEORY

If the biological and psychological "flight" response to danger (whether real or just perceived), is taken to its absolute extreme in the context of this book what would that mean? It would mean that the Brethren would want not just to flee the immediate vicinity of Babylon (in her religious, epistemological and secular forms), but would want to fly physically as far away as possible. They would want to leave the world entirely, to escape completely, to be taken out of "Babylon" altogether. And the most extreme way that this could be realized is through a "rapture" or taking up of the saints to heaven. Nebeker has noted,

> Political, ecclesiastical and theological factors notwithstanding, personal temperament, emotional conflicts and psychopathologies may also serve as the impulses behind one's eschatological expectations . . . some observers of Darby have noted that his life reflected a certain psychological complexity. One might suspect that the traumas of life and other psychological factors lent expression to the otherworldliness of his hope.[22]

Darby is widely regarded among millennial and apocalyptic historical scholars as being one of the key figures in the development of the doctrine of the "rapture of the church." Although Nebeker suggests that "Darby, from the best historical evidence . . . appears to be the principle architect of . . . the pretribulational rapture,"[23] it is perhaps better to take a more conservative stance and state, as does Coad, that "Darby had adopted the doctrine of 'the Secret Rapture of the Saints.'"[24] For certain Darby was a major player, perhaps *the* major player in the formulation, refinement and propagation of the doctrine, but it was by no means his original idea. Before some of the influences on Darby *vis-à-vis* Brethren rapture theory are examined, a definition of rapture theory must be proposed.

In chapter 4 of this book the Brethren concept of the "Secret Rapture of the Church" was explained in some detail as essentially the removal or translation of the saints on earth to heaven. Nebeker uses the Pauline analogy of the church as Christ's bride to define the rapture, and uses the phrase "nuptial mysticism" to refer to the union between the church and Christ at the rapture: "When Christians were conformed into the likeness of Christ's heavenly glory . . . the nearness of the rapture, by virtue of its pretribulational sequence, lent urgency to one's yearnings for ultimate union with

22. Nebeker, "Ecstasy of Perfected Love," 71–71.

23. Ibid., 69.

24. Coad, *Prophetic Developments*, 129.

Christ."[25] Thus in a sense it could be said that "rapture serves as the entryway into the consummation of love between Christ and His Church in the heavenlies."[26] Some historical background to how the rapture theory entered into the Brethren movement was given earlier in chapter 4, but exactly how the Brethren took that idea and developed a peculiarly and particularly nuanced rapture doctrine is summed up well by Coad. The Second Advent would take place in two stages: first there would be a quiet

> appearance—the "presence"—of Christ, when all true Christians, the true church, would be removed from the earth. This was the "rapture of the saints" . . . [only then] would Antichrist arise. His rule would be brought to an end by the second stage of the Advent—the public "appearing" of Christ [and the saints] in Glory.[27]

The divergence from a general "rapture theory" to a particularly Brethren "secret rapture theory" is essentially found in the timing of the rapture. For those who adhere to a single rapture doctrine, the saints remain on earth during the tribulation at the end of which Christ appears, destroys Babylon and the antichrist, then the saints are raptured. However the Brethren secret rapture theory deviates from this view insofar as Christ appears in secret and takes the true saints from the earth. This first stage of the second coming Darby and Kelly refer to as the *parousia* or "the coming." Only after that point is Babylon destroyed, while the saints are in the air with Christ. Some time after either three and a half or perhaps seven years the second stage of the second coming occurs. Darby and Kelly refer to this as the *epiphaneia*, or "the appearing."[28]

The first influence on the development of Brethren rapture theory was that of the Jansenists. The Jansenists were a partisan Catholic sect, led by Cornelius Jansen, (1585–1638), Bishop of Ypres, who were condemned by Pope Innocent X in 1653 for believing a Calvinistic doctrine of predestination and a Semipelagian interpretation of the doctrine of grace. The group rebelled against the anathema and attempted to remain a distinct sect *intra muros* of the Catholic Church, however, persistent condemnation from Rome combined with disapproval from Louis XIV, and persecution during the French Revolution caused the group to diminish greatly.

25. Nebeker, "Ecstasy of Perfected Love," 84.

26. Ibid., 69.

27. Coad, *Prophetic Developments*, 130.

28. Darby, "Appearing, Manifestation and Presence," 151–53; Also Darby, "Rapture of the Saints," 180. "The rapture of the saints before the appearing of Christ." Kelly, "Answers to Questions," *BT*, 16.222.

While it is not clear whether earlier forms of Jansenism had developed a doctrine of the "rapture" it is the case that they were to do so by the mid-nineteenth century when Darby arrived in Paris and came into contact with Jansenists, in particular, the congregation of the Sisters of St. Martha and the group *La Petite Eglise*. Much has been made of this visit to Paris in early 1830. On this trip Darby encountered "a Jansenist community that had been engaged in a vigorous debate about the timing of the rapture."[29] From within the group two major views contended for dominance. Agier (1748–1823) and some of the Jansenists, influenced by the earlier work of the Jesuits Ribera and Lacunza, had argued for a one-stage rapture. Whereas the Jansenist group *La Petite Eglise* and the Dominican writer Bernard Lambert (1738–1813) "argued that Christ's coming must occur in two stages, with an initial gathering of believers preceding Christ's coming to inaugurate the millennium."[30] Although Darby could not have personally come into contact with Lambert, who died in 1813, he would have come into contact with his circle who would have promulgated his view that the "millennial reign of the saints is yet to come—to be introduced by the personal advent of Christ, the destruction of Antichrist with his apostate church and Babylon."[31] What is certain is that Darby would have been aware of both of these Jansenist views, as Brethren Hebraic scholar Tregelles noted: "Lambert and Agier were the writers Mr. J. N. Darby studied earnestly before he left the Church of England. I remember his speaking much about them in 1835."[32]

The next significant influence on the formation of Darby's, and thus Brethren, rapture doctrine, came through contact with Scottish Presbyterian secessionist Edward Irving. Grass has noted that an "early formulation of the concept of the rapture of the believers makes its appearance" in Irving's work,[33] and Stunt has noted that there is no doubt "that at some stage in 1827 or 1828 he [Darby] read Irving's translation of *La Venida del Mesias en Gloria y magestad*."[34] The reading of the English version of *La Venida* would have meant for sure that Darby was familiar with Lacunza's one-stage rapture hypothesis. However, familiarity with a hypothesis and adoption of that

29. Gribben and Stunt, *Prisoners of Hope?*, 13.

30. Ibid., 13.

31. Lambert, in Froom, *Prophetic Faith*, 3.325.

32. Tregelles, quoted in Stunt, "Influences in the Early Development of J. N. Darby," 62–63. Stunt notes here that "Lambert expects the [rapture] event to be in two stages and foresees an immediate coming . . . when Christ will first gather his saints," whereas "by 1818 Agier had abandoned a two-stage rapture hypothesis."

33. Grass, "Edward Irving," 101.

34. Stunt, "Influences in the Early Development of J. N. Darby," 57.

hypothesis are entirely different things, and although it has been suggested by some that Darby "took" his pretribulational rapture view from Irving (or someone in "Irving's circle") it must be remembered that Irving's rapture theory was based on a one-stage return whereas Darby's rapture theory was based on a two-stage return. As Burnham has astutely noted: "a comparison of the eschatological systems of Darby and Irving yields far more differences than similarities."[35]

Another significant difference between Darby and Irving's rapture theories is based on the overall timing of the rapture. Darby, and the Brethren, it will be clear by now, were futurists, whereas Irving, through his contact with Frere,[36] understood the rapture from a historicist hermeneutical stance.[37] The Irvingite historicist stance in relation to the rapture can be seen in the work of the prominent Irvingite Robert Baxter who believed the 14th of July 1835 to be the date of "the rapture or translation of believers before the Second Coming, but which Catholic Apostolics afterwards referred to [as] the, 'Separation of the Apostles.'"[38] As such Darby cannot have taken his rapture doctrine from Irving as the specifics differ too greatly. The very most one can conclude is that Darby was aware of Lacunza, Agier and Irving's one-stage rapture hypothesis and rejected it in favor of his own development of Lambert's two-stage rapture hypothesis.

The importance of the Powerscourt and Albury conferences as a melting pot for the dissemination and formulation of prophetic ideas cannot be undermined. As noted in chapter 4 above, Powerscourt was the place where Darby first came into contact with Irving,

> though the precise date remains uncertain, it appears that at some point between the 1832 and 1833 Powerscourt conferences Darby began to promote his unique view of the pretribulational rapture of the church . . . by the third Powerscourt conference,

35. Burnham, *Story of Conflict*, 124.

36. James H. Frere, who occupied a "leading place" among the Historicist School of interpreters of the Apocalypse, along with Edward Irving and Lewis Way formed the Society for the Investigation of Prophecy in June 1826. See Froom, *Prophetic Faith*, 3.499. They were all familiar with Lacunza's *La Venida*, and the one-stage rapture hypothesis, as Way, who was minister of the English Church in Paris in the 1820s, had read the Jansenist Agier's French translation of that book, See Gribben and Stunt, *Prisoners of Hope?*, 64, and Way in his monthly publication, the *Gallican Watchman*, draws attention to "a society of one hundred Jansenist women in Paris" who shared "an indubitable persuasion of Christ's second coming to establish his personal reign on earth." Way, in Froom, *Prophetic Faith*, 3.425.

37. See ch. 1 above for definitions.

38. Grass, "Edward Irving," 116.

he had come fully to acknowledge a futurist perspective which included the pretribulational rapture of the church.[39]

Darby's prominence at these conferences, combined with his "dominant personality and masterful will,"[40] would certainly have meant that his own version of the rapture, that is a two-stage rapture beginning with a secret pretribulation *parousia* followed by a visible post tribulation *epiphaneia*, would have been promulgated and propagated successfully and forcefully.

Later on in the year 1830, Darby was yet again exposed to the two-stage rapture hypothesis that he had first come across in the *La Petite Eglise* and the work of Lambert, when he, along with Wigram, travelled to Row (now Rhu) in Scotland to witness the controversial prophecies of Margaret MacDonald. MacDonald and her brothers, like the Irvingites, would prophecy utterances in "tongues" or *glossolia* which would be followed by interpretations. They were presided over by John McLeod Campbell who was originally the Church of Scotland minister in Row, but in 1830 was ejected from the Establishment for heresy.[41] Darby described Campbell as "a very estimable person" but overall he was very unimpressed with the exercise of prophetic tongues. He draws an analogy to the meetings in Row and the Babel of Genesis 11 (which, for course, Darby links to Babylon),[42] writing:

> God had confounded their pride . . . There was a pretended interpretation . . . one, if not more, of the texts was quoted wrongly . . . The excitement was great, so that, though not particularly an excitable person, he [Darby refers here to himself] felt its effects very strongly. It did not certainly approve itself to his [Darby's] judgment . . . It was too much of a scene . . . delusion . . . female vanity, and very distinct worldliness . . . the tongues . . . have allied themselves with other influences suited to the world.[43]

Regardless of Darby's views on the authenticity of MacDonald's prophecies, they were, nonetheless, widely circulated at the time, and were undoubtedly influential on the development of Irving's ecclesiology in particular the Irvingite practice of *glossolia*.

It is highly unlikely though that MacDonald or Campbell's rapture theory played any significant role in the development of Darby's two-stage secret rapture theory. In addition to Darby's dismissal of the authenticity

39. Burnham, *Story of Conflict*, 122.

40. Ibid., 43.

41. Froom, *Prophetic Faith*, 3.595.

42. See ch. 7 above.

43. Darby, "Irrationalism of Infidelity," 447–50.

of the prophecy, Campbell clearly differed to Darby on the details of the rapture. In 1830, the year that Darby and Wigram visited Row, Campbell based many of his sermons on "the hour of his judgment has come . . . Fallen is Babylon the Great" (Rev 14:7–8), thus locating the fall of Babylon in the present before the rapture of the saints, whereas, quite importantly, as we shall see in the remainder of his chapter, the timing of Darby's rapture is crucially placed *before* the fall of Babylon.[44] In addition to this, although some, such as MacPherson have suggested that the MacDonald home was where Darby learned this teaching,[45] Stunt has convincingly argued that MacDonald's prophecy "is so very confused that it hardly provides a basis for constructing a coherent eschatology," and there is no evidence at all from contemporary sources that she "proclaimed a new doctrine."[46] Indeed, such prophecies were perceived by Darby as emanating from Babylon.

By the middle of the nineteenth century many Christians had come to expect and wait for some kind of rapture event. Darby's two-stage rapture theory, with its initial secret rapture removing the saints before the tribulation, followed by a second appearing of Christ and the saints, was gaining wide spread support as the nascent Brethren movement itself was growing. Those outside the Brethren movement would also have been aware of a one-stage rapture theory through the work of Irving, Frere and Way. The question that remains to be answered is "why did such a theory explode in French and English exegesis at that time?"

On one level the answer is clearly down to the social, political and religious unrest of the time, the details of which have been noted already above. Events such as the French Revolution, cholera epidemics, widespread war and the like were perceived as real and immediate dangers to everyday people at the start of the nineteenth century. Such threats must clearly be understood in light of the biological and physiological processes described earlier on in this chapter. As such, rapture theory provides a physical escape mechanism from this dangerous world wrapped up in religious and biblical language. As Nebeker has noted, the rapture may be seen as "the aesthetic attraction that heavenly imagery provides for those living in tumultuous social contexts, or even in states of lasting emotional deprivation."[47] For

44. In this respect excommunicated Brethren author Newton was closer to the one-stage rapture doctrine of Campbell, Irving, Agier, and Lacunza, in that he too expected the fall of Babylon to be before the rapture of the saints. See, e.g., Newton, *Thoughts on the Apocalypse*, 295–300. Also Newton, *Babylon*, vii; Newton, *Harlot of Babylon*, 12.

45. MacPherson, *Rapture Plot*, 133–38.

46. Stunt, "Tribulation of Controversy," 93.

47. Nebeker, "Ecstasy of Perfected Love," 71.

the Brethren authors such as Darby, who employed such a highly literalistic interpretation of Scripture, the threat of some apocalyptical enemy such as Babylon, would be just as real as the more immediate threats of revolution, war and cholera, and would thus evoke the same biological and psychological responses. It has been noted that "Darby's pretribulational rapture theory was nothing more than an acute form of escapism,"[48] a statement which is truer in a more literal sense than the author who made that claim originally intended, for tribulation escapism, is as much of an entirely valid and reasonable reaction to the apocalyptic imagery of Revelation as the physical escapism of a person fleeing from a dangerous confrontation with a grizzly bear through fear.

THE *WIRKUNGSGESCHICHTE* OF THE "WHORE OF BABYLON" IN THE FORMATION OF BRETHREN RAPTURE THEORY

Darby

It has already been demonstrated that Darby distinguishes between a primary *parousia* or "coming" and a secondary *epiphaneia* or "appearing." The question to be answered here is that of the extent to which and ways in which the Whore of Babylon motif influenced his development of the Brethren secret rapture of the church doctrine. The question is not an idle one given the truly phenomenal importance of "Rapture Culture" in the contemporary world, particularly, perhaps in the United States.[49]

The destruction of Babylon plays an important role in the timing of Darby's twofold rapture theory. The secret *parousia* of Christ occurs, and the saints are raptured, crucially, before Babylon is judged and destroyed. In general terms the whole of Darby's hermeneutical approach to Revelation is futurist insofar as he states that: "In the third part, we have that which takes place after the church has been removed (chapters 4–22)."[50] More specifically, in commenting on Revelation 18:4–6, Darby informs us that when the voice from heaven cries "come out of Babylon . . . this warning, though placed in the account *after* the judgment of Babel, is addressed to the saints *before* the judgment [of Babylon]."[51] Here Darby is stating that although the physical geographical entity of Babylon has already been judged according

48. Ibid., 70.
49. See Frykholm, *Rapture Culture.*
50. Darby, "Notes on the Revelation," 126.
51. Darby, "On the Apocalypse," 536, my own italics.

to the Genesis account, the apocalyptic Babylon will not be judged until after the *parousia* when the saints have left the earth. The distinguishing between Old Testament forms of Babylon, destroyed in the historical past, and the destruction of the apocalyptic Babylon to be destroyed in the future, is continued when Darby turns to the Babylonian empire of the book of Daniel and states that "the times of the Gentiles began in Babylon . . . The times of the Gentiles [i.e., the Babylonian kingdom] will not end at the same time with the church, but go on a little *after* we are caught up."[52] In both cases Darby describes the past destructions of Babylon, both in Genesis as the Tower of Babel, and Daniel as Nebuchadnezzar's kingdom, and goes on to conclude that the final destruction of Babylon will occur post-rapture, when the saints will have been gathered into the sky with Christ, safe from her bloodthirsty and pernicious threats.

He continues with this line of interpretation when he writes that the judgment and destruction of the Apocalyptic Babylon, which occurs at the hand of the beast and the ten kings, is restrained for the moment by "God . . . [who] holds the bridle till the church is gathered,"[53] after which point Babylon is destroyed and the tribulation begins. The judging of Babylon is not an event that should cause the believer to be afraid or worried, on the contrary it is something that should be looked forward to with great expectation, because the eschatological hope of the true church is that they will have quitted the earth *before* Babylon is judged. Thus Darby writes that for the Brethren their "hope is, the coming of the Lord to take the saints, already called, into glory with Himself . . . [then] the nominal church, not members of Christ, will be spued out of His mouth: Babylon judged . . . and glory for the church."[54]

This first stage of the rapture process can be understood as Darby's flight response to danger. The overall impression that one gets from his compiled works is that here is a reader who adheres to a highly literalistic interpretation of Scripture. Darby would, upon reading about such destruction,

52. Darby, "On the Gospel according to John," 360. N.B., again my italics.

53. Darby, "Fragmentary Thoughts," 344.

54. Darby, *Letters of J.N.D.*, 2.361. The sequence of an initial rapture before the destruction of Babylon can also be seen in Darby, "Progress of Democratic Power," 510–11; Darby, "On the Apocalypse," 534–35. "Hence it is finished—Nothing remains but the coming of the Son of man . . . this book shews us also the end of all things . . . the rapture . . . blessing is on high, judgment below." Darby, "Meditations on the Acts of the Apostles," 492–94. "The rapture of the Saints to be with Jesus . . . God gathers the joint heirs with Christ, who are not of this world . . . they will reign with Him." Darby, "Character of Office," 142–43. The Church belongs to "the heavenlies . . . Christ who is our life shall appear." Darby, "Sketch of Joshua," 512, "Rome is Babylon thus viewed. The Church of God is heavenly and we Christians must have heavenly things."

sin and judgment to be imminently served up to Babylon, understand this in literal terms, as a dangerous and unpredictable situation. On a biological level, Darby would unconsciously respond to such a text by his adrenal medulla releasing adrenal into his body causing a heightened state of alertness, fear, stress, anger, anxiety and nausea. Developing a belief that he and his Brethren would fly away from the earth to the safety of their Lord in the sky, in order to escape Babylon, can be seen simply as the most appropriate physical response to a text which describes such a dangerous entity.

The second stage of Darby's two-stage rapture theory is the visible *epiphaneia* of Christ with his saints, which occurs, significantly, after Babylon has been judged and destroyed. Thus in commenting on Revelation 19, that is the chapter that comes chronologically immediately after chapters 17 and 18, and the marriage of the Lamb to his wife the church, Darby stresses that this apocalyptic nuptial union occurs "after the judgment of Babylon." The Church "may be said to be espoused or destined for him, but the marriage is not yet come. This takes place on being united to Him in that day when He shall appear in His glory, when He calls them up into the air."[55] The chronological sequence can be seen further when Darby writes that first there is "the complete pulling to pieces of Babylon. She is destroyed . . . [by the] different nations," then next, "the Lamb overcomes them, but you have saints coming with Him."[56] Thus the second stage of the rapture, the *epiphaneia*, is a returning to the earth of Christ newly married to his bride the church, after Babylon's destruction, to destroy the beast, the false prophet and the kings of the earth.

Stage two of the rapture can be understood as Darby's psychological responses to the Whore of Babylon. On this level the text can be seen to have absorbed Darby's imagination because the author of Revelation has reacted and responded to the threat of the world around him in the same way that Darby responds and reacts to danger and perceived threats, that is their "defences have been matched."[57]

The text informs us that the dangerous character of Babylon has been destroyed in a most horrific way, she has been stripped, burnt and eaten. It is possible that Darby fits into the category of archetypal reader that Holland

55. Darby, "Scriptural Criticisms," 18.

56. Darby, "Further Notes on the Revelation," 154. Further examples of the second stage of the rapture, after the destruction of Babylon, that is the, *epiphaneia*, the visible return of Christ with the saints, can be seen in Darby, "Thoughts on Isaiah," 339; Darby, "Psalm 93," 162, "Babylon, the Mother of Harlots . . . the Lord coming in judgment . . . we shall be caught up before He comes, and when He comes to reign we come with Him to reign."

57. Holland, *Five Readers Reading*, 115.

identifies as "Saul" whose unconscious responses to danger involve feelings of unhappiness from "father's absence,"[58] feelings that mother figures are "frightening [and] terrible,"[59] and an expectation of "threat from a large sadistic person, most likely a woman."[60] If he could not match or overcome the woman, "he would avoid the whole situation, physically or psychically, and look for a world of safe precision elsewhere."[61] These feelings can be clearly seen in Darby's writings about Babylon. His unhappiness about Jesus' absence from the church can only change when the church rises to meet him for the heavenly marriage, after the large sadistic whore has been avoided by leaving the world which she inhabits.

Darby's exegesis of this text also has some similarities with the archetypal reader "Shep." This reader coped with the world's dangers in a way remarkably similar to how Darby copes with the danger from Babylon. When confronted with danger, usually a sexualized mother figure,[62] Shep "either hid or he fled to a point from which he could fight."[63] We have just seen Darby's responses to the Mother of Harlots. First of all he hides, through a secret rapture, which will not be seen by those outside of the Brethren, then after Babylon is destroyed, an advantageous point from which he could fight arises, thus he, with his Brethren and Christ return to fight against the beast, the false prophet and the kings of the earth.

Kelly

Like Darby, Kelly also believed that there would be a two-stage rapture and differentiated between a primary *parousia* and a secondary *epiphaneia*. The first stage of the rapture is for Kelly an event that should provide comfort and reassurance to those who, upon reading about the dangerous and threatening Whore, feel a sense of anxiety or worry. He writes,

> In the midst of such a dreary future, what a comfort that we shall be with Him then! You, if you love the Lord, will be with Him. . . . It will not then be a question of gathering His people to Himself. Not a hint of such a removal is given in this context.

58. Ibid., 78.
59. Ibid., 80.
60. Ibid.
61. Ibid.
62. Ibid., 85.
63. Ibid., 82.

The faithful are *already* with Him. They had been therefore
caught up to Him before.[64]

Although Babylon is an object "of judgment . . . the great harlot . . .
the Lord is leading His own to expect their removal to heaven to meet the
Bridegroom."[65] Those who belong to God will be safe in the arms of the
heavenly husband while Babylon is being judged. He reiterates this removal
from danger when he writes, "The heavenly saints will be taken away before the judgment falls upon Babylon. They are not referred to in that word
'Come out of her, my people.'"[66] The Brethren will not be on the earth when
the time of danger reaches its zenith.

Showing an awareness of Irving's one-stage rapture hypothesis, which
was itself a development of Lacunza and Agier's eschatology, Kelly writes
that Babylon will be judged in the future, only *after* "the translation of the
heavenly saints found in Him [are] caught up to the throne of God . . . the
saints can be caught up and thus seen mystically in Him."[67] This contrasts
clearly with a one-stage rapture theory in which Babylon is judged and destroyed, *and then* the true church will be gathered out of the earth to meet
the Lord in heaven.

Again, this first stage of the Brethren rapture theory, can be seen as the
biological response to a physical threat. Kelly, like Darby reads Scripture in
a highly literalistic way. The threat of Babylon is a real and physical threat,
and as she cannot be overcome by the church, that is, as a fight response
would fail, then the only physical option left to maintain safety is the flight
response.

Kelly may have felt the emotional rush associated with adrenaline preparing the body to react to a dangerous situation, his writings clearly show
that he experienced strong subjective feelings of anxiety and excitement
towards such a threat, and believing that the imminent future destruction
of Babylon could only be avoided by flight, developed the doctrine of the
secret rapture as a coping strategy to the text.

The second stage of the rapture for Kelly involved a visible return
of Christ to the earth, with his saints, to judge and destroy the remaining
powers of evil and wickedness. Kelly writes: "The judgment of Babylon

---

64. Kelly, *Babylon and the Beast*, 12.

65. Kelly, *Prospects of the World*, 56–58.

66. Kelly, *Lectures on the Book of Revelation*, 387.

67. Kelly, "Catholic Apostolic Body," *BT*, 18.124–36. For further examples of Kel-
ly's first stage of the rapture sequence before Babylon's judgment, see also Kelly, *Lectures
Introductory . . . Acts*, 559; Kelly, "The Coming," in *Three Prophetic Gems*, 45; Kelly,
"Christian Hope," 366.

will involve in it the humiliation and punishment of all the different parts of professing Christendom . . . just before Christ appears. The downfall of Babylon is just before He comes for the judgment of the world . . . before the brightness or appearing of the Lord's coming."[68]

Kelly distinguishes between the hidden and revealed aspects of the rapture. He writes of the difference between the manifestation which "distinctly calls for 'every eye' to see it," and the rapture which "excludes every eye." There will be a gathering "into the air to meet Him . . . out of the vision of those on the earth," then, after those hidden events preceding the destruction of the Great Whore, the visible events may occur: "The final judgment on earth of Babylon . . . Only then is the visible display of the Lord and of the glorified saints who follow Him out of the opened heavens."[69]

Thus the first stage of the rapture, which is hidden and secret precedes the destruction of Babylon, but Kelly asks the question "What follows the kings' destruction of Babylon?" He answers: "'These shall make war with the Lamb.'. . The saints then come from heaven, being with the Lamb when the conflict arrives . . . being changed, they are to be forever with the Lord and thus follow Him out of heaven."[70] Thus although the saints do not fight against Babylon, there is a role for them to fight against the remaining coalition of evil that succeeds Babylon. Of the Brethren's role in judging and destroying, Kelly writes that "Babylon's fall . . . [is] before the Lord appears from heaven followed by the glorified saints . . . to execute the closing judgment and to bring in the millennial reign."[71]

This description of a second stage of the rapture reveals something of Kelly's psychological responses to reading Revelation chapters 17–18. This text would be of particular significance to Kelly as he responds and reacts to the danger and threat of Babylon in the same way that the author, John, responds and reacts to Babylon. Kelly and John of Patmos' defense mechanisms have been matched. Kelly's archetypal reading style is the same as Holland's reader "Shep," insofar as there is a dual response to the sexualized mother figure. The similarities are remarkable: Shep hides from her, and Kelly "excludes every eye" when he escapes her. Shep extracts himself from danger to a place from which he can fight, and Kelly visibly follows the Lord out of heaven to fight in the Lamb's army. Yet Kelly also demonstrates

68. Kelly, "Micah," in *Minor Prophets*, 256–57.

69. Kelly, "Heavenly Hope," in *Three Prophetic Gems*, 59.

70. Kelly, "The Coming," in *Three Prophetic Gems*, 75.

71. Kelly, "Catholic Apostolic Body," *BT*, 18.27–44. Further examples of the second stage of Kelly's rapture theory, the *epiphaneia* or "appearing" with the saints after Babylon's destruction, can be seen in Kelly, *Christ for the Saint*, 19–21; and Kelly, *Purpose of God*, 41–42.

similarities with the archetypal reader group Holland identifies as "Saul": Saul desires that the polluted devil woman be "treated aggressively lest she prove to be destructively sexual,"[72] while Kelly, after the Whore's destruction, desires to be involved in "conflict" and to "execute the closing judgment."[73] There is also something of the "Sam" archetypal response to Babylon in Kelly's desire to see the judgment of Babylon expressed as the simultaneous "humiliation and punishment of all the different parts of professing Christendom."[74] Holland writes that a reader like Sam has a defense mechanism based around "wishes to take in or get out, taking in passively or getting out actively."[75] While passivity is somewhat synonymous with humiliation, Sam's simultaneous desire to "assert power and gratify drives to express his manliness,"[76] particularly with regards to a dangerous sexual woman, is synonymous with Kelly's description of the concurrent humiliation and punishment of the Great Whore.

Trotter

William Trotter, whom Coad describes as "Darby's own follower," did indeed follow in Darby's footsteps when it came to the newly emerging, uniquely Brethren, two-stage rapture hypothesis. Trotter adamantly believed that before Babylon could be judged and destroyed the Brethren must evacuate the earth. He writes:

> From this vast system . . . the saints of God are called to withdraw. "Come out of her, my people" . . . the true Church [is] . . . translated to its home and dwelling place in heaven [whereas] the false professing body will still be found in unhallowed alliance with the wealth and greatness of this world.[77]

However we see some divergence here from Darby's other major disciple, Kelly, in that it will have been noted above that Kelly doesn't consider the call to "come out" to be a call to the saints to be raptured literally out of the earth (although he does think that there will be a rapture, he doesn't use Revelation 18:4 to argue for it), whereas Trotter clearly does think that "come out" is a call to be raptured.

72. Holland, *Five Readers Reading*, 338–39.
73. Kelly, "Catholic Apostolic Body," *BT*, 18.27–44.
74. Kelly, "Micah," in *Lectures Introductory . . . Minor Prophets*, 256–57.
75. Holland, 75.
76. Ibid.
77. Trotter, "Recapitulation," 428.

This rapture is in itself the precursor to Babylon's judgment, that is, she cannot be destroyed until the true saints have been "changed at Christ's coming, and with the departed saints caught up to meet the Lord in the air. Judgment will afterwards fall on the false professing body which will be left on earth [mystic Babylon]."[78] This rapture event then paves the way for Babylon's terrible and sudden demise, yet all the time this is unfolding there is no risk or danger to the Brethren as they are safe with Christ. He writes,

> The translation of the Church to heaven, at the descent of the Lord Jesus into the air . . . The removal of the true Church may be immediately followed by this judgment on the false one [i.e., Babylon] . . . The only place in which the Church is seen from Rev. 4: 1 to Rev. 19: 14, is in heaven.[79]

However, for all the confidence and certainty that Darby and Kelly show towards the details of the rapture, Trotter does retain a little hesitance and uncertainty as to the exact details. He writes, "The doom of Babylon the Great . . . The crisis hastens . . . Where to place the translation of the church to meet her Lord, we know not. It may be the very first stage of the crisis. Perhaps. It will be so. Are we ready for it?"[80]

What Trotter is clear on is that for the duration of Babylon's destruction and judgment, the Brethren will not be on the earth, they will be out of harm's way, awaiting the heavenly union and observing events on the earth with great interest. We read: "During this period, the true Church is in heaven . . . deeply interested in the action which takes place on earth . . . When Babylon's overthrow has taken place, the marriage of the Lamb is celebrated in heaven."[81]

Trotter's views on the first stage of the rapture process, of an initial exiting from the world to maintain a safe distance from Babylon's destruction, can be understood simply as a physical flight response to a real and imminent danger. To a reader like Trotter, for whom Scripture must be literally fulfilled, the image of Babylon would be terrifying indeed, and promote feelings of anxiety and stress, as well as feelings of fear and a desire to escape to safety. The only way to escape the threat and danger of Babylon is through flight, that short term, adrenaline-fuelled response to danger, and for Trotter, flight means rapture, flying (quite literally in the context of 1 Thess 4:16–17) into the arms of Jesus.

---

78. Trotter, "Christ and the Church," 119.

79. Trotter, "Apocalyptic Interpretation," 356.

80. Trotter, "Predicted Corruption of Christianity," 209.

81. Trotter, "Apocalyptic Interpretation," 360.

The second stage of the Brethren two-stage rapture process begins, for Trotter, after "He has thus taken away the true Church." At this point we have "the doom of Babylon," after which stage two begins: "He will descend, accompanied or followed by His glorified saints, to execute the judgments . . . which will shortly burst upon an astonished and affrighted world."[82] Thus, although the saints do not destroy Babylon, they do on the second stage of the rapture return with Christ to destroy the kings of the earth, the beast and the false prophet at the post-tribulation battle of Armageddon. Such apocalyptic enemies can be overcome by the church, therefore rather than promoting a flight response, a similar biological process would promote a fight response. The dual flight-fight responses can be seen in the two-stage rapture process in Trotter's writings. The first stage *parousia* elicits a flight response to avoid a confrontation with Babylon, whereas the second stage *epiphaneia* elicits a fight response, whereby the Brethren actually engage in conflict with the coalition of evil. Trotter writes, "The apostle distinguishes between the *parousia* (coming) of Christ, when the saints, whether raised or changed, shall be translated to meet Him in the air, and the *epiphaneia* of His coming, by which the man of sin is to be destroyed."[83] A supernatural transformation or changing has occurred at some point between stage one and stage two of the rapture process which enables the Brethren to fully engage in the apocalyptical battle.

Eminent psychologist C. G. Jung (1875–1961) notes that when faced with all the "horrid" images in the book of Revelation, and the "drastic events" also contained in that book "man's terrified consciousness quite understandably looks round for a mountain of refuge, an island of peace and safety,"[84] and it is to the heavens, united with Christ, that Trotter turns for such solace. Jung describes the Whore of Babylon as a symbol which can have "several aspects of meaning and can therefore be interpreted in different ways."[85] Jung is, of course, most concerned with the psychological effect of Babylon. The psychological effect that the Whore of Babylon text has on Trotter is similar to that of Darby and Kelly and includes personifying the enemy as an overtly sexual mother figure, which must be simultaneously hidden from and escaped from in order to recoup and fight from a place of strength, combined with a simultaneous sadness at the heavenly groom's absence coupled with a fear of a large sadistic woman. Jung describes such

82. Trotter, "Approaching Judgments," 35.

83. Trotter, "Ecclesiastical Corruption," 241. See further: Trotter, "Last Days of Gentile Supremacy," 26; and Trotter, "Church Removed Before the Apocalyptic Judgments," 275–92.

84. Jung, *Answer to Job*, 136.

85. Ibid., 138–39.

characters as Babylon in terms of the author's (*vis-à-vis* reader-response criticism, the reader's) own "dark counterpart, i.e. the Shadow,"[86] a primitive part of the subconscious ego which symbolizes both the instinct for survival and desire for sexual reproduction. A reader who belongs to the same archetypal reading group as Holland's "Shep" would find the "Shadow" side of their ego coming to the surface as they read about the Great Whore and feel threatened by a "mother" type figure who is believed to exert control, cause pain, anger, and resentment in return for some type of sexual gratification.[87] It is perhaps to this archetypal reading group that Totter belongs.

Wolston

Wolston takes up the Brethren two-stage rapture hypothesis in his apocalyptic writings but his focus is much more firmly placed on the first stage of the doctrine, that is, the secret rapture, which will remove the Brethren from the earth, so as to avoid the danger and destruction that the judgment of Babylon poses. In a lecture given on the Second Coming of Christ he turns to Revelation chapter 18, and interprets the passage in terms of those who are and those who are not raptured, that is, those who do and those who do not escape Babylon's downfall. We read of

> the fall of Babylon . . . if any of you are unsaved, and want to know what you are hastening on to, I recommend you, without delay, to read these chapters [i.e., Rev 17–18] . . . you will have a very fair idea of what your portion is to be, if not caught up at the rapture. If the Lord Jesus came now, if the true saints were called up at this moment into glory, I will tell you what you would have to face immediately thereafter.[88]

The clearest answer to what will happen after the initial secret rapture of the saints is found in another publication, this time on the book of Daniel, in which Wolston states "you will find Babylon is judged in Revelation 18 . . . when the Church has been taken away."[89] Once again the development of such a theory must be viewed in light of the biological and psychological reactions that a literalistic reading of the Revelation would promote. Wolston is clearly reacting according to a physiological flight response to danger, and even goes so far as using the threat of such danger to warn those

86. Ibid., 139.

87. Holland, *Five Readers Reading*, 85.

88. Wolston, "Stone Cut Out," 126–27.

89. Wolston, *Night Scenes of Scripture*, 262–36.

who are "unsaved" of what hazards are in store for them if they do not "come out" of Babylon. It is entirely possible that in an emotionally charged and psychologically tense atmosphere, such as a Brethren sermon on prophecy would have been, that Wolston's exegesis of the text would have resulted in a release of adrenaline from the adrenal medulla of those who were listening, resulting in the classic fight-flight physiological responses of gooseflesh, hair standing on end, nausea, fear and stress.

As we have seen in chapters 6 and 7, Wolston identifies Babylon as the church in Thyatira (Rev 2) thus linking the prophetess Jezebel with the apocalyptic Whore of Revelation chapters 17–18. Concerning Jezebel he writes: "Jezebel is going ahead with leaps and bounds in this present day in the British Isles. This will continue till the rapture of the saints—the removal to heaven of God's Assembly—and then Babylon the great . . . will be destroyed."[90] Thus this evil woman will continue to be successful with her seductive teaching until the rapture of the church, at which point she, as representative of Babylon, will be destroyed. Of this woman Jezebel in Revelation chapter 2, Jung asks:

> Who wants to throw "the woman Jezebel" on a sickbed and strike her children dead? Who cannot have enough of her bloodthirsty fantasies? Let us be psychologically correct: it is not the unconscious mind of John that thinks up these violent fantasies, they come to him in a violent 'revelation.'"[91]

Wolston, in placing an importance on the destruction of Babylon is demonstrating his own desire to see Jezebel destroyed, and he like Holland's archetypical reader "Saul," shows a desire for the destruction of the "devil woman,"[92] and like the archetypal reader "Shep" shows an underlying fantasy about violence, killing and blood.[93]

Continuing with the churches in Revelation chapters 2–3, Wolston writes:

> The moment of the Rapture . . . when the Lord takes away the candlestick . . . that frightful church-world system afterwards portrayed in Babylon and its judgment . . . all who are His are

---

90. Wolston, "Established and Endowed," 98.

91. Jung, 144.

92. Cf. the pope's "ecclesiastical mistress," in Trotter, "Established and Endowed," 97.

93. Cf. Wolston, "Candlestick and the Bride," 197.

taken out of it . . . The rapture is before . . . Laodicea . . . [is] judged as Babylon.[94]

It is perhaps enough to note here that Wolston demonstrates a response to danger similar to four of the five archetypal readers that Holland identifies. When experiencing the threat from a feminine, sexualized enemy, Saul, Sam, Shep and Sebastian all express emotion of fear, and respond according to their own defense mechanism. Wolston, in focusing primarily on the first stage of the two-stage rapture theory, that is the *parousia*, rather that on the second stage of the two-stage rapture theory, that is the *epiphaneia*, shows that his defense mechanism is primarily a flight mechanism, not a fight mechanism.

Other Authors

The trend in Brethren exegesis has now become clear. The Brethren adhered to a two-stage rapture hypothesis, the first stage being a hidden *parousia*, the second being a visible *epiphaneia*. Such a belief was in part the result of an exegesis of the Babylon motif, for the true church could not overcome this bloodthirsty entity, thus on both a physical and psychological level the appropriate response to her could only be rapture. Any group, when faced by a hidden risk, has to weigh up whether that danger is something that can be faced or whether risk aversion needs to occur. In Douglas and Wildavsky's essays on technological and environmental danger, those groups who perceive the world as inherently dangerous and risky see themselves as "involuntary visitors on this planet, [where] every conceivable damage they sustain could be attributable to unwished-for destructive agencies . . . involuntary inhabitants in their own bodies, totally withdrawn to social life."[95] Although the authors of this publication are referring to those in the modern United States concerned with environmental and technological disaster the theory may be applied to the group here in focus. The Brethren also see themselves as involuntary visitors on this planet and they too attribute danger to an unwished-for and hidden destructive agency: Babylon.

A number of other Brethren authors link Babylon with the rapture but in no way as comprehensively as Darby, Kelly, Trotter and Wolston above. Dennett, for example, whose work we have seen to be of great importance within the Brethren interpretative community, uses the image of Babylon to argue for a secret rapture on a number of occasions. For him the important

94. Ibid.
95. Douglas and Wildavsky, *Risk and Culture*, 20.

stage is part one: the *parousia*, whereby on "the eve of Babylon's destruction . . . there can be no Christians in Babylon" as "the church is already in heaven."[96] He paints a picture of a "left behind" world of "mere nominal believers" who remain on earth after the saints have been "caught away" from Babylon, "caught up in the clouds to meet the Lord in the air."[97] The process is "the rapture of the Church."[98] He does not however connect Babylon's destruction with the second stage of the rapture: the *epiphaneia*, as those noted above do. Bellett, on the other hand, places a greater stress on the second stage of the rapture process: the *epiphaneia*, in relation to Babylon, noting that "during the tribulation" the Brethren are with Christ, before Babylon is judged and then "the heaven is opened to let down the white horsed rider and his army."[99] Of the first stage: the *parousia*, Bellett vaguely notes that "at any time . . . the saints may be taken up to meet the Lord in the air."[100]

Lincoln clearly distinguishes between a first stage of the Lord's coming (or *parousia*) "after the Lord has taken up the church to be with himself, then . . . Revelation *xiii* to *xviii* will be fulfilled," and a second stage of his appearing (or *epiphaneia*) when "at last He will come down, but not alone; but we with him."[101] In like manner Newberry sees a remnant of "professing Christianity . . . Babylonish in its character" left behind after the "true believers . . . are caught up to meet the Lord in the air."[102] Bland notes that the church will have been raptured before the tribulational events,[103] as does Snell, who notes that those who suffer will not be the Brethren for "we shall have been caught up, to meet the Lord in the air."[104]

SOME CONCLUDING REMARKS ON "BABYLON" AND THE SECRET RAPTURE OF THE CHURCH

The biological origins, mechanisms and outcomes of extreme fear, shyness and social phobia have been studied in detail by developmental psychologists and behavioral neuroscientists who have noted a number of typical

96. Dennett, *Visions of John in Patmos*, 232, 235.
97. Dennett, *Blessed Hope*, 62.
98. Dennett, *Daniel the Prophet*, 79, 125, 180. See also Dennett, *Scripture*, 18.26.
99. Bellett, *On the Return of the Lord Jesus Christ*, 26.
100. Bellett, "Potter's Broken Vessel," 32.
101. Lincoln, "Rapture of the Church," 6.1.
102. Newberry, *Notes on the Book of Revelation*, 97.
103. Bland, "Babylon," 51–53.
104. Snell, *Notes on the Revelation*, 165.

responses to extreme fear and stress.[105] Of the variety of responses demonstrated there are two that are of relevance here in this book, namely "withdrawal" and "avoidance." Social withdrawal, it has been argued, develops as a result of the fear of strangers. Whereas social avoidance, or reticence, it has been argued, emerges from the development of a conflict avoidance strategy to cope with the fear of unknown and potentially dangerous social encounters.[106] Such characteristics are clearly visible in the above examined Brethren exegesis. The secret rapture theory can be understood simply as a social withdrawal strategy developed to combat a real fear of the "mystery" (Rev 17:5), or "stranger," that is Babylon. The unwillingness to engage with so-called "worldly" pursuits, even socially beneficial ones, can be seen as a form of social reticence, which when the above theory is applied, arises as a form of conflict avoidance. The timing of the Brethren rapture, which removes the saints from the earth before the great tribulation and the destruction of Babylon, can be seen as simply a way of avoiding conflict, in order to assuage fears of what could be, if a literalistic reading of Revelation chapters 17–18 is held, quite a bloody encounter.

The Brethren cannot fight against such a "real" danger as Babylon, thus a biological flight response occurs: an adrenaline rush, gooseflesh, a cold sweat, and nausea. This is channeled through the pen into what would become an internally coherent doctrine of escapism: the "Secret Rapture." The Brethren also experience a psychological reaction to the danger of Babylon, as they read the text they find in it a description of their own situation. They respond to religious and secular competitors in the same way that the earliest Christians to whom John wrote responded to danger, for there are, as has been demonstrated throughout, remarkable similarities in the *Sitz im Leben* of the two groups. The Brethren fit easily into Holland's male archetypal reading groups as they write about the threat that Babylon poses and the response which the Brethren should take. With such terrifying images and hidden dangers permeating the book of Revelation it is perhaps only to be expected that a group like the Brethren should seek out safety and protection, and this they do. They fly away from Babylon, this world with its corrupt religion and confused doctrine, to the celestial nuptial embrace of Christ in the heavens.

---

105. Schmidt and Schulkin, *Extreme Fear*.

106. Schmidt and Fox, "Conceptual, Biological and Behavioral," 48–51.

Concluding Remarks
on Babylon and the Brethren

In the previous chapter the central importance of the doctrine of the secret rapture of the church in the Brethren movement was noted in detail.
That the Brethren had such a doctrine has of course been noted before, and
others have given some account and explanation of it, although some of
the authors that have been examined above have not prior to this present
piece of research been studied in detail before. However, such explanations
have been largely related to tracing the historical antecedents of the theory
and have hence placed its presence in the work of the early Brethren movement in a historical context. This book has done more. It has explained the
origin, or at least the appeal, of the doctrine of the secret rapture within
early Brethren circles by showing how both biological and psychological responses to the image of the Whore of Babylon found in Revelation chapters
17–18 have directly influenced the development of this "escapist" doctrine.

While there is no space here to argue this in detail, one potentially
important contribution to learning that this book makes, therefore, is that
it sheds light on the wider context of, and the reasons for, the appeal of the
doctrine of the secret rapture in early Brethren sources. The importance of
this finding is not limited to those concerned with Brethren history alone,
for it is certainly the case that "rapture culture" (as it has become known)
is a significant force in the world today, especially in contemporary North
American popular biblical exegesis. What should be noted here is that a
clear trajectory of ideas can be traced from Darby, and his circle, and their
biological and psychological reaction to the Babylon motif, to such commentators as Scofield, Gaebelein, Lindsey and LaHaye and Jenkins, who
also, it may be argued, responded on both a physiological and psychological
level to the text and desired to be "raptured" beyond the threats and dangers
of their own day.

This book has also made a contribution to learning in a number of other ways. Perhaps most obviously in the very extensive archival research that has been undertaken, the extent of which will by now be apparent. This has brought to the surface substantial new factual information. From this information a number of hypotheses have emerged. For example, it has been shown that the Babylon motif has a significant impact on Brethren ecclesiology. The impact of the Babylon motif on Brethren ecclesiology is by no means less profound than the impact that the Babylon motif had on the formation of Brethren eschatology and the two-stage secret rapture doctrine. Just as the early Christian community for whom the Revelation was originally written used the text as a form of vituperative rhetoric to castigate their enemies both near and distant, both external and internal, so too the Brethren turned the text against their own enemies. The use of the text in this way is analogous to a series of concentric circles. Just as in geo-metrical terms, the closer to the "fixed-point" or "center-point" each circle gets the smaller its circumference becomes, so too the exegesis of Babylon gets gradually more sectarian and exclusive as it becomes closer and closer to the author until what was once only an external and distant threat (Papal Rome) becomes a much more imminent threat (Protestantism). The rings of exegesis tighten and Babylon is then to be found *intra muros*, within the Brethren community itself in the form of confused doctrine.

The intention of this book has been to examine the use made of the Whore of Babylon motif and the influence that this image exerted upon the readers of that text, namely, the Christian Brethren of the nineteenth century. Such a book, embodying the results of significant primary archi-val research, has been presented in the material above and is an original contribution to learning in that the use of the particular text of Revelation chapters 17–18 within the specific community of the Brethren has not be-forehand been undertaken. The work presented here is hence both com-prehensive and original. Furthermore it is hoped that the data procured from the archive has been presented clearly, coherently and systematically. It should be noted that the Brethren authors were certainly not short of things to say about Papal Rome, other Christian denominations, heresy and the world in which they lived. However, this book has been confined solely to those publications which explicitly connect such things with "Babylon the Great." Thus while the strength of the scope of the book is in its broad-ness and comprehensiveness, some claim to exhaustiveness can be made as every reference made to Babylon from Brethren authors in the specified time period has been examined.[1]

---

1. At least at the time of writing, and in terms of what may reasonably be expected

Whereas traditional historical-critical writings on Revelation follow a somewhat standard outline, this book has foregone such a structure, for the argument has centered upon a well-defined community of readers and the use made of a specific text by those largely noncritical, albeit intelligent, readers. Thus traditional historical-critical issues relating to the origin of the book of Revelation and its own *Sitz im Leben* have been of only limited importance and little space has been given over to them. It is, however, of utmost importance to note that the Brethren writers examined above had a *Sitz im Leben* that was, in many ways, similar to that of the community to which John originally wrote his Revelation, and because of this the Brethren were drawn into John's apocalyptical, visionary world in such a way, and to such an extent, as to see the great end-time enemy called "Babylon" all around them. John Wesley's remarks on the book of Revelation are relevant here: "It was given to a banished man; and men in affliction understand and relish it most."[2] The Brethren also perceived themselves both spatially and temporally (i.e., as a true remnant, end-time church) as a banished and afflicted community.

No claim to absolute originality can be made for the first two chapters of the book. Rather, these narrowly focused chapters were designed primarily to set the context of that which followed so that the Brethren readings examined later in the book could be placed in a much broader theoretical framework. However, the use of reader-response theories when applied to the Revelation in general and Babylon in particular has enabled the connection of previously unrelated facts and methodologies in a novel way. As such the interdisciplinary nature of the book comes to the fore even at such an early stage of the work.

In chapter 3, a systematic overview of the exegesis of the Babylon text, a historical survey of the afterlife of the Whore of Babylon motif from the second to nineteenth century CE was carried out. In that chapter all the various ways (but by no means all the various interpreters) in which the text has been historically interpreted have been elucidated, and the conclusion was made that the standard interpretation was, historically, of Babylon as a cryptogram for Pagan or Imperial Rome in the Pre-Reformation time period, and of Papal Rome in the Post-Reformation era. A number of less common interpretations did exist, and these were investigated as they arose. Such a chapter helped us note the similarities and differences in the underlying thought patterns of Christian writers throughout the history of

---

within the confines of the appropriate period of research required for the award of a PhD degree.

2. Wesley, *Explanatory Notes Upon the New Testament*, 654.

the church and then enabled us to see precisely where the Brethren writers fitted onto the hermeneutical map.

Chapter 4 briefly tracked the major people and events associated with the origins of the Christian Brethren movement in order to make the *Sitz im Leben* of the readers there examined plain. This was an important chapter for in the overall process of reading it was noted that the reader approaches the text from within a very specific social, religious and historical context and that this context will affect in significant ways how the text functions within the community. These preliminary chapters also enabled the question of how Brethren exegesis related to that of those who went before them to be answered.

Chapters 5 to 9 of this book are its heart. These chapters have yielded the fruits of a detailed examination of the archival material and, it is suggested, are an original contribution to learning. Chapter 5 revealed that, for the Brethren authors, Babylon was Papal Rome. The conclusion made from such an identification was that this exegesis enabled them to identify themselves with the broader Protestant interpretive community's normative hermeneutical schema. A form of Fish's reader-response critique was used to explain why the Brethren identified Babylon in this way. However, the Brethren authors did break some new ground insofar as they did not identify Babylon as *the* pope or *a* pope in an individualistic sense, but rather as the whole papal system. Furthermore the Brethren projected the fulfillment of the passage into the future, albeit very near future, unlike the Protestant Reformers before them, who, although interpreting this passage as being papal, did so according to a historicist rather than futurist framework. A futurist hermeneutic made such an identification rather vague, unspecific and difficult to prove wrong on a historical level. It was shown in that chapter that the Brethren used the Whore of Babylon motif as a form of vituperative rhetoric, to castigate the extreme outsider: Papal Rome. The language of "Babylon" was extremely useful to the Brethren in this vitriolic activity.

In chapter 6 the concentric hermeneutical circles tightened, for in that chapter it was shown that the Brethren also interpreted Babylon as all of corrupt Christendom. Babylon, for the Brethren, was not just a symbol of the Roman church but of every other church (except the Brethren church of course). Textually, the reason for this was to be found in a literalist reading of the word "mother" (Rev 17:5), which the Brethren presumed must mean that Babylon had given birth to other corrupt churches. The reason for such an identification, it was suggested in that chapter, was because of a highly sectarian ecclesiology. Chapters 5 and 6, when taken together, demonstrated how the Brethren used the Whore of Babylon motif, *extra muros*, to define the "self" through vilifying the "religious other." However, whereas in the previous chapter the distant outsider (Papal Rome) was the Babylonian enemy, in chapter 6 the accusation becomes closer, directed at the nearest outsider, other Protestant denominations, whom the Brethren traduced using the convenient language John had provided in Revelation chapters 17–18.

Chapter 7 examined the identification of Babylon in Brethren writings as doctrinal confusion. Babylon was, for the Brethren, a metaphor or symbol for either believing, holding onto or accepting corrupt or heretical doctrinal teaching. For Darby and the Exclusives this identification of Babylon became the basis for the "Doctrine of Contamination" theory, which gave biblical sanction to that group to excommunicate individuals and whole congregations who held onto any perceived unorthodox teachings. This interpretation had strong implications in the formation of Brethren sectarian factions who placed a high importance on the "correct" interpretation of Scripture. In that chapter we saw the way that the Brethren used the Whore of Babylon motif, *intra muros*, to define the "self" through vilifying the "epistemological other" or the enemy within. Babylon was contagious and her germs of heretical doctrine could be transmitted from individual to individual and congregation to congregation, and thus she must be avoided at all costs.

Chapter 8 was devoted to secular identifications of Babylon in Brethren sources. In general terms it became clear that Babylon represented worldliness, but a number of authors took up a few more specific secular interpretations, including the antitypical idea of the geographical kingdom of Babylon *redivivus*, and indeed some were so specific in their interpretation that contemporaneous events such as the Great Exhibition were held to be the literal fulfillment of prophecy. It was concluded in that chapter that due to a high priority placed on the corruption of the world, and the perceived corruption of all other churches, the call of Revelation 18:4 to "come out of her" formed something of a *Clavis Interpretum* to understanding Brethren ecclesiology. The findings of this chapter were related to the general body of knowledge in the subject insofar as anthropological and sociological theories, normally used for examining cultures, were applied to explain how the Brethren used the Whore of Babylon motif to define the "self" through vilifying the "secular other." In that chapter it was shown that in the interplay between the text, the reader and the context in which the reading takes place, it is often far from clear which has the upper hand in the determination of presumed "meaning." What was clear was that Brethren eschatology was feeding Brethren ecclesiology to the extent that a picture developed of an end-time, true remnant church who have to stand against the world in order to retain their status as a pure bride awaiting Christ's imminent return.

Chapter 9 focused on the response that needs to be made to the previously identified religious, epistemological and secular "other." The key, again, is Revelation 18:4: "come out of her." It was suggested that the secret rapture doctrine which was developed and popularized to a wide audience through Brethren authors, emerged as a direct result of Brethren exegesis of the Babylon motif. Although the rapture doctrine may not have had its sole origin with the work of the Brethren, it was they who gave it a real presence in the millennial marketplace and a solid, internally logical and consistent scriptural basis through their use of Babylon. Here we see a real example of the *Wirkungsgeschichte* or "impact" of a text on a community, rather than simply "use" or *Auslegungsgeschichte*, for the reason this eschatological doctrine was formulated and developed by the Brethren can be understood as a direct "fight or flight" response in biological terms to the Whore of Babylon and also as a psychological "fear-fantasy" response to the text.

These archival chapters do not, therefore, break new ground only by presenting new information from previously unexamined sources; they also contribute to knowledge in that various methodologies have been applied to the reading of Revelation 17–18 connecting together previously unrelated facts in an interdisciplinary way. Methodological approaches from anthropology, sociology, psychology, and even biology have been applied to both the text examined and the group studied.

Throughout this book the Brethren have been in focus, though much of what has been said above will have been of value in the broader context of "sectarian" biblical exegesis more generally.

For modern students of theology, steeped in the techniques of the historical-critical school, and who have learned to maintain a professional distance from the text, the question of how Brethren exegesis may be of relevance to the present day and of what can be learned from those Brethren authors is a difficult question to answer. One may learn from their zealous inaugurated eschatology that to live one's life on earth as though each day may be the last is to bring purpose and reason into each day, while to live one's life with the heartfelt assurance that death is not the end of life may bring hope to those who are suffering or have been bereaved. One may learn from the passion of early Brethren ecclesiology something of the fellowship that can come from breaking down denominational barriers and joining together in an ecumenical celebration of faith. From their sectarian ecclesiological tendencies, however, one may learn something of how quickly such utopian ideals can disintegrate, and of how the language of Revelation can be used, not to bring hope and comfort, but to castigate and vilify those who practice a different form of Christianity or hold different beliefs about their faith. The book has also raised some difficult questions regarding the ethics of reading, for those who would argue that the "true" meaning of the text is in no way confined by the intentions of the author have to contend with the moral problem of the text being used in such vitriolic and painful ways.

And so to conclude; notable Baptist author C. H. Spurgeon long ago remarked: "Ye men of Plymouth, why stand ye gazing into heaven?"[3] This book has at least given a partial explanation for such a heavenly preoccupation. As the authors examined above struggled to find their place in this world, replete as it was with danger, risk and fear, they too, like the first apostles in the book of Acts (Acts 1:11) turned their eyes skywards, and believing that there would be no amelioration of the current world situation, they awaited their rapture and consequent millennial bliss.

3. Spurgeon, *Lectures to My Students*, 2.65.

Bibliography

Addaeus the Apostle. "Memoirs of Edessa." In *ANF*, 8:645–720.

Alcazar. *Vestigatio Arcani Sensus in Apocalypsi* (1615). In Froom, *Prophetic Faith of Our Fathers*, 2:507–10.

Ambrose. "On Repentance." In *NPNF*, 2.10:327–58.

———. "On the Christian Faith." In *NPNF*, 2.10:242–43.

Apocalypse of Baruch. Translated by R. H. Charles. London: SPCK, 1917.

"Apocalypse of Daniel." Translated by G. T. Zervos. In *The Old Testament Pseudepigrapha*, edited by J. H. Charlesworth, 1:755–70. 3 vols. Garden City: Doubleday, 1983.

Athanasius. "Circular Letter." In *NPNF*, 2.4:500–539.

Audisio, G. *The Waldensian Dissent: Persecution and Survival c. 1170–1570*. Cambridge: Cambridge University Press, 1999.

Augustine. *City of God*. Translated by G. G. Walsh. New York: Doubleday, 1958.

———. *Expositions of the Psalms*. Translated by M. Boulding. 6 vols. New York: New City Press, 2000–2005.

———. "Expositions on the Book of Psalms." In *NPNF*, edited by P. Schaff and H. Wace, 1.8:1–683. 28 vols. Edinburgh: T. & T. Clark, 1886–1900.

———. *On Christian Doctrine*. Translated by J. F. Shaw. N.pl.: Aeterna, 2015.

———. *On the Catechising of the Uninstructed*. Translated by S. D. F. Salmond. In *NPNF*, 1.3:277–314.

———. *The Thirteen Books of the Confessions of St. Augustine*. Translated by R. S. Pine-Coffin. London: Penguin, 1961.

Aune, D. *Revelation*. 3 vols. WBC. Nashville: Nelson, 1997–98.

Backus, I. *The Infinite Importance of the Obedience of Faith, and of Separation from the World*. 1767. Reprinted Boston: Samuel Hall, 1791.

Bailey, W. A. "Tebel." In *New International Dictionary of Old Testament Theology and Exegesis*, edited by W. VanGemeren, 1:663–64. 5 vols. Grand Rapids: Zondervan, 1997.

Baines, T. B. "The Church of God." Section 3 of *The Lord's Coming, Israel, and the Church*, 253–447. 4th ed. London: Broom, 1881.

———. "The Glorious Coming and Kingdom of Christ." Section 3 of *The Revelation of Jesus Christ*, 124–310. 4th ed. London: Broom, 1879.

———. "The Hope of Israel and Creation." Section 2 of *The Lord's Coming, Israel, and the Church*, 95–252. 4th ed. London: Broom, 1881.

———. "Preliminary Judgments." Section 2 of *The Revelation of Jesus Christ*, 67–123. 4th ed. London: Broom, 1879.

———. "Revelation." *NW* 15 (1885) 140–42.

Bauckham, R. *The Climax of Prophecy: Studies on the Book of Revelation.* Edinburgh: T. & T. Clark, 1993.

Beagley, A. J. *The Sitz im Leben of the Apocalypse, with Particular Reference to the Role of the Church's Enemies.* New York: de Gruyter, 1987.

Beale, G. K. *The Book of Revelation.* New International Greek Testament Commentary. Carlisle: Paternoster, 1999.

———. *John's Use of the Old Testament in Revelation.* Sheffield: Sheffield Academic, 1998.

Bellett, J. G. "Babylon, Rev 17, 18." In *Musings on Scripture,* 1:26–27. 3 vols. London: Walters, 1885–87.

———. *Belshazzar's Feast in Its Application to the Great Exhibition.* London: Morrish, n.d.

———. "An Extract, Fragment." *CF* 18 (1891) 190–97.

———. "Extracts from Letters." *CF* 12 (1885) 25, 166–67.

———. "Extracts from Unpublished Letters." *CF* 11 (1884) 37.

———. "An Introduction to Isaiah." *BT* 4 (1863) 229–45.

———. "A Letter—Jeremiah." *CF* 14 (1887) 29.

———. "The Mornings of Scripture." In *Short Meditations,* 5–8. Dublin: Cavenagh, 1866.

———. *Notes from Meditations on Luke.* London: Crocker & Cooper, ca. 1870.

———. *Notes on Joshua: An Outline Study of the Book of Joshua.* Kilmarnock, Scotland: Ritchie, 1938.

———. "Obadiah." In *The Minor Prophets,* 34–42. Glasgow: Allan, 1870.

———. *On the Return of the Lord Jesus Christ from Heaven to Meet His Saints in the Air.* Manchester: Horner, n.d.

———. "The Potter's Broken Vessel, Jeremiah 18, 19." *CF* 7 (1880) 32–35.

———. "Revelation: A Book of Conquerors." *NW* 8 (1878) 86–88.

———. "Rightly Dividing the Word of Truth." In *Miscellaneous Papers,* 87–90. Glasgow: Allan, n.d.

———. "Ruth." In *Musings on Scripture,* 3:117–18. London: Walters, 1885–87.

———. *Witnesses for God, in Dark and Evil Times: Being Studies and Meditations on the Books of Ezra, Nehemiah, and Esther.* Kilmarnock: Ritchie, n.d.

———. *Woollen and Linen.* London: Morrish, n.d.

———. "Zechariah." Section 11 in *The Minor Prophets,* 99–114. Glasgow: Allan, 1870.

Bennett, A. *Readers and Reading.* London: Taylor & Francis, 1995.

Bergin, F. "Babylon to Be Rebuilt and Destroyed." 1893. Reprinted in *Watching and Waiting* 10 (1937) 161–64.

Bérubé, M. "There Is Nothing Inside the Text." In *Postmodern Sophistry,* edited by G. A. Olson and L. Worsham, 11–26. Albany: SUNY, 2004.

Bland, E. A. "Babylon, Past and Future: With Remarks on Babylon, the Metropolis of Satan, by A. R. Habershon." *Dispensational Series* 5. London: Holness, n.d.

Bland, F. C. "Babylon." *NW* 9 (1879) 51–35.

Block, Jack, and Jeanne Block. "An Investigation of the Relationship between Intolerance of Ambiguity and Ethnocentricity." *Journal of Personality* 19 (1951) 301–11.

Boesack, A. A. *Comfort and Protest: Reflections on the Apocalypse of John of Patmos.* Edinburgh: St. Andrew's University Press, 1987.

Bonar, A. A. *The Development of Antichrist.* 1853. Reprinted Chelmsford: SGAT, n.d.

Bonar, A. A., and R. M. McCheyne. *Narrative of a Mission of Inquiry to the Jews from the Church of Scotland in 1839.* Edinburgh: n.pubs, 1842.

Boyer, P. *When Time Shall Be No More: Prophecy Belief in Modern American Culture.* Cambridge: Harvard University Press, 1992.

Boxall, I. "The Many Faces of Babylon the Great: *Wirkungsgeschichte* and the Interpretation of Revelation 17." In *Studies in the Book of Revelation,* edited by S. Moyise, 51–68. Edinburgh: T. & T. Clark, 2001.

Bridget of Sweden. *Leben und Offenbarungen der heiligen Brigitta,* edited by L. Clarus [pseud.]. Regensburg: Manz, 1856.

Brothers, R. *Revealed Knowledge of the Prophecies and Times.* London: n.pubs., 1794.

Brown, F. *Joanna Southcott: The Woman Clothed with the Sun.* Cambridge: Lutterworth, 2002.

Brunton, C. "The Land of Shinar." *ChW* 4 (1837) 281–84.

Burgh, W. *An Exposition of the Book of the Revelation.* 5th ed. Dublin: Hodges & Smith, 1857.

Burnham, J. D. *A Story of Conflict: The Controversial Relationship between Benjamin Wills Newton and John Nelson Darby.* Milton Keynes: Paternoster, 2004.

Burrage, C. *The True Story of Robert Browne (1550–1603), Father of Congregationalism.* Oxford: Oxford University Press, 1906.

Caldwell, J. R. "Separation from the World." *NW* 8 (1878) 81–83.

Calvin, J. *Institutes of the Christian Religion.* Translated by Henry Beveridge. 4 vols. Edinburgh: Calvin Translation Society, 1845.

Chadwick, O. *The Victorian Church.* 3rd ed. Vol. 1. London: Black, 1971.

Charles, R. H. *A Critical and Exegetical Commentary on the Revelation of St. John.* 2 vols. ICC. Edinburgh: T. & T. Clark, 1920.

Chrysostom. "Homilies on the Epistle to the Hebrews." In *NPNF,* 1.14:333–522.

———. "Homilies on the Gospel of St. John." In *NPNF,* 1.14:1–332.

Clarke, A. *Clarke's Commentary on the NT.* 8 vols. London: 1810–1826.

Coad, F. R. *A History of the Brethren Movement: Its Origins, Its Worldwide Development and Its Significance for the Present Day.* 2nd ed. Exeter: Paternoster, 1976.

———. *Prophetic Developments: With Particular Reference to the Early Brethren Movement.* London: Christian Brethren Research Fellowship, 1966.

Cohn, N. *The Pursuit of the Millennium: Revolutionary Millenarians and Mystical Anarchists of the Middle Ages.* London: Paladin, 1970.

Collins, A. Y. "The Apocalypse (Revelation)." In *The New Jerome Biblical Commentary,* edited by R. Brown et al., 994–1016. 2nd ed. London: Chapman, 1996.

———. *Crisis and Catharsis: The Power of the Apocalypse.* Philadelphia: Westminster, 1984.

———. "Insiders and Outsiders in the Book of Revelation." In *To See Ourselves as Others See Us,* 187–218. Chico, CA: Scholars, 1985.

———. "Vilification and Self-Definition in the Book of Revelation." *HTR* 79 (1986) 308–20.

Commodianus. "Instructions of Commodianus in Favour of Christian Discipline." In *ANF,* 4:199–219.

Cranmer, Thomas. *Writings and Disputations Relevant to the Lord's Supper,* edited by J. E. Cox. Cambridge: Cambridge University Press, 1844.

Cross, E. N. *Irish Saint and Scholar: A Biography of William Kelly.* London: Chapter Two, 2004.

Cullmann, O. *Peter: Disciple, Apostle, and Martyr; A Historical and Theological Study.* Translated by F. V. Filson. Philadelphia: Westminster, 1953.

Darby, J. N. "The Altar of Abraham (1850)." *CW* 16 (1883) 102–14.

———. "Analysis of Dr. Newman's, 'Apologia Pro Vita Sua,' with a Glance at the History of Popes, Councils and the Church." *CW* 18 (1883) 145–248.

———. "Appearing, Manifestation and Presence." *NC* 4 (1902) 151–53.

———. "The Bethesda Circular." *CW* 15 (1883) 253–58.

———. "A Brief Outline of the Books of the Bible." *CW* 19 (1883) 75–79.

———. "The Character of Office in the Present Dispensation (1838)." *CW* 1 (1883) 141–60.

———. "Christian Liberty of Preaching and Teaching the Lord Jesus Christ (1834)." *CW* 1 (1883) 108–19.

———. "Christianity Not Christendom (1874)." *CW* 18 (1883) 249–75.

———. "'The Church and Its Friendly Subdivisions' in reply to Mr. R. W. Monsell (1849)." *CW* 4 (1883) 203–52.

———. "The Claims of the Church of England Considered: Being the Close of a Correspondence . . . (1842)." *CW* 14 (1883) 284–350.

———. *The Closing Days of Christendom.* London: Hammond, n.d.

———. *Commentary on Greek New Testament.* 4 vols. MSS, vol. 4, 1818.

———. "Considerations on the Nature and Unity of the Church of Christ (1828–1834)." *CW* 1 (1883) 20–35.

———. "The Counsel of Peace, Zechariah 6:13." *CW* 12 (1883) 308–14.

———. "Dialogues on the Essays and Reviews." *CW* 9 (1883) 1–633.

———. "Edinburgh Meeting: Address, Titus 2:11–15." *NJ* (1931) 68–81.

———. "Evangelical Protestantism and the Biblical Studies of M. Godet (1875)." *CW* 23 (1883) 234–72.

———. "Evidence from Scripture of the Passing Away of the Present Dispensation." *CW* 2 (1883) 149–80.

———. "Examination of the Book Entitled 'The Restitution of All Things.'" *CW* 31 (1883) 120–68.

———. "An Examination of the Statements Made in the 'Thoughts on the Apocalypse,' by B.W. Newton . . . (1848)." *CW* 8 (1883) 1–498.

———. "Exposition of the Epistle to the Romans (1843)." *CW* 26 (1883) 113–99.

———. "Familiar Conversations on Romanism." *CW* 22 (1883) 1–334.

———. "Fragmentary Thoughts on Revelation." *CW* 34 (1883) 263–366.

———. "Further Note on Isaiah." *NC* 4 (1902) 83–85.

———. "Further Notes on the Revelation." *NJ* (1931) 135–57.

———. "General Remarks on the Prophetic Word (continued)." *CW* 30 (1883) 361–70.

———. "Genesis, Typically Considered." *NC* 1 (1884) 111–60.

———. "God For Us." *CW* 31 (1883) 246–52.

———. "Hints on the Book of Genesis: Being the Substance of Remarks at a Scripture Reading (1852)." *CW* 19 (1883) 106–62.

———. "An Introduction to the Bible." *CW* 34 (1883) 1–43.

———. "The Irrationalism of Infidelity: Being a Reply to 'Phases of Faith,' by F. W. (1853)." *CW* 6 (1883) 237–595.

———. "Isaiah." *NC* 4 (1902) 7–19.

———. "Jeremiah." *NC* 4 (1902) 90–95.

———. "Joshua Chapter 1–13." *CW* 19 (1883) 305–9.

———. "A Letter to a Clergyman on the Claims and Doctrines of Newman Street." *CW* 15 (1883) 16–32.

———. "Letter to the Saints Meeting in Ebrington Street . . ." *CW* 20 (1883) 3–11.

———. *Letters of J. N. D.* Vols. 1–3. Kingston on Thames: Stow Hill, 1832–1882.

———. "The Living Water, John 7: 37–39, Notes of Sermons (1838)." *CW* 12 (1883) 19–31.

———. "Meditations on the Acts of the Apostles." *CW* 25 (1883) 480–510.

———. "Miracles and Infidelity." *CW* 32 (1883) 274–328.

———. "The Mystery." *NC* 2 (1887) 108–14.

———. "Narrative of the Facts Concerned with the Separation of the Writer from the Congregation Meeting in Ebrington Street (1846)." *CW* 20 (1883) 36–108.

———. "Notes of a Lecture on Revelation 3:7–13, 1863." *Words in Season* 6 (1892) 264–65.

———. "Notes on Isaiah." *NC* 4 (1902) 23–62.

———. "Notes on the Apocalypse, Gleaned at Lectures in Geneva, Revelation 18, No. 3 (1842)." *CW* 5 (1883) 1–106.

———. "Notes on the Revelation (1839)." *CW* 2 (1883) 42–142.

———. "Observations on a Tract Entitled, 'Remarks on the Sufferings of the Lord Jesus': A Letter Addressed to Certain Brethren and Sisters in Christ by Mr. B. W. Newton (1847)." *CW* 15 (1883) 34–96.

———. "On 'Days' Signifying 'Years' in Prophetic Language (1830)." *CW* 2 (1883) 20–62.

———. "On the Apocalypse." *CW* 28 (1883) 515–37.

———. "On the Gospel according to John: Notes of Remarks Made . . . at a Conference (1871)." *CW* 25 (1883) 338–433.

———. "Outline of the Revelation." *CW* 5 (1883) 369–87.

———. "Practical Reflections on the Proverbs (1866)." *CW* 17 (1883) 139–56.

———. "Practical Reflections on the Psalms (1860)." *CW* 17 (1883) 1–222.

———. "Presbyterianism: A Reply to 'The Church and the Pulpit' (1868)." *CW* 14 (1883) 493–523.

———. "Progress of Democratic Power and Its Effects on the Moral State of England." *CW* 32 (1883) 507–11.

———. "The Proverbs." *NC* 3 (1889) 290–93.

———. "Psalm 93." *CW* 30 (1883) 161–65.

———. "The Psalms." *NC* 3 (1889) 128–47.

———. "Rapture of the Saints and the Character of the Jewish Remnant, Shewing the Position Which the Scriptures Give to the Remnant in Israel. . . ." *CW* 11 (1883) 180–229.

———. "Reading at Notting Hill on 1 Corinthians 1." *NJ* (1931) 113–25.

———. "Reading on 1 Peter (1879)." *CW* 28 (1883) 238–49.

———. "Readings on Joshua." *NJ* (1931) 400–52.

———. "Reading on the Fifth Book of Psalms." *NJ* (1931) 200–208.

———. "Readings on the Seven Churches." *NJ* (1931) 335–72.

———. "Remarks on the Pamphlet of Mr. F. Olivier Entitled, 'An Essay on the Kingdom of God' . . . (1843)." *CW* 1 (1883) 428–57.

———. "Reply to an Article in the 'Zionsbote' upon 'Darbyism.'" *CW* 33 (1883) 19–28.

———. "Reply to the Remarks in Two Leading Articles of the Christian Journal Entitled 'Our Separating Brethren' (1871)." *CW* 14 (1883) 200–259.

———. "Revelation." In *Synopsis of the Bible*, 5:516–602. 2nd ed. 5 vols. London: Morrish, n.d.

———. "Romanism; or, An Answer to the Pamphlet of a Romish Priest, Entitled 'The Law and the Testimony' (1870)." *CW* 18 (1883) 30–144.

———. "Ryde Address: Repentance and the Kingdom." *NJ* (1931) 55–60.

———. "Scriptural Criticisms (1834)." *CW* 13 (1883) 4–24.

———. "Second Address to His Roman Catholic Brethren by a Minister of the Gospel." In *CW* 18 (1883) 11–29.

———. "A Short but Serious Examination of the Fundamental Principles Issued by Mr. Gaussen in His Book Entitled 'Daniel the Prophet' (1850)." *CW* 11 (1883) 63–108.

———. "Sketch of Joshua." *CW* 19 (1883) 503–13.

———. "Some Further Development of the Principles Set Forth in the Pamphlet, Entitled 'On the Formation of Churches.'" *CW* 1 (1883) 250–99.

———. "The Sufferings of Christ." *BT* 2 (1859) 203–10.

———. "Testimony of God: Or the Trial of Man, the Grace and the Government of God (1861)." *CW* 22 (1883) 508–69.

———. "Thoughts on Isaiah the Prophet." *CW* 30 (1883) 265–347.

———. "Thoughts on Romans 11, and on the Responsibility of the Church in Reference to a Pamphlet of Mr. F. Olivier." *CW* 1 (1883) 474–514.

———. "Thoughts on the Present Position of the Home Mission (1833)." *CW* 1 (1883) 79–106.

———. "The Vaudois (1871)." *CW* 20 (1883) 534–41.

———. "What Has Been Acknowledged? or, The State of the Controversy about Elders . . . (1852)." *CW* 4 (1883) 448–68.

———. "What Is the Church, as It Was at the Beginning? And What Is Its Present State? (1866)." *CW* 14 (1883) 121–34.

———. "What Is the World, and What Is Its End? A Serious Question for Those Who Are Of It (1862)." *CW* 34 (1883) 176–87.

———. "Zechariah." *NC* 4 (1902) 215–23.

Daubney, C. *The Fall of Papal Rome: Recommended to the Consideration of the English.* London: Cadell & Davies, 1798.

Davis, R. C., and R. Schleifer. *Contemporary Literary Criticism: Literary and Cultural Studies.* 3rd ed. London: Longman, 1986.

Dennett, E. *The Blessed Hope: Being Papers on the Lord's Coming and Connected Events.* London: Broom, 1879.

———. *Daniel the Prophet, and the Times of the Gentiles.* London: Rouse, 1893.

———. "Expository Jottings 1: Keeping the Word of Christ." *CF* 9 (1882) 205–7.

———. *The House of God: Traced through the Scriptures.* Reprinted from *CF.* Morganville, NJ: Present Truth, 1991.

———. *Pilgrim Songs: Being the Songs of Degrees.* London: Rouse, 1897.

———. *The Rapture, the Appearing of Christ and the Eternal State.* London: Morrish, n.d.

———. *Recovered Truths: Being Letters to Certain Believers.* London: Broom, 1885.

———. "Revelation—Scripture Notes part 2." *CF* 18 (1891) 24–26.

———. *The Visions of John in Patmos: Being Notes on the Apocalypse.* London: Rouse, 1892.

———. "Widows Indeed." *CF* 9 (1882) 123–25.

———. *Zechariah the Prophet: Being an Exposition.* London: Broom, 1888.

Dickson, N. T. R. *Brethren in Scotland, 1838-2000: A Social Study of an Evangelical Movement*. Milton Keynes: Paternoster, 2002.

Douglas, M. "Pollution." In *TIESS*, 12:336-42.

———. *Purity and Danger: An Analysis of the Concepts of Pollution and Taboo*. London: Routledge, 1966.

———. *Risk and Blame: Essays in Cultural Theory*. London: Routledge, 1992.

Douglas, M., and A. Wildavsky. *Risk and Culture: An Essay on the Selection of Technical and Environmental Dangers*. Berkeley: University of California Press, 1982.

Dunton, H. "Millennial Hopes and Fears: Great Britain 1780-1960." *Andrews University Seminary Studies* 37 (1999) 181-210.

Duppa, R. "Anecdotes Respecting Pius VI." In *The European Magazine*, 34:5-8. London: Sewell, 1798.

———. *A Brief Account of the Subversion of the Papal Government: 1798*. London: Robinson, 1799.

Embley, P. L. "The Early Development of the Plymouth Brethren." In *Patterns of Sectarianism*, edited by B. R. Wilson, 225-30. London: Heinemann, 1967.

———. "The Origins and Early Development of the Plymouth Brethren." PhD diss., University of Cambridge, 1967.

Evans, G. R. "Meaning." In *A Dictionary of Biblical Interpretation*, edited by R. J. Coggins and J. L. Houlden, 435-38. Philadelphia: Trinity, 1990.

"F.G." [full name not given]. "Babylon." *ChW* 3 (1836) 277-87.

Figal, G. "The Doing of the Thing Itself." In *The Cambridge Companion to Gadamer*, edited by R. J. Dostal, 102-25. Cambridge: Cambridge University Press, 2002.

Fish, S. *Is There a Text in This Class? The Authority of Interpretive Communities*. Cambridge: Harvard University Press, 1980.

Flindall, R. P., ed. *The Church of England 1815-1948: A Documentary History*. London: SPCK, 1972.

Ford, J. Massyngberde. *Revelation: A New Translation with Introduction and Commentary*. Anchor Bible Dictionary. New York: Doubleday, 1975.

Freeman, S., ed. *Biological Science*. 2nd ed. Upper Saddle River, NJ: Prentice Education, 2005.

Freund, E. *The Return of the Reader*. Abingdon: Routledge, 1987.

Froom, Le Roy Edwin. *The Prophetic Faith of Our Fathers: The Historical Development of Prophetic Interpretation*. 4 vols. Washington, DC: Review & Herald, 1950-54.

Frykholm, A. J. *Rapture Culture: Left Behind in Evangelical America*. New York: Oxford University Press, 2004.

Gadamer, H. G. *The Philosophy of Hans-Georg Gadamer*. Library of Living Philosophers 24. Chicago: Open Court, 1997.

———. *Truth & Method*. London: Sheed & Ward, 1975.

Garrett, C. *Respectable Folly: Millenarians and the French Revolution in France and England*. Baltimore: Johns Hopkins University Press, 1975.

Geertz, C. *The Interpretation of Cultures*. London: Hutchinson, 1975.

Gerard of Borgo San Donnino. *Liber Introductorius in Evangelium Aeternum*. Edited by H. Denifle. Berlin: Weidmannsche Buchhandlung, 1885.

Graff, G. Headnote to "Is There a Text in This Class?" Chapter 2 in *The Stanley Fish Reader*, edited by H. A. Veeser, 38-39. Oxford: Blackwell, 1999.

Grant, F. W. *A Divine Movement and Our Path with God Today*. New York: Loizeaux, ca. 1894.

Grass, T. "Edward Irving: Eschatology, Ecclesiology and Spiritual Gifts." In Gribben and Stunt, *Prisoners of Hope?*, 95–121.

Green, W. S. "Otherness Within: Towards a Theory of Difference in Rabbinic Judaism." In *"To See Ourselves as Others See Us": Christians, Jews, and "Others" in Late Antiquity*, edited by Neusner, J. and E. Frerichs, 49–69. Chico, CA: Scholars, 1985.

Gregory Nazianzen. "Select Orations." In *NPNF*, 2.7:185–434.

Gregory of Nyssa. "Against Eunomius." In *NPNF*, 2.5:33–248.

———. "Oratorical: On Meletius." In *NPNF*, 2.5:509–13.

Gribben, C., and T. C. F. Stunt, eds. *Prisoners of Hope? Aspects of Evangelical Millennialism in Britain and Ireland, 1800–1880*. Carlisle: Paternoster, 2004.

Groves, A. N. *The Letter from A. N. Groves to J. N. Darby, March 10th, 1836*. Bristol: E.C.L., n.d.

Hale, A. "Letter to Mr. Pond," *Signs of the Times and Expositor of Prophecy*, edited by J. V. Himes and J. Litch, 34:41–44. Boston: Dow & Jackson, 1843.

Harris, H. *The Tübingen School*. Oxford: Clarendon, 1975.

Harris, J. L. "On the Increase in Popery." *ChW* 4 (1837) 1–15.

———. "Religious Societies" *ChW* 4 (1837) 86–100.

———. *The Sufferings of Christ as Set Forth in a Lecture on Psalm VI*. London: Campbell, 1847.

Holland, N. *Five Readers Reading*. New Haven: Yale University Press, 1975.

———. *The I*. New Haven: Yale University Press, 1985.

Hippolytus. "Extant Works and Fragments." In *ANF*, 5:9–266.

Innocent III. "*Sicut universitatis conditor*" (1198). In *The Christian Theology Reader*, edited by A. E. McGrath, 470–71. 2nd ed. Oxford: Blackwell, 2001.

Irving, E. "An Interpretation of the Fourteenth Chapter of the Apocalypse." In *The Morning Watch; or, Quarterly Journal on Prophecy*, 6:18–44; 262–450. London: Fraser, 1833.

Iser, W. *The Act of Reading: A Theory of Aesthetic Response*. Baltimore: Johns Hopkins University Press, 1978.

Jerome. "Jerome's Apology in Answer to Rufinus." In *NPNF*, 2.3:482–542.

———. "Lives of Illustrious Men." In *NPNF*, 2.3:349–402.

———. "Principle Works." In *NPNF*, 2.6:1–502.

Joachim of Fiore. *Concordia Novi ac Veteris Testamenti*. Frankfurt: Minerva, 1964.

———. *De articulis fidei di Gioacchino da Fiori*. Edited by E. Buonaiuti. Rome: Istituto Storico Italiano, 1936.

———. *Liber Concordia Novi et Veteris Testamenti*. Venice: n.pubs., 1519.

Jung, C. J. *Answer to Job*. Translated by R. F. C. Hull. London: Hodder & Stoughton, 1965.

Kelly, W. "Answers to Questions." *BT* 11 (1877) 47–288.

———. "Answers to Questions." *BT* 16 (1886–87) 209–25.

———. "Answers to Questions." *BT* 18 (1891) 224–320.

———. "Answers to Questions." *BT* N1 (1897) 45–368.

———. "Answers to Questions." *BT* N2 (1898) 15–335.

———. *Babylon and the Beast*. London: Broom, 1872.

———. *The Brethren and Their Traducers: A Refutation of Rev. F. Whitfield's Letter to Rev. O. Dobree*. London: Morrish, n.d.

———. *Christ for the Saint and Christ for the Sinner*. London: Weston, 1907.

————. "The Christian Hope Consistent with Events Revealed in Prophecy." *BT* 9 (1872–73) 153–272.

————. *The Church of God and the Ministry of Christ, with Collateral Points: In Reply to the Rev R. P. Carey's "Remarks."* London: Morrish, 1863.

————. "The Churches and the Church." In *The Kelly Collection*, edited by L. Hodgett, 1–16. Ramsgate: Stem, 1998.

————. "Daniel 7." In *CA* 6 (1856) 61–62.

————. *The Doctrine of Christ and Bethesdaism.* Bristol: n.pubs., 1848.

————. *Eleven Lectures on the Book of Job Delivered at Blackheath in 1903.* London: Race, 1919.

————. "Encyclical Letter of Pope Leo XIII, on the Unity of the Church, June 29th 1896." In *The Kelly Collection*, n.pg. Ramsgate: Stem, 1998.

————. *Exposition of the Acts of the Apostles with a New Version of a Corrected Text.* 2nd ed. London: Race, 1914.

————. *Exposition of the Book of Isaiah.* London: Weston, 1897.

————. *Exposition of the Epistle of James: With a Translation of an Amended Text.* London: Hammond, 1913.

————. *Exposition of the Epistle of Paul to the Thessalonians.* London: Cheverton, 1893.

————. *Exposition of the Epistle of Paul to Titus.* London: Weston, 1901.

————. *Exposition of the Gospel of John: Edited with Additions by E. E. Whitfield.* London: Stock, 1908.

————. *Exposition of the Gospel of Luke: Edited with Annotations by E. E. Whitfield.* London: Holness, 1914.

————. *Exposition of the Gospel of Mark.* London: Stock, 1907.

————. *Exposition of the Second Epistle to Timothy.* London: Race, 1913.

————. *The Feasts in Deuteronomy XVI.* London: Weston, 1906.

————. *The First Epistle of Peter.* London: Weston, 1904.

————. *God's Inspiration of the Scriptures.* London: Weston, 1903.

————. *The Hope of Christ, Compatible with Prophecy.* London: Weston, 1898.

————. *The Interpreter: A Church Monthly Magazine.* Vol. 1, no. 1, January 1905.

————. *Is the Anglican Establishment a Church of God?* London: Broom, n.d.

————. *Jeremiah: The Tender Hearted Prophet of the Nations.* London: Hammond, 1938.

————. "Jesus the Son of God: John 1:29–43." In *BT* N11 (1917) 197–202.

————. "Jonah." In *Lectures Introductory on the Minor Prophets*, 206–23. London: Broom, 1871.

————. "Joseph (1871)." Republ. Ramsgate: Stem, 1998. 561–647.

————. *The Judgment, Not Reunion, of Christendom.* London: Hammond, 1963.

————. *The Known Isaiah: A Defence of Its Unity.* London: Cheverton, 1874.

————. *Lectures Introductory to the Study of the Acts, the Catholic Epistles and the Revelation.* London: Broom, 1870.

————. *Lectures Introductory to the Study of the Earlier Historical Books of the Old Testament.* London: Broom, 1874.

————. *Lectures Introductory to the Study of the Gospels.* London: Broom, 1867.

————. *Lectures Introductory to the Study of the Minor Prophets.* London: Broom, 1871.

————. *Lectures on the Book of Revelation.* London: Broom, 1897.

————. *Lectures on the Church of God.* London: Broom, 1890.

———. *Lectures on the Epistle of Paul, the Apostle, to the Ephesians, with a New Translation*. London: Morrish, n.d.

———. *Lectures on the Epistle of Paul, the Apostle, to the Galatians*. London: Morrish, 1865.

———. *Lectures on Ezra and Nehemiah*. London: Race, 1921.

———. *Lectures on the Gospel of Matthew*. London: Morrish, 1868.

———. *Lectures on the Second Coming and Kingdom of the Lord and Saviour Jesus Christ*. London: Broom, 1865.

———. *A Letter on the Church of the Scriptures*. London: Broom, n.d.

———. *The Lord's Supper, 1 Cor. XI*. London: Baldwin, n.d.

———. "Matthew 16:28." *CA* 6 (1856) 337–41.

———. *The Mystery of Godliness: A Discourse on 1 Tim. iii:16*. London: Shorto, 1895.

———. "Nebuchadnezzar's Dream and Daniel's Vision: Daniel 2:7." *BT* N1 (1896–97) 4–7.

———. *Notes on Ezekiel*. London: Morrish, 1876.

———. *Notes on the Book of Daniel: With an Introduction in Review of Dean Farrar's Work on the Prophet. . . .* London: Carter, 1897.

———. *Notes on the Second Epistle of Paul the Apostle to the Corinthians with a New Translation*. Oak Park, IL: Bible Truth, 1975.

———. "Obadiah." In *Lectures on The Minor Prophets*, 134–230. London: Broom, 1871.

———. *The Offerings of Leviticus: An Exposition of Leviticus 1–7*. London: Weston, 1899.

———. "'On the Millennium': A Review of the Late Bishop of Lincoln's Two Lectures." *BT* N1 (1875) 252–57.

———. "Philadelphia and Laodicea: Revelation 3:7–22." *BT* 16 (1886–87) 268–86.

———. *The Plymouth Brethren: A Reply to the Christian Observer Art. II, December 1866*. London: Morrish, ca.1867.

———. *The Priesthood, Its Privileges and Its Duties: An Exposition of Leviticus 8–15*. London: Race, 1902.

———. *The Prospects of the World according to the Scriptures*. Manchester: Horner, ca. 1872.

———. *The Proverbs with a New Translation*. Oak Park, IL: Bible Truth, 1967.

———. *The Purpose of God for His Sons and Heirs*. London: Weston, 1906.

———. "Receive Ye the Holy Ghost." In *Lectures on the Doctrine of the Holy Spirit*, 130–37. London: Broom & Rouse, 1867.

———. "Revelation 14:19." *CA* 6 (1856) 51.

———. *The Righteousness of God: What Is It?* London: Broom, 1865.

———. "The Salt of the Earth." *BT* N5 (1904) 86–87.

———. *Sanctification*. London: Broom, 1872.

———. "The Scripture of Truth: Daniel 11 and 12." *BT* N1 (1896–97) 6–163.

———. "The Second Advent Before, Not After, the Millennium." *BT* 17 (1888–89) 4–137.

———. *The Second Epistle of Peter*. London: Weston, 1906.

———. *Three Prophetic Gems, 1903–1904*. Republished. Sunbury, PA: Believer's Bookshelf, 1970.

———. *Two Lectures on the Song of Solomon*. London: Race, 1917.

———. *The Unity of the Spirit: And What It Is to Keep It; Being Notes of a Lecture, by W. K.* London: Horner, 1882.

———. "What Is God's Kingdom Like? Luke 13:18–21." *BT* N1 (1896–97) 319–57.

———. "Zechariah." In *Lectures Introductory on the Minor Prophets*, 441–81. London: Broom, 1871.

Kimball, J. W. *Biology*. 4th ed. Reading, MA: Addison Wesley, 1965.

King, E. *Remarks on the Signs of the Times*. Philadelphia: Humphreys, 1800.

Knox, R. A. *Enthusiasm: A Chapter in the History of Religion with Special Reference to the 17th and 18th Centuries*. Oxford: Clarendon, 1951.

Kovacs, J., and C. Rowland. *Revelation*. Oxford: Blackwell, 2004.

Lacunza, M. *La Venida del Mesias en Gloria y Magestad*. London: Ackermann, 1826.

Levinson, D. J. "Projective Questions in the Study of Personality and Ideology." In *The Authoritarian Personality*, edited by T. W. Adorno et al., 545–602. New York: Harper, 1950.

Lincoln, W. *Address of the Rev. W. Lincoln, to the Congregation of Beresford Episcopal Chapel on November 23rd, 1862, on the Occasion of His Quitting the Communion of the Established Church*. London: Paul, 1862.

———. "The Book of the Revelation: Some Clues to Its Principles and an Outline of Its Contents." *Lincoln's Leaflets* 10. London: Yapp & Hawkins, 1874.

———. "On the Value of the Third Epistle of John: And More Especially in These Closing Days of Christendom." *Lincoln's Leaflets* 8. London: Yapp & Hawkins, 1874.

———. "The Rapture of the Church at Christ's Second Coming." *Lincoln's Leaflets* 6. London: Yapp & Hawkins, 1874.

Lindsey, H. *The Late Great Planet Earth*. Grand Rapids: Zondervan, 1970.

Longley, C. *Chosen People: The Big Idea That Shapes England and America*. London: Hodder & Stoughton, 2002.

Luther, M. "The Babylonian Captivity of the Church" (1520). In *The European Reformations Sourcebook*, 38. *LW* 36. Oxford: Blackwell, 2000.

———. "A Treatise on Goods Works" (1520). Translated by C. M. Jacobs. *LW* 44. Philadelphia: Fortress, 1966.

Luz, U. *Matthew in History: Interpretation, Influence and Effects*. Minneapolis: Fortress, 1994.

———. *Matthew 1–7: A Commentary*. Translated by Wilhelm C. Linss. Edinburgh: T. & T. Clark, 1990.

Mackintosh, C. H. *The Assembly of God; or, the All-Sufficiency of the Name of Jesus*. London: Morrish, 1868.

———. *Discipleship in an Evil Day: Lectures on the Book of Daniel*. London: Morrish, 1859.

———. "Fifteenth Letter to a Friend." *Things New and Old: A Monthly Magazine* 18 (1875) 7–16.

———. "A Fifth Letter to a Friend." *Things New and Old: A Monthly Magazine* 17 (1874) 317–24.

———. *Jehoshaphat: A Word on World-Bordering*. London: Morrish, n.d.

———. "Letters to a Friend on the Present Condition of Things." *Things New and Old: A Monthly Magazine* 17 (1874) 197–201.

———. *The Life and Times of Josiah*. Oak Park, IL: Bible Truth, n.d.

———. *The Miscellaneous Writings of C. H. M.* Vol. 5. 7 vols. Neptune, NJ: Loizeaux, 1898.

———. *Notes on the Book of Numbers*. London: Morrish, 1869.

————. *Occasional Papers*. London: Broom, 1877.

————. *The Remnant: Past & Present*. London: Morrish, n.d.

————. *Thou and Thy House: or, The Christian at Home*. London: Morrish, n.d.

————. *Work in Its Right Place; or, Reflections on the Life and Times of Hezekiah*. London: Morrish, 1862.

MacPherson, D. *The Rapture Plot*. Simpsonville, SC: Millennium III, 1995.

Macrae, G. "Messiah and Gospel." In *Judaisms and Their Messiahs at the Turn of the Christian Era*, edited by J. Neusner et al., 169–86. Cambridge: Cambridge University Press, 1987.

Madaule, J. *The Albigensian Crusade: An Historical Essay*. Translated by Barbara Wall. New York: Fordham University Press, 1967.

Maier, H. O. *Apocalypse Recalled: The Book of Revelation after Christendom*. Minneapolis: Fortress, 2002.

Mather, I. *Ichabod, or the Glory of the Lord, Is Departing from New England*. Boston: Green, 1702.

Mayhew, J. *Discourse Occasioned by the Earthquakes in November 1755*. Boston: Eddes & Gill, 1755.

————. *Popish Idolatry*. Boston: Draper, 1765.

McGinn, B., ed. *Apocalyptic Spirituality: Treatises and Letters by Lactantius, Adso of Montier-en-Derl, Joachim of Fiore, the Spiritual Franciscans and Savonarola*. London: SPCK, 1980.

————. *The Calabrian Abbot: Joachim of Fiore in the History of Western Thought*. New York: Macmillan, 1985.

McKnight, E. V. "Reader-Response Criticism." In *A Dictionary of Biblical Interpretation*, edited by R. J. Coggins and J. Houlden, 370–73. Nashville: Abingdon, 1999.

Methodius. "Banquet of the Ten Virgins." In *ANF*, 6:309–63.

Miller, A. *The Brethren: A Brief Sketch of Their Origin, Progress and Testimony*. London: Morrish, 1879.

————. *Meditations on the Beatitudes of Matthew V, as They Present to Us the Main Features of the Saviour's Life*. Glasgow: Pickering & Inglis, 1878.

————. *Short Papers on Church History*. 3 vols. London: Wheeler, 1873–78.

Miller, A., and W. Kelly, eds. *The Collected Works of J. N. Darby*. 34 vols. Dublin: Morrish, 1879–1883.

Milton, John. *The Poems of John Milton*. Edited by J. Carey and A. Fowler. London: Longmans, 1968.

Mounce, R. H. *The Book of Revelation*. Grand Rapids: Eerdmans, 1998.

Moyise, S. *The Old Testament in the Book of Revelation*. Sheffield: Sheffield University Press, 1995.

Mwombeki, F. R. "The Book of Revelation in Africa." *Word & World: Theology for Christian Ministry* 15 (1995) 145–50.

Neatby, W. B. *A History of the Plymouth Brethren*. London: Hodder & Stoughton, 1901.

Nebeker, G. L. "'The Ecstasy of Perfected Love': The Eschatological Mysticism of J. N. Darby." In *Prisoners of Hope?*, edited by C. Gribben and T. C. F. Stunt, 69–94. Carlisle: Paternoster, 2004.

Newberry, T. *Notes on the Book of Revelation, Taking Up Each Chapter in Order*. Kilmarnock: Ritchie, ca.1890.

Newport, K. G. C. *Apocalypse and Millennium: Studies in Biblical Eisegesis*. Cambridge: Cambridge University Press, 2000.

————. *The Branch Davidians of Waco: The History and Beliefs of an Apocalyptic Sect.* Oxford: Oxford University Press, 2006.

Newton, B. W. *Answers to Questions on the Propriety of Leaving the Church of England.* London: Wertheimer, 1841.

————. *Babylon: Its Future, History and Doom, with Remarks on the Future of Egypt and Other Eastern Countries.* London: Houlston, 1890.

————. *Doctrines of the Church in Newman Street Considered.* N.pl.: n.pubs., ca. 1835.

————. *God and the Heathen.* Aylesbury: Hunt & Barnard, n.d.

————. *The Harlot of Babylon: Revelation Chapter Seventeen in Conversation.* Chelmsford: Sovereign Grace Advent Testimony, n.d.

————. "Is the Exercise of Worldly Authority Consistent with Discipleship?" *ChW* 4 (1837) 251–55.

————. *Observation on a Tract Entitled, "The Sufferings of Christ as Set Forth in a Lecture on Psalm VI," Considered.* London: Campbell, 1847.

————. *The Olive Tree and Its Branches.* Aylesbury: Hunt & Barnard, n.d.

————. *The Probable Course of Events up to the Time of the End.* Aylesbury: Hunt & Barnard, n.d.

————. *The Prophecy of Habakkuk.* Aylesbury: Hunt & Barnard, n.d.

————. *The Time of the End: A Resume of Prophetic Truth.* Aylesbury: Hunt & Barnard, n.d.

————. *Thoughts on the Apocalypse.* London: Hamilton & Adams, 1844.

Noel, N. *The History of the Brethren.* 2 vols. Denver: Napp, 1851.

Norman, E. "Church and State since 1800." In *A History of Religion in Britain*, edited by S. Gilley and W. J. Sheils, 277–90. Oxford: Blackwell, 1994.

Oliver, W. H. *Prophets and Millennialists: The Uses of Biblical Prophecy in England from the 1790s to the 1840s.* Auckland: Auckland University Press, 1978.

Origen. "Origen Against Celsus." In *ANF*, 4:395–669.

————. "*Origen de Principiis.*" In *ANF*, 4:239–384.

Osborn, E. *Irenaeus of Lyons.* Cambridge: Cambridge University Press, 2001.

Peter of les Vaux-de-Cernay. *Historia Albigensis; or, The History of the Albigensian Crusade.* Translated by W. A. Sibly and M. D. Sibly. Woodbridge: Boydell, 1998.

Philos [pseud.]. "The Catholic Church." In *The Christian Observer*, 5.25:198–99. London: Hatchard & Son, 1842.

Pickering, H. *Chief among Brethren: One Hundred Records and Photos.* 2nd ed. Glasgow: Pickering & Inglis, 1931.

Powerscourt, T. A. W. *Letter and Papers.* London: Broom, 1872.

Puccius, A. "*Oratio Antonii Pucii.*" In *Sacrorum conciliorum nova, et applissima collection*, edited by J. D. Mansi, 32:887–97. 53 vols. Paris: Welter, 1901–27.

Rad, G. von. *Holy War in Ancient Israel.* Translated by M. J. Dawn. Grand Rapids: Eerdmans, 1991.

Räisänen, H. "The 'Effective History' of the Bible: A Challenge to Biblical Scholarship?" *Scottish Journal of Theology* 45 (1992) 303–24.

Reeves, M. *The Influence of Prophecy in the Later Middle Ages: A Study in Joachimism.* Oxford: Clarendon, 2000.

————. *Joachim of Fiore and the Prophetic Future: A Study in Medieval Millennialism.* Stroud: Sutton, 1999.

Reeves, M., and B. Hirsch-Reich. *The Figurae of Joachim of Fiore.* Oxford: Oxford University Press, 1972.

Reisser, H. "Porneuo." In *The New International Dictionary of New Testament Theology*, edited by C. Brown, 1:494–97. Carlisle: Paternoster, 1988.

Remigius. "Libellus de tribus epistolis." In *Patrologia Latina*, 21:985–1068. Paris: Bibliotecha Universalis, 1852.

Ribera. *In sacrum Beati Ioannis Apostoli, & Evangelistae Apocalypsin Commentarij.* Lugundi: Ex Officina Iuntarum, 1593.

Roberts, A., and J. Donaldson, eds. *The Ante-Nicene Fathers: Translations of the Fathers Down to A.D. 325.* 10 vols. Grand Rapids: Eerdmans, 1968–1971.

Rorty, R. *Objectivity, Relativism and Truth.* Cambridge: Cambridge University Press, 1991.

Rosenbaum, A. S. *Coercion and Autonomy: Philosophical Foundations, Issues and Practices.* New York: Greenwood, 1986.

Rossier, H. L. *Le Livre du Prophete Habakuk.* Vevey: Guignard, 1916.

———. *Meditations sur le Seconde Livre de Chroniques.* Vevey: Guignard, 1913.

Rowdon, H. H. *The Origins of the Brethren, 1825–1850.* Glasgow: Pickering & Inglis, 1967.

Rowland, C. *The Open Heaven: A Study of Apocalyptic in Judaism and Early Christianity.* London: SPCK, 1982.

Sacchoni, R. "Treatise on the Cathars and Waldensians" (1250). In *The Birth of Popular Heresy*, edited by R. I. Moore, 132–44. London: Arnold, 1975.

Sandeen, E. R. *The Roots of Fundamentalism: British and American Millenarianism, 1800–1930.* Chicago: University of Chicago Press, 1970.

Sandys, E. *Europae Speculum; or, A Survey of the State of Religion in the Westerne Parts of the World.* London: Cotes, 1638.

Schaff, P., and H. Wace, eds. *A Select Library of Nicene and Post-Nicene Fathers of the Christian Church*, 1st series. Grand Rapids: Eerdmans, 1956.

———. *A Select Library of Nicene and Post-Nicene Fathers of the Christian Church*, 2nd series. Grand Rapids: Eerdmans, 1957.

Schmidt, L. A., and N. A. Fox. "Conceptual, Biological and Behavioral Distinctions among Different Categories of Shy Children." In *Extreme Fear, Shyness and Social Phobia: Origins, Biological Mechanisms and Clinical Outcomes*, 47–66. Oxford: Oxford University Press, 1999.

Schmidt, L. A., and J. Schulkin, eds. *Extreme Fear, Shyness and Social Phobia: Origins, Biological Mechanisms and Clinical. Outcomes.* Oxford: Oxford University Press, 1999.

Schüssler Fiorenza, E. *Revelation: Vision of a Just World.* Edinburgh: T. & T. Clark, 1991.

Seventh-day Adventists Believe: A Biblical Exposition of 27 Fundamental Doctrines. Washington, DC: Ministerial Association, 1988.

Sheppard, G. T. "Biblical Interpretation in Europe in the 20th Century." In *Historical Handbook of Major Biblical Interpreters*, edited by D. K. McKim, 401–540. Leicester: InterVarsity, 1998.

Sibly, W. A., and M. D. Sibly. *The History of the Albigensian Crusade.* Woodbridge: Boydell, 1998.

The Sibylline Oracles. Translated by H. N. Bale. London: SPCK, 1918.

Signor Pastorini. *See* Walmsely, C.

Simmel, G. *Conflict.* Translated by Kurt H. Wolff. Glencoe, IL: Free Press, 1955.

Simonde de Sismondi, J. C. L. *History of the Crusades against the Albigenses, in the Thirteenth Century.* London: Wightman & Camp, 1826.

Simonetti, M. *Biblical Interpretation in the Early Church: An Historical Introduction of Patristic Exegesis*. Edinburgh: T. & T. Clark, 1994.

Smith, H. *Haggai: The Messenger and His Message*. Edinburgh: Reid, n.d.

———. *Open Brethren: Their Origin, Principles and Practice*. Weston-super-Mare: Smith, 1930.

Snell, H. H. *Notes on the Revelation: With Practical Reflections*. London: Broom, 1866.

Spurgeon, C. H. *Lectures to My Students*. 2 vols. New York: Carter & Brothers, 1890–1889.

Strayer, J. R. *The Albigensian Crusades*. Michigan: University of Michigan Press, 1992.

Stunt, T. C. "Influences in the Early Development of J. N. Darby." In *Prisoners of Hope? Aspects of Evangelical Millennialism in Britain and Ireland, 1800–1880*, edited by C. Gribben and T. C. F. Stunt, 44–68. Carlisle: Paternoster, 2004.

———. "The Tribulation of Controversy." *Brethren Archivists and Historians Network Review* 2 (2003) 91–98.

Surridge, R. "Seventh-day Adventism: Self-appointed Laodicea." In *Studies in the Book of Revelation*, edited by S. Moyise, 21–27. Edinburgh: T. & T. Clark, 2001.

Sweet, J. P. M. *Revelation*. Westminster Pelican Commentaries. Philadelphia: Westminster, 1979.

Taylor, C. "Gadamer on the Human Sciences." In *The Cambridge Companion to Gadamer*, edited by R. J. Dostal, 126–42. Cambridge: Cambridge University Press, 2002.

Tertullian. "Writings of Tertullian." In *ANF*, 3:17–710.

Theodoret. "Ecclesiastical History of Theoderet." In *NPNF*, 2.3:33–159.

Thompson, D. M. "The Religious Census of 1851." In *The Census and Social Structure: An Interpretive Guide to Nineteenth Century Censuses for England and Wales*, 241–88. London: Cass, 1978.

Thube, C. G. *Ueber die nächstkommenden vierrzig Jahre*. Schwerin: Bödner, 1798.

Tregelles, S. P. *Codex Zacynthius. Greek Palimpsest Fragments of St. Luke*. London: Bagster, 1861.

———. *A Collation of the Critical Texts of Griesbach and Others*. London: Bagster, 1841.

———. *Genesius' Hebrew and Chaldee Lexicon*. London: Bagster, 1881.

———. *Hebrew Reading Lessons with a Grammatical Praxis and Interlinear Translation*. London: Bagster, 1860.

Trotter, W. "Apocalyptic Interpretation." *PPPS* 16 (1854) 341–60.

———. "Approaching Judgment." *PPPS* 2 (1854) 21–40.

———. "Christ and the Church." *PPPS* 5 (1854) 81–100.

———. "The Coming Crisis and Its Results." *PPPS* 3 (1854) 41–60.

———. "The Doom of Christendom; or, Why Are the Judgments Coming?" *PPPS* 4 (1854) 61–80.

———. "Ecclesiastical Corruption and Apostacy." *PPPS* 11 (1854) 201–20.

———. "Israel in the Approaching Crisis." *PPPS* 12 (1854) 251–60.

———. "The Last Days of the Gentile Supremacy." *PPPS* 13 (1854) 261–70.

———. "The Millennial Reign of Christ, and the Universal Blessing of the Earth, Connected with the Restoration of the Jews." *LP* 4 (1890) 81–119.

———. "The Spared Remnant." *PPPS* 14 (1854) 271–80.

———. *The Origins of (So-Called) Open Brethrenism: A Letter by W. Trotter Giving the Whole Case of Plymouth & Bethesda*. Otley, July 15th 1849. Kingston: Stow Hill, n.d.

————. "The Predicted Corruption of Christianity and Its Final Results." *LP* 6 (1890) 191–219.

————. "A Recapitulation; or, Outline of Prophetic Truth." *PPPS* 19 (1854) 421–29.

————. "The Second Coming of Christ Pre-millennial." *LP* 2 (1890) 41–59.

————. "The Times of the Gentiles: The Character and Doom of the Great Gentile Powers." *LP* 7 (1890) 210–21.

Trump, R. F., and D. L. Fagle. *Design for Life*. New York: Holt, Rinehart & Winston, 1963.

Turner, W. G. *John Nelson Darby: A Biography*. London: Chapter Two, 1990.

Tweedie, T. "Mystery, Babylon the Great." *NW* 9 (1879) 94–95.

Valpy, R. *Sermons Preached on Public Occasions*. London: Longman, 1811.

Victorinus. "Commentary on the Blessed John." In *ANF*, 7:344–60.

Wainwright, A. W. *Mysterious Apocalypse: Interpreting the Book of Revelation*. Nashville: Abingdon, 1993.

Walmsely, C. [pseud.]. *The General History of the Christian Church, from Her Birth to Her Final Triumphant State in Heaven. . . .* Wigan: Ferguson, 1782.

Warnke, G. "Hermeneutics, Ethics and Politics." In *The Cambridge Companion to Gadamer*, 79–101. Cambridge: Cambridge University Press, 2002.

Weber, E. *Apocalypses: Prophecies, Cults and Millennial Beliefs throughout the Ages*. London: Hutchinson, 1999.

Wesley, J. *Explanatory Notes on the New Testament*. New York: Carlton & Porter, 1754.

————. *The Works of John Wesley*. Vol. 1. Nashville: Abingdon, 1984.

West, D. C., and S. Zimdars-Swartz. *Joachim of Fiore: A Study in Spiritual Perception and History*. Bloomington: Indiana University Press, 1983.

Wigram, G. V. *An Answer of G. V. Wigram, to "Mr. H. Craik's Letter, Dated 15th November, 1848."* London: Campbell, 1848.

————. *An Appeal to Saints That Remain Still in Bethesda and Salem, as to Certain Bad Doctrine*. London: Campbell, 1848.

————. "The Church: Its Present State and Prospects." In *Selections from the Writings and Ministry of G. V. Wigram*, 99–118. London: Horner, 1874.

————. "The Coming Kingdom: Being an Outline on Revelation." Lecture 2 in *Notes of Three Lectures, Delivered in Georgetown, Demerara, 11th, 18th & 25th Jan. 1876*, 29–66. London: Morrish, 1876.

————. "God's System of a Church." *BT* 16 (1886–1887) 199–201.

————. *A Letter Dated March 8th 1846*. London: n.pubs., 1846.

————. "Marks whereby the Assembly of God and the Table of the Lord Were and Are to Be Known." In *Selections from the Writings and Ministry of G. V. Wigram*, 119–36. London: Horner, 1874.

————. "Notes on Scripture: Lectures and Letters." In *Memorials of the Ministry of G. V. Wigram*, 1:1–425. London: Broom, 1881.

————. *The Present Question (1848–1849)*. Letters 1 & 2. London: Campbell, 1849.

————. *To the Christians in New Zealand*. Christchurch: W.C. Nation, 1874.

Wittgenstein, L. *Philosophical Investigations*. Translated by G. E. M. Anscombe. Oxford: Blackwell, 1958.

Wolston, W. T. P. "The Candlestick and the Bride." *CNT* 8 (1905) 172–93.

————. "Established and Endowed." *CNT* 4 (1905) 69–92.

————. *"Handfuls of Purpose" Let Fall for Eager Gleaners: Thirty Addresses on Various Scripture Truths and Incidents*. Edinburgh: Gospel Messenger, 1899.

———. "The New Jerusalem . . . Behold the Bridegroom!" *CNT* 9 (1905) 194–216.

———. *Night Scenes of Scripture: Seventeen Bible Night Scenes, Illustrating and Elucidating Various Truths of the Gospel.* Edinburgh: Gospel Message, 1896.

———. "The Stone Cut Out Without Hands . . . Behold the Bridegroom!" *CNT* 6 (1905) 121–42.

———. "The Times of the Gentiles . . . Behold the Bridegroom!" *CNT* 3 (1905) 43–68.

W.P.L. [pseud.]. "Love of the World." *NW* 9 (1879) 76–79.

Wrangham, F. "Rome Is Fallen." In *Thirteen Practical Sermons*, 213–66. London: Gillet, 1802.

Subject Index

Lightning Source UK Ltd.
Milton Keynes UK
UKOW01f2038121215

264622UK00001B/7/P